Voices

Voices

The Educational Formation of Conscience

Thomas F. Green

University of Notre Dame Press
Notre Dame, Indiana

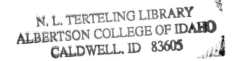

Library of Congress Cataloging-in-Publication Data

Green, Thomas F.
    Voices : the educational formation of conscience / Thomas F. Green.
       p.   cm.
    Includes bibliographical references and index.
    ISBN 0-268-01924-X (alk. paper)
    1. Moral education.   I. Title.
  LC268.G667   1999
  370.11′4—dc21   98-50201

Contents

Preface

Whatever coherence exists among the essays assembled here is a late discovery in the history of their composition. They have come together, not out of some generative plan of inquiry, but simply from the gropings now of several decades to understand the practices of education in ways that can be described as philosophical. Yet this is a deceptive formulation. It is not as though I ever thought it possible to 'apply' philosophy to the practices of education or that philosophy might provide a guide to policy or to pedagogy or to the organization of schools and schooling. As Collingwood once observed, it is a fundamental task of every society to empty the nursery and, I would add, to populate the commons. Every society must do it or perish. The point is not that philosophy can tell us just how that ought to be done. The point is rather that anyone who attends to doing it will encounter a nearly endless tangle of problems of the sort that we typically describe as philosophical. They include the need to grasp the nature of duty and virtue, but also of authority, social order, work, and so forth. Instead of attempting to apply philosophy to the conduct of education, I have tried, over these many years, simply to unravel what of philosophical interest is already implicit in the social necessity of education.

So these essays begin by asking about the topic of discussion. What are we to understand by 'moral education'? How are we to *think* about it? An answer is provided toward the end of chapter 1, explicated in chapter 2, and extended in chapters 3 and 4. The answer offered is that moral education is the formation of conscience (What does that mean?) and that the formation of conscience occurs by the acquisition of norms (What is that?). It cannot be stressed too much nor stated too often that the focus of attention throughout is on the *acquisition* of norms, not their vindication or their logical or ontological status. These first four chapters can be construed as Part I. The next three chapters, constituting Part II, extend the analysis in various directions. Chapter 5 scrutinizes a claim made early on that the idea of moral education as something called 'teaching values' is a cruel deception. Yet the notion has become so widespread and has come to seem so natural that an account of what might be meant by it is sorely needed. Following this are two chapters extending the idea of norm acquisition first to the creation of a public through public speech and finally to the office of citizen.

It may seem odd that notions of 'citizen', 'public', and 'public speech' should be accorded such prominence in a work openly concerned with moral education. Indeed the fittingness of that inclusion was not merely a late decision in the order of these essays. It was, in fact, the last discovery. That moral education might be construed as the formation of conscience is a view that I first explored in the John Dewey lecture of 1983. The idea was attractive primarily because it gave breadth to the subject, allowing the notion of moral education to embrace excellence in the exercise of the intellectual virtues as well as the crafts and various practices of the professions. I did not then fully grasp, however, that by norm acquisition I had in mind how reflexive self-governance makes its appearance, on the one hand in the self-governance of individuals, but also in the self-governance of a people, in their institutions of government as well as in the professions and practices of the arts and sciences. I sought the account of a kind of seamless progression from the reflexive government of individuals to the activities of citizenship and thus to the conduct of government, all under the rubric of moral education. It may be this inclusiveness of excellence in conduct over such a continuous span of activities both intellectual and political that constitutes the distinctive contribution of these essays.

It is also important to note that in these essays, such a perspective is matched also by a particular and very old conception of the nature of philosophy. The idea is that philosophy aims simply at 'unwrapping the ordinary'. What this means, however, can become clear only in context. It needs argument much less than it needs a kind of 'showing'. This approach to philosophy is better simply revealed than paraded; still, there are signs of its presence to which we can be alerted.

The first is its neutrality with respect to philosophical doctrine. I have always envied those academics who know just what their field of scholarship is about and just how to go about it. Such confidence provokes both my admiration and my skepticism: admiration because I have never been able to muster much confidence in my grasp of the nature of philosophy, skepticism because of doubts that anyone so confident could possibly have got it right. So, without exception, to proponents of the various 'ists', 'ites', and 'isms'—modernists, postmodernists, Deweyites, Marx-ists—I would apply a test of common sense and ask whether their doctrine aids in unwrapping the ordinary, whether it helps in grasping what I and others know to be true in ordinary experience. Some may find here influences of pragmatism in one or another of its various forms. If that is so, it would not surprise me. The resemblance provides no evidence for the truth of what is argued either here or elsewhere. Nor does it matter, apart from the need to locate arguments in the intellectual landscape, whether the argument offered here fits this or that research program or paradigm of inquiry.[1]

This attitude of thought, or something very like it, recurs in the history of philosophy, always producing a distinctive formulation of what might be called the philosophical project. The significance of philosophical systems, a feature not to be confused with their consistency or completeness, lies in their capacity to elucidate, clarify, and set in ordered array the everyday problems implicit, but often concealed, in the daily experiences of life among ordinary persons. Their significance, in other words, lies in their capacity to explicate the experience of common sense. By such a view, philosophy cannot teach anyone anything they do not already know, but it may call to their attention what they had not noticed, remind them of what they had forgotten, and bring to understanding what had been taken for granted. In this project of 'unwrapping the ordinary' are many surprises. As far as I can discern, no philosophical doctrine is implicit in such a project, nothing, at least, that can be translated into a school of philosophy, another of those 'isms', 'ists', or 'ologies'.

This look into the conduct of moral education is neutral in the further sense that it advances no particular *moral* doctrine. It matters little to the central claims of these essays whether one is a Democrat, Marxist, libertarian, Christian, Muslim, Jew, or something else. It does not matter whether one is philosophically a utilitarian, an intuitionist, or a deontologist. That is, it does not matter to the central thesis. Moral education, from any of these perspectives, will remain an effort at fostering the acquisition of norms. The question of how norms can be said to govern conduct will remain, whatever one's moral position. The libertarian, for example, will need to ask not so much whether the libertarian stance is true, is useful, or can be framed as a political platform, but the awkward questions, What are the norms of libertarianism? What is a libertarian conscience? In other words, I have eschewed advocating any particular moral system, not only because I believe that I have no privileged access to moral truth, but even more because I believe that whenever philosophers take on the role of priests, gurus, missionaries, and evangels, they are an embarrassment to their 'calling'.

To these considerations of method, offered here so that they may shape the reading as they have the writing, some remarks should be added on the overall plan of which these essays are only a part. To this book, *Voices: The Educational Formation of Conscience,* is to be added a second volume, already well underway, called *Walls: Education in Communities of Text and Liturgy.* The sectarian claims I would make are reserved for this second volume. Discussion there flows from the conviction that in a highly pluralistic world in which commons and sect are separated by walls of one sort or another, the health of the commons depends upon the possibility of strong sectarian education. At the same time, the bare possibility of strong sectarian education depends for its continued existence upon maintaining the viability of the commons. Yet it occurs to me—more as conjecture than conviction—that the necessary elements of *any* moral education may be discoverable only in the context of sectarian education, that is to say, it will be understood only by examining education in a setting where adults are able to say to youth with confidence, with clarity, and for a very long time, "This is who we are and this is why we do these things." Any awkward hesitation or apology in this presentation either on the grounds that it is too complex a story for children to grasp or that there are alternatives among which an eventual choice must be made—any such hesitation will spell disaster for attempts at moral education. Such a context for education is paradigmatically a community of text and liturgy, even when the text is a constitution and the liturgy is found in a variety of civic rites.

To these remarks should be added the further hint, later elaborated, that these essays on moral education as the acquisition of norms are prompted by a growing conviction that in America we may have reached a point at which the romance of the public school *movement* has played out its story and is now in that fading-away in which all romances end. Faced with such a prospect, we must be at the difficult business of building once again a public commitment to education in the commons, but this time out of a deeper understanding of the mutual need of sect and commons. The sect, on the one hand, offers the moral resources that the commons needs but by itself cannot provide; the commons, on the other hand, affords the protection of all partial communities and views of life, so that the fevers always provoked when such advocates meet nose to nose and toe to toe may be cooled and kept at a distance.

Acknowledgments

A book like *Voices* lurks in the darkness of one's mind for years before becoming bold enough to announce its presence. It sits there, a timorous thing, seeking shelter from even the most cursory inspection of strangers and too shy to come forward and be known. The story of its coming to life is the story of accretions, the accumulation of ideas, counter-intuitions, doubts, and declared absurdities that in time take on the appearance of transparent truths. The accretions include seminar discussions, correspondence, objections from the Internet and from the reading of colleagues, and whole paragraphs deposited and waiting to be rediscovered, reworked, and placed side by side with other thoughts to be tested by still other readings. The indebtedness to students, friends, and even to participants in casual conversations becomes too great to even consider drawing up an exhaustive list.

Still, there are special debts that one acknowledges with a pleasure that can only come from deep affection. Among them is the thorough reading of Dr. Robert Daly, who observed early on, quite rightly, "This book does not yet know where it wants to go," and who, with a later draft in hand, helped enormously to discern the right order that whole sections ought to assume. Along the same lines, I owe a substantial debt to Stephen Macedo, who also read an early draft and declared his difficulty in discerning what this book is about, and who by that declaration pushed me to think all over again how to state the central issues. Also from within the Syracuse community are Manfred Stanley, whose helpful reading and approval did much to push that shy creature to see the light of day, and Gerry Grant, whose perceptive comments from the vantage of an acute observer helped greatly. For years, Gary Fenstermacher endured the arguments as they took shape out of that morass of accumulated thought. For his steady interest and active support, I am deeply grateful. As in all things I have written, I owe a special debt of thanks to Emily Robertson, who unfailingly seems to know what I mean even when it is not what I have written and who, in pointing it out, points also in directions the better to escape misunderstanding. For the same reason, I acknowledge my debt to the students in a seminar of hers who voiced their doubts about substantial portions of the manuscript. Other seminar discussions assembled at a variety of universities include those of Randall Curren at the University of Rochester, Nancy Beadie at the University of Washington, Gary Fenstermacher at the University of Michigan, William Hunter at the University of Calgary, and Arthur Brown at Wayne State University. I acknowledge my debt to these colleagues, their students, and their respective institutions with grateful thanks.

Clearly, such acknowledgments stir recollections of nearly a lifetime of work in which one's indebtedness only grows. Many, though not participating directly in the movement from draft to draft, have nonetheless remained exemplars and guides, colleagues who embody the standards that one seeks to satisfy and who therefore preside over such a work simply by being there. First among them is Maxine Greene, who showed me years ago that to be a student of education is demanding enough to enlist all the philosophical acumen one can muster, important enough to stir all one's passion, consequential enough to demand the most careful attention to the details of ordinary life, and broad enough in its reach to open all the academic disciplines to thoughtful study. Likewise, there is Jerome Bruner, whose agility of mind, leaping from the particular details of human growth to the most general principles and describing it always, from principle to particular, with clarity and grace, offers a model of thoughtful and lucid composition and integrity. If it is usually supposed there are but three ways to describe a particular phenomenon, Jerome Bruner will offer five. And finally, there is Robert Lynn, vice president of the Lilly Endowment at the time of his retirement. For nearly thirty years he prodded and offered encouragement and concrete assistance in the struggle to find a voice with which to express my interest in the contributions of theology and biblical studies to the conduct of every kind of education. I hope that these, my masters and tutors, will be pleased by what they find in these pages.

To all of them I gratefully offer my thanks, and to each the usual absolution of responsibility for any errors or downright foolishness that remains.

Chapter I

The Project: A Matter of Governance

These essays aim to formulate a coherent and inclusive view of moral education, or more precisely, a view as to how we ought to *think* about moral education. That is how things stand. It is not how they began. At the beginning, even to entertain such large purposes would have seemed indecent. Such aims were nowhere in sight. Instead, there was only a series of random attempts to calm a vague unease over a point here and a point there in what seemed the received wisdom of moral education. That vague and scattered unease grew in depth and scope, however, until it turned into a nagging conviction that we need to revise our ways of dealing with moral education. And if it is true that the act is offspring of the thought, then how much greater is the need to revise our very vocabulary for thinking about moral education. That revision of our vocabulary is one way of stating what these essays are about.

The conduct of moral education is crucial, which is to say, it is a problem situated at a point where many fundamental matters intersect. Any view suited to the revisionary task will touch an enormous range of problems, many seldom examined in detail. Problems necessarily touched upon include the need to note with care where the limits of education lie as well as the limits of morality, and what is still another matter, the limits of moral education. We cannot suppose that education can make saints of ordinary human beings. It is not by education that heroes are made heroes, assuming heroes are made at all. Education is a weak instrument with which to undertake the moral reformation of the world. If, in some foolish fit of absentmindedness, we were to attempt it, then by any account of education or of sainthood I can think of, we would need other means than education to accomplish it. The mere thought pushes forth a need to distinguish those human aspirations for which education is a suitable tool and those for which it is not. Mark out the boundaries, and you are likely to discover that they circumscribe an enterprise of fairly modest dimensions.

Much the same can be said of the limits of morality itself. Not every question of conduct is a moral question. Just as we ought to note with care the limits of education, so also we ought to note that not every human aspiration can be subjected to moral appraisal. Whether we squander our resources, for example, either personal or communal, can be viewed as calling for the exercise of purely prudential judgment. It is entirely a matter of wise management, and therefore, so the argument would go, not a subject of moral significance. Can or must moral education include lessons in budgeting? If so, why? If not, why not? Let it be conceded that the management of resources is entirely a prudential matter and thus, by some views, beyond the ken of morality. Even so, cultivating such prudential wisdom may remain a fit concern for moral education. How to mark the reasonable limits of education and the reasonable bounds of morality and mark off both from the appropriate domain of moral education—these are topics seldom considered. Yet they are forced upon us by any attempt to think thoroughly and carefully about the nature and practices of moral education, especially if we ponder how we ought to *think* about the matter. That such questions will inevitably appear is only one clue that the topic is crucially situated.

I. A Matter of Governance

It is correct to say that these are essays exploring how to think about the conduct of moral education, but that is not the most helpful formulation. A more satisfying account, one affording a slightly different angle of vision, would say simply that these are essays on governance. Governance lies at the heart of all education; it is quite possibly the constitutive problem of moral education. By 'governance' I mean the *effective* regulation of conduct, but conduct of many sorts. By 'governance' is meant more than the governance of a society through its system of law and its political institutions. These are means of ordering conduct, yet they are not the sole instruments of governance.

By 'governance' must be meant the self-governance of persons. And thus we quickly enter the domain of ethics, the effective regulation of conduct. By 'governance' must also be meant the governance of belief and, therefore, the effective conduct of inquiry. By 'governance' is meant the governance of various practices among human beings. It extends, therefore, to the governance of conduct in the professions. In short, by 'self-governance' is here meant the regulation of conduct in the exercise of every craft and profession and in the maintenance of every civilizing practice. Education to the arts and crafts as well as excellence in their exercise, like education to the office of citizen and to all the disciplines of inquiry, is also education whose aim is governance, the effective regulation of conduct.

By this word 'effective' I mean to direct thought beyond the problem of producing right behavior, and even beyond the matter of having at hand right reasons for conduct. We may get right conduct without any formed capacity for its rational appraisal, and get a capacity, even a sophisticated capacity, to engage in moral reasoning without any formed propensity to act as reason would direct. It is a folksy dictum, certainly trite, but at the same time quite possibly true, that one must not only "talk the talk but also walk the walk." To suit the point at hand, I would revise the slogan: one must not only talk the walk, but walk the talk. The *effective* governance of conduct—the central aim of moral education—is not simply comprehension, that is, the capacity to talk the talk of ethics and set out in argument the proper path of conduct. Moral education has to do with an acquired temper of the self by which the talk is brought to actually govern conduct and can be discerned to do so, even when the conduct itself falls short of all we think it ought to be.

The point is of sufficient weight to bear yet another formulation. When it comes to moral education, we are all of us behaviorists in the sense that our concern is the governance of conduct, not simply its understanding. It is partly this emphasis upon actual behavior that I mean to stress by emphasizing effective governance. We are not behaviorists, however, if by that is meant that thought or reason has *no* role in governing conduct. That would be a view impoverished beyond imagination. It would be a view that limits our interests to the control of behavior instead of extending to the governance of conduct. In saying that moral education has to do primarily with the problem of governance, I aim to focus attention—and to fix it stubbornly—upon the relation of thought to conduct, that is, upon the question what it means to say that thought governs conduct, no matter what may be the moral qualities of the thought that governs or the conduct that issues, whether it can be described in general, for example, as imbued with saintly charity or as nothing more than the cautious and cunning protection of self-interest. Each may be an expression of governance, each a consequence of moral education. It is this relation of thought to conduct that I mean to identify as effective governance and not the moral quality of the thought or the moral rectitude of the conduct.

If governance so conceived is the central problem of education, then any philosophy of education must include some carefully wrought account of what it means to say that conduct is governed and not merely shaped. Such an account will have to include some appraisal of the springs of conduct. Here then are two additional problems, one to describe the *springs* of behavior, the other to describe the *governance* of conduct. The difference is hinted at in the simple linguistic contrast already employed. Behavior has its *springs;* conduct its governance.

Do we think of human beings as driven, on the whole, by their sentiments and feelings? Are they first and foremost emotional beings? Are these the springs of behavior? Then attend to the governance of the emotions, either to their cultivation or their control. Is it in human interests, even in keenly calculated and parochial interests, that we shall find the springs of behavior? Then perhaps for an education aimed at the governance of conduct we must aim at an education in rational prudence, an education in properly estimating probabilities. Perhaps the behavior of human beings is to be understood as springing, on the whole, from their attachments. Then for the governance of conduct, attend not to this or to that set of rules but to nurturing the ties of family, community, neighborhood, region, and country. Cultivate the ligaments of loyalty. Perhaps, on the other hand, we shall find the springs of behavior in the fantasies that human beings harbor, the soap operas of the soul, the frontier westerns, and knightly sagas of everyday life by which even the streets of lower Manhattan, in Walter Mitty fashion, can turn into the streets of Loredo. Perhaps it is true that human beings are creatures pushed, pulled, or directed by those carefully cultivated narratives of justice, prosperity, love, and tenacity that provide for each the visions of the best they can imagine for themselves and others. The springs of behavior, in other words, might be discovered in a composition of various romances. Perhaps governance will come, then, through the critique of such romances.

This focus upon governance is but the first approximation of a formulation aimed at drawing attention away from either what is done or what is thought and toward the relation between thought and conduct, toward a distinction between the springs of behavior and the governance of conduct. Such a formulation is meant not merely to hint at the complexities of what is yet to come, but to frame those complexities in a quite specific way. The announcement was that in the idea of governance will be found the unifying element in all that follows, and it will take all that follows to make it plain. The notion needs a thorough explication. Since such a formulation was a late discovery in the actual composition of these essays, there may be no better way to grasp its importance than to revisit the path of its discovery. It begins in simplicities. How does this revisionary project take shape? Out of what illusions about the limits of education, of moral philosophy and moral education, out of what appraisal of the springs of human action does this matter of governance come to center stage? How might one fully grasp the claim that the presiding concern of a philosophy of moral education is simply governance?

II. The Fears and Illusions of Moral Education

Each person will have some idea of what moral education is about, but those ideas will differ so much that one can hardly hope to discover any common conception of the subject. What does it include? What does it exclude? What is its domain? The idea of moral education is not simply vague or ambiguous; it is also frightening. To many persons the very idea stirs images of authoritarian politics, religious intolerance, oppression, propaganda, indoctrination, manipulation, and thought control. It provokes fears.

Fears of Repression

Some will think of moral education as aimed primarily at forming right belief; others at forming right behavior; and still others as practice in making autonomous decisions. The problem is not that there is anything wrong in seeking to transmit right belief or inculcate right behavior, nor any fault in seeking to shape autonomous agents. Each of these is a legitimate aim of moral education, or for that matter, of any education. Despite the fact that each represents, at best, a partial view of moral education, nevertheless, each is sometimes advanced as though it were the whole. That is when problems begin. When that happens, each view threatens. The view that moral education is entirely a matter of forming right belief offers grounds to fear that orthodoxy will become its end and indoctrination its means. How do we settle on right belief? Whose shall it be? And if moral education be conceived simply as shaping right behavior, then we have reason to believe that its goal will be conformity and the development of unthinking habits, sustained by a variety of sanctions. 'Education', it is feared, will become simply another name for oppression. The idea of moral education aiming simply at forming right behavior or implanting right belief provides a defective picture, partly because of what it says, but even more because of what it won't allow us to say. Such a view leaves no place for the virtues, for example, since the possession of virtue can never be summed up as right opinion or as right action.

We run still other risks when moral education is viewed as practice in making principled decisions. Fanatics act on principle, but their principles are always too few and their application of them always too inflexible. Adherence to principle is no doubt a good, but not an unlimited good or the whole good. Sometimes we are justly encouraged to rise above principle. Besides, statements sufficiently general to be called moral principles almost certainly will be insufficiently contextual to provide much guidance in actual situations. Like that rationally fundamental rule of justice that similar persons should be treated similarly, moral principles will invariably lack content, saying little—to preserve the example—about which persons are to be regarded as alike and what will count as like treatment. Such a view also, except in praise of conscientiousness, is unlikely to allow any mention of forming the virtues. Yet their cultivation must surely be a large part of moral education.

If it be a fault to neglect the formation of virtue, then how much more at fault must be any view that sums up the moral life as though it consists of making judicial-like decisions in the face of moral dilemmas? Moral dilemmas arise, to be sure, but rarely. When they do, we may have to make decisions. To suppose that these rare occasions can provide the model for all of moral education, however, is to commit a kind of part-whole fallacy. It is to suppose that all of moral life can be modeled after a bit of it. Though there are times when we must make moral decisions from among difficult alternatives, the fact remains that our moral lives neither consist of making such decisions nor are they defined by or limited to such decisions.

The Illusion of the Autonomous Self

That moral education is an education in how to choose, and how to choose independently and autonomously, is a view driven no doubt by a commitment to the sovereignty of reason. This commitment is likely to be unbounded by limitations of age. It is likely to assume uncritically that reason can be a sufficient guide to conduct equally at every age. If we see things in this way, then we must ask whether parents and teachers are to remain silent on which choices are wise or efficient or prudent—much less morally superior—and which unwise, inefficient, or foolish. Must we eschew all comment on these matters in deference to the child, retreating altogether from such questions out of fear that comment will abridge someone's freedom of choice? Such evasion is no doubt rooted also in the idea that a moral agent is always an autonomous agent, and so moral education must not abridge that autonomy. It must avoid intrusion on the agent. Except for the sweet voice of reason, by such a view, interventions are forbidden. Who can doubt that autonomy is a good thing and that it ought to be encouraged? Autonomous choices, we are told, are superior to any, if any there be, that are not autonomous. Yet who knows what such advice amounts to? 'Autonomous choice' is a redundancy. What is 'non-autonomous choice'? Is it also a kind of choice? Such talk, no matter how appealing, is so obscure as to offer hardly any clear direction in which to understand the conduct of moral education.

We can agree that persons must be allowed to choose what kind of life they wish to live. Not even from such agreement, however, does it follow that children should be allowed such liberty at every age. Sometimes it is argued that if persons are to choose what kind of life they want to live, then their choice must not be predetermined. Yet such matters are almost never entirely open to choice at any age. Whether we have in mind the sort of belief we call propositional or the more expansive kind that we sometimes call faith, in neither case is belief a willful thing. That is to say, we cannot believe about the world just whatever we wish to believe. We cannot will the world to conform to our desires. Nor can we shop around among the world's traditions of faith and choose which to 'buy' or which to live by. We are not free, in short, to choose just whatever we want to believe. To suppose that we are free in this sense is to pursue a purely fictional liberty and then to compound the error by supposing that from this imagined freedom can be derived a view that moral education is merely education to prepare us for the exercise of choice. To refrain from comment or decline to offer any guidance that some choices are more worthy and some more foolish, and to do so out of respect for such a liberty, is to abdicate a large chunk of educational responsibility. Surely we seek to develop persons who, as adults, will assume responsibility for their beliefs and actions and even for the formation of their own character insofar as that is possible. But it is risky, perhaps not even intelligible, to rest our view of moral education on the assumption, first, that such a good demands liberty of choice at every age or perfect liberty at any, and secondly, that such liberty is an unlimited good. We misrepresent the moral life in still other but related ways when we present it simply as a continual process of rank ordering things.

The multiplicity of these views confuses. Each of them is no doubt true—within limits. But the opposite of each—within other limits—is also true. Up to a point, each of these views ought to be accepted, and beyond some point each ought to be resisted. Such a bewildering array obstructs the possibility of any clear understanding of moral education. Nevertheless, I have no doubt that each of the views I have briefly sketched, with its distinct and partial portrayal of moral life, is currently proposed by someone as though it were the whole, and each, I suppose, is actually being practiced somewhere. Its practice may not appear in the bald form in which I have sketched it. However, competing alternatives in both practice and theory often turn upon these different points of emphasis: whether moral education ought to aim at autonomous choice, as in the case of 'values clarification'; at principled decision, as in Kohlbergian stage theory; at right belief, as occurs in various forms of religious education; or at right behavior, as is often stressed in appeals to patriotism and civic order. None of these alternatives, *taken by itself*, can define the domain of moral education in ways that escape public opposition. Nor can any one of them be advanced as though free of serious intellectual fault.

What is the teacher, the parent, or the principal to do? Surely, whatever we mean by moral education must include attention to right belief, but not if that means sacrificing liberty of belief, nor if it means tolerating just any belief or forsaking attention to good reasons for belief. Surely we want moral education that shapes good behavior, but not if that means sacrificing the critical capacity to appraise behavior, and not if developing right behavior means reducing conduct to the routines of unthinking habit. Surely we desire to educate persons who will appeal to principle, but not to such an extent that appeals to principle displace appeals to ideals and relationships, or pleadings of simple good sense. There are times when, because of one's ideals, certain cherished principles may need to be set aside, even if only for a moment.

The Illusions of Teaching Values

One path appears to overcome these difficulties. We could conceive of moral education simply as the formation of values. To take a stand against teaching values is virtually impossible. Yet it is easy to imagine a person, even a person of deep and sincere religious convictions, for example, being suspicious, even deeply offended, upon learning that his or her children are being taught something called religious values in school. Such a person might legitimately wonder what that could be. It is also easy to imagine another religiously sensitive person objecting because the schools do *not* teach religious values. Even in this case, there seems no prospect of agreement on what moral education means and what it includes.

Yet, in a pluralistic society, something described as teaching values is probably the perspective most often expected to provide answers to the dilemmas of moral education. It is a point of view supposed to offer escape from controversy. Persons can differ in their values and still get along. I can have my values, you yours, and no conflict results from this apparent difference among us. Differences in our values remain of the same logical status as many other differences. Not that one of us is right and the other wrong or that one person's values are better or worse than another's. By such a flaccid yet popular point of view, values turn out to have the same logical force as differences of taste, or custom, or mere preference. With such a view, it is supposed, the school can engage in moral education and still remain neutral between contending views of what is valuable, prudent, or wise. Such a perspective apparently offers a way to escape from the contentiousness generated, for example, by conflicting sectarian religious views confronting one another in the public schools. We can retreat to something like the formation of moral or religious values. Retreat to such a level of generality will exact its price, however, and the price will be the sacrifice of any semblance of thoughtful moral clarity, much less precision. Such a view says nothing of offense because it says virtually nothing of any deep significance. If the expression 'autonomous choice' is a masterwork of obscurity, then how much more obscure it is to speak of 'the formation of values'.

Perhaps such talk reduces simply to another version of the formation of beliefs, behavior, habits, dispositions or mere preferences. Maybe by 'teaching values' is to be understood the formation of personality, which marks a person as one who values some things over others and responds with favor to certain events and not to others. If that is the intended meaning, then teaching values will get, and richly deserve, the undying opposition of thousands of parents who resist the idea that strangers might be authorized to preside over the formation of their children's personality, however professional they claim to be. Understood in this way, the idea of teaching values in the school will be viewed by many as among the most offensive and intrusive ideas of an already presumptuous cadre of persons who call themselves 'educators'.

Being the most general and the most encompassing of all approaches to the nature of moral education, this perspective also is the most attractive in meeting certain difficulties. Its attraction stems almost entirely from the fact that it commits us to so little, and because of this, allows us to speak of moral education in ways that appear to achieve agreement. That is only appearance, however. Things look that way only as long as we are allowed to be indefinite in our meaning. In fact, to adopt the view that moral education consists simply in teaching values is to elevate evasion to the level of a policy. Habits, virtues, beliefs, and preferences are different sorts of things. They are formed differently, taught differently, modified differently, and they function differently in the lives of persons. Any perspective that obscures these differences by subsuming them all under a single notion of 'teaching values' evades discussion exactly where discussion is most needed and where it ought to be rampantly pursued. It will become apparent throughout these essays, in fact, that we can do very well without the view that moral education is the formation of values. These essays, in a way, constitute a demonstration of how much can be said about moral education without ever introducing the idea that persons *have* values.[1]

III. The Utopian Threat: Conservatives, Liberals, Radicals

In addition to these controversies over the aims of moral education as right belief, right behavior, or induction into some ideology or religious faith, and in addition to the vacuous claim that moral education is simply the formation of values, other fears are excited by the prospect of moral education. Whenever the topic is broached, some will suspect, and with considerable reason, that another utopian scheme is about to be unpacked, one of those stories of a social order whose fulfilling promise is more apparent to its author than to any who might actually have to live there. Utopias are always concerned with moral education. They cannot avoid it. Moral education, that is, forging good people and good lives, is simply what utopias are about, though utopia cannot be what any useful view of moral education is about. The list of utopian thinkers includes figures whose social proposals remain fairly unattractive to most modern, liberal-minded persons. Think of Plato, Hitler, and Mao Tse Tung, all moralists of a utopian bent. Call to mind some of the more unhappy aspects of Calvin's Geneva and Cromwell's England. Such utopian thinkers, such seekers after perfection, do much to give moral education a bad name.

Among utopian advocates are those convinced that if the descent of the heavens tarries and the delay is too much to endure, then its coming must be encouraged, if not by persuasion then by the point of a sword. Such utopian seekers usually fail to notice that among the most prominent features of the world is its complexity. Human affairs are filled with irony. We are reminded along Freudian lines, for example, that the consequence of inevitable repression is sublimation. Culture is both the presupposition and the consequence, both cause and result, of repression. We are to believe that in civilizing the human animal, base energies, being put down, are redirected along higher and more noble paths, thus producing the arts, manufacture, scholarship, and civic life, which achievements, to endure, require repression all over again, and the cycle is repeated. But paths of sublimation need not be lofty. Think of the ubiquity of simple human cussedness. Even in a benign setting like that described in Skinner's Walden II, it is practically certain that someone will tinker with the thermostat in the nursery just for the fun of it, and everything in consequence will be changed. In Paul Tillich's world where people have "the courage to be," it is practically certain that some will find attraction, if not fulfillment, in the courage *not* to be. Social perfection, planned for and educated for, is hard to come by except through suppression, censorship, or violence of some kind. Anyone embarking on a program of moral education, provided it amounts to anything at all—anything of definite content, that is—is likely to harbor visions of social perfection and yearnings after some kind of evangelical victory. If human beings were only angels. Yes, and if pigs could fly. . . .

Those who carry around in their bags some program of moral education will need unusual assurance about what ought to be taught and what ought not. They will need an image of angelic virtue and of pigly flight. In education, as in other realms of public life, utopian proposals stem mostly from a radical temperament, but there are other habits of thought, other temperaments described as conservative or liberal, that also give expression to programs of moral education. Moral education is an especially difficult subject for those of liberal temperament. The others, both radicals and conservatives, occupy the field of contention because, though persuaded in different ways, they are at least persuaded, often passionately so. They seem assured in their knowledge of where rectitude lies. They alone seem able to muster certainty and to point with clarity and assurance to the moral direction along which educational thought and practice ought to run.

Oddly enough, the assurance of conservatives seems to spring from a kind of doubt, a skepticism that human beings can ever, merely by taking thought, devise humane and lasting forms of public life. In proportion as their skepticism is strengthened, so also, it seems, is their reliance upon tradition. Although tradition is capable of rational amendment, it is practically impossible to justify apart from the simple claim that it is, after all—well, traditional. Those of conservative temperament are likely to sum up tradition as experience tested by the centuries, and to let the matter rest. That which takes years to produce, they will say, ought not to be replaced in a moment of anger or even in a moment of rare collective good sense, if it is guided by some merely rational construction. "Rage and frenzy," writes Edmund Burke,

> will pull down more in half an hour, than prudence, deliberation, and foresight can build up in a hundred years. The errors and defects of old establishments are visible and palpable. It calls for little ability to point them out; and where absolute power is given, it requires but a word wholly to abolish the vice and the establishment together. . . . No difficulties occur in what has never been tried. Criticism is almost baffled in discovering the defects of what has not existed; and eager enthusiasm and cheating hope have all the wide field of imagination, in which they may expatiate with little or no opposition.[2]

The conservative sees the task as the slow, halting, often devious, but always incremental pursuit of justice and a civilized order within the limits of what is already given. The work of public life is likely to be a patient adding-on. The conservative knows what to teach. Teach the tried and true, teach what has been tested and proved. Teach the tradition, in other words, and its wisdom.

Those of radical temperament, on the other hand, seem to draw assurance not from skepticism but from the rational certainty of some social diagnosis. As Burke would have noticed, they are better at describing the pathologies of society than they are at the patient and often dull task of social reconstruction. If they know anything at all, the radicals, of every stripe, know what is wrong with us and with our world—parental neglect, government meddling, the media, the capitalist state, the liberal state, sin. They are tireless in pointing it out. Theirs is a cry, often strident, against injustice, and injustice is always more definite, more specific, and known with more certainty than the claims of justice. Injustice is painful and pain is particular, so their cries can be focused easily. Justice, however, is not particular. It often goes unnoticed, and perhaps it ought to. In a world where justice prevails, it will be the normal thing and thus will be quite unremarkable. It will not call out for comment, much less provoke loud cheers to match the strident protests always provoked by the pain of injustice.

Such moral certainty! This radical and fixed gaze at injustice, as well as its consequences for self-criticism, are beautifully captured by William Lee Miller when he considers how another kind of revolutionary—James Madison—offers sober contrast to this radical temperament. "The world has had a plentiful supply of revolutionaries since Madison's day," he writes:

> The modern revolutionary with his clenched fist and his barricades, his marching songs and his banners, has characteristically attributed the perennial problems of politics to the corrupt old order that he clenches his fist against; once that is overthrown, he implies, then humankind will awake in the springtime of the human spirit, when the problems of power, conflict, and interest have evaporated. Once the colonial oppressor is cast into the sea, once the royal tyrants are overthrown, once the dispossessors have themselves been dispossessed, once the working men of the world have united and thrown off their chains, once the white man with his racism has been replaced, once the arrogant males with their violence have been tamed by the soft sound of another voice, once the last king has been hanged in the entrails of the last priest, *then* the problems of power, the problems of self-interest, perhaps even the fact of social *evil* itself will be gone. It will depart with the departing oppressors and their evil system.[3]

A loud, but not a likely prospect. "If you attribute the entire stock of the world's social evil to the particular order you seek to overthrow," observes Miller, "then you and your movement are, by implication, altogether exculpated." You needn't look within yourself, much less upon the vices of the past. You are excused. Eyes fixed firmly upon the objects of reform are likely to shun the inward view and thus remain unacquainted with the egotism and arrogance found there. Such eyes are unlikely to be practiced at gazing upon the conflicts and power plays of one's own movement. They are eyes unlikely to note in such precincts the plain evidence of the old political problems being reborn. The sacrifice of reflective scrutiny is the price paid by those of radical temperament to purchase their admirable moral certainty.

Faced with so much conviction on what should be the content of moral education, those of liberal temperament stand in a particularly vulnerable position. They share the conservative skepticism of all rational utopias, but not the conservative confidence in and reliance on tradition, or the conservative assurance that they know just what this or that tradition includes. They share, on the other hand, the radicals' passion against injustice, but not their faith in rational utopias or their apparent affection for uprooting things. Hence, those imbued with the liberal temperament often appear to conservatives and radicals on either side of them to be simply uncertain. The liberal position must seem to them a variety of spineless flexibility, a sort of tolerance that makes disciples reluctant to take any stand with much conviction except for a general and abstract stand against injustice.

This description, of course, is a caricature. The liberal posture is actually quite a substantive one. Still, in every caricature are the elements of an accurate description. For all its rejection of rational utopias, there is, nonetheless, a place in the liberal temperament, a very large place, for the play of reason. But it belongs to individuals. Individuals are rational; societies are not. Societies are too complex. It follows that in the pantheon of the liberal imagination, liberty holds a favored place. Social arrangements are devised with an eye on preserving liberty. And so the essential expression of justice turns out to be procedural rather than either substantive or meritorious. The view is not that in a just society persons will get what they merit or even what they need, but rather that whatever they get is simply whatever they have gotten by a fair procedure.

Thus for individuals, according to the liberal, there is a presumed efficacy of reason. But against this play of reason the liberal temperament also involves a strong skepticism that anyone can claim to know what is good for everyone with anywhere near enough assurance to do it to them. The liberal temperament is a modest one. The point is not, therefore, that it entails some doubt about what the good life requires, but rather that it entails a reluctance to impose any particular version of the good life upon the collective. So what may appear a kind of flabby, empty tolerance is in fact a principled defense of liberty.

Among the utopian or evangelical responses to the threats of moral education, consider also the common observation that education is a public affair but our moral lives are and must remain essentially private. Such a divided world is familiar to those of liberal temperament because theirs is a spirit that often seems bent on constructing a world of boundaries—some have said walls or spheres—separating church and state, state and family, state and economy, education and the market, the public and the private sectors. Flowing from such divisions of the world is the view that unless moral education is limited simply to education for the office of citizen, we ought to keep it out of the schools. It belongs with the private, with those things beyond the sphere of education, at least insofar as that education is public. Persons must be free to find their own good, including the liberty to craft their own moral lives and to make their own mistakes. We do not know what goods there can be if we do not allow the pursuit of happiness the liberty it needs. So our liberal inheritance includes an insistence on pluralisms of many sorts, a tender appreciation of variety together with a tough-minded insistence on preserving those arrangements that prevent a few, any few, from imposing their image of the good life upon us all.

Thus the utopian threat stems from the fact that if it amounts to anything at all, that is, anything of definite moral substance, then moral education must aim at propagating some already formed opinion of the good life. And that formed vision is likely to be the world as imagined either by reformers responding to the visible faults of what already exists and seeking the remedy of some alternative, or the world as imagined by others aiming to keep in place a tradition formed in their imagination as an Eden or Arcadia. When confronted with such certainties, it is easy to retreat altogether and rely upon an education in liberty, an education aimed not at doing as much good as can be imagined but at doing simply as little harm as can be managed in order that the private search for the good life can go on in all its marvelous variety.

IV. Moral Philosophy and Moral Education

Discerning the limits of morality, and hence the limits of moral education, is as difficult a problem as discerning the limits of education. Clearly, the domain of whatever might be called moral education is ill

defined. Frame the subject as a program and your program will provoke a
variety of fears. Defend your program, and you are likely to find it rooted
in one or another of an apparently endless series of utopian visions that
human beings hanker after. To find some rescue from these difficulties,
one's first inclination, perhaps, is to turn to moral philosophy or if not to
moral philosophy strictly speaking, then to the vast body of moral reflection of which we are heirs. If we need a philosophy of moral education,
how could we do better? But alas! The prospects are dim.

The relation between moral philosophy and a philosophy of moral
education is by no means clear. There may be only the most fragile connection or there may be none at all. The study of moral philosophy no
doubt has its benefits. But we may doubt that moral improvement is
among them. To have been a student of moral philosophy might add to
one's moral education, but no more than the study of literature, or law, or
even economics. Whatever the moral character of professors of ethics, it
can hardly be attributed to their mastery of the subject. Indeed, they are
unlikely to be any more inclined to moral excellence than, say, professors
of economics or history. Nor are members of any such group likely to be
much distinguished in moral character from the rest of mankind. It
would never occur to professors of ethics that their teaching ought to be
evaluated by measuring the moral improvement of their students. It
seems plain, in short, that the study of moral philosophy offers no path of
special merit for the conduct of moral education.

Moral philosophy and the philosophy of moral education are distinct
projects. If moral philosophy is concerned with the architecture of the
moral institution of life, then the philosophy of moral education deals
with how we enter it; if moral philosophy studies the shape and content
of a mature conscience, then a philosophy of moral education asks how
we come to own that kind of conscience; if moral philosophy addresses
the nature of virtue, then a philosophy of moral education is concerned
with how virtue is spread and the worldly conditions of its spread. It is
one thing to know what courage is, another to know how it is acquired. It
is one thing to ask on what rational grounds our moral principles can be
understood to rest; another to ask by what path we acquire such principles. The first in each of these pairs poses a problem of moral philosophy,
the second, a problem for the philosophy of moral education. The rational foundations of our moral principles may differ from and even conceal
the educational path trod in their acquisition.

These contrasts suggest that moral philosophy and the philosophy of moral education, being different sorts of projects, have different starting points and different ends. If we think of the formation of desirable human characteristics, such as truthfulness, generosity, gentleness, sobriety, reliability, and the like, then it is universally agreed that such qualities are acquired. And if we think of that side of the moral life that deals with principles, rules, duties, rights and the like, it is also universally agreed that their corresponding virtue of conscientiousness is acquired. If we think of those qualities of moral discernment or what might be termed 'moral perception', qualities essential to a praiseworthy character, it will be agreed that they too are acquired. And finally, if we consider that side of the moral life that calls for prudence, it will be universally confessed that foresight is an acquired capacity. Virtue, in short, if not exactly learned, is at least acquired in some way. So, although moral philosophy may begin by *assuming* the presence of the moral institution of life, and proceed to forge its description and its foundations, the philosophy of moral education cannot. A philosophy of moral education must aim to understand the nature of moral *learning*. Moral philosophy, for example, may reveal to us reasons for the sacrifice of self-interest in the face of duty, even morally good reasons. But moral education asks not for that, but for the actual sacrifice of self-interest. No one, as I have suggested, would suppose that success in teaching moral philosophy to young people can be measured by measuring its moral effects. Moral philosophy is a subject and a tradition, an entire range of traditions, in fact. None should expect instruction in it to make anyone morally better. *But making persons morally better is precisely what moral education is about* and understanding the nature of that practice is what a philosophy of moral education must be about.[4]

This contrast between moral philosophy and a philosophy of moral education can be discovered in yet another way. Moral education must include an education in prudence, and thus any philosophy of moral education must find a prominent place for its formation. Yet considerations of prudence are placed beyond the moral by certain strains of modern moral theory. Bernard Williams, in his *Ethics and the Limits of Philosophy*,[5] marks a useful distinction that I shall employ throughout these essays, between the broad domain of the ethical and the more narrow limits of the moral, suggesting that the word 'morality' has taken on a rather specialized meaning in Western philosophy. Western philosophy, he says, "emphasizes certain ethical notions rather than others, developing in particular a special notion of obligation. It is, in fact, morality, the special system," he continues, "that demands a sharp boundary for itself (in demanding 'moral' and 'nonmoral' senses for words, for instance)." By forcing such a distinction upon us, this special system, as Williams calls it, places morality and prudence in opposition to one another.

A part of this opposition stems from the fact that prudence and morality, construed as interest and duty or as desire and obligation, can conflict. But this opposition of prudence and morality stems also from another direction, in particular from the claim that the moral quality of any life—in contrast to whatever other qualities it may possess—should not be dependent upon mere luck or good fortune. It should be unconditioned by the circumstances of life, that is, it should not be dependent upon wealth, station, or other gifts of life, partly because to say of someone that he or she is fortunate is not a moral commendation, and partly because the moral quality of a life must be something durable, whereas the gifts of wealth, station, health, reputation, good fortune, and the like are notoriously fragile, even fleeting. Prudence, insofar as it is rooted in self-interest, can be viewed largely, though not entirely, as aimed at gaining and securing such conditions of a good life, whereas the moral estimate of that life must concern itself with qualities that are unconditioned. Thus prudence, in consequence of its inherent nature, comes to fall on one side of a divide of which morality is found only on the other. Or so the argument goes.

Such considerations have played a major role in the history of moral philosophy to shape the divide separating morality and prudence as seen from the perspective of moral philosophy. Thus, What is my duty? is made, by many accounts, the entry question into philosophical ethics. For a philosophy of moral education, however, entry is gained more fully through the Socratic question, How ought one to live? I do not mean that a philosophy of moral education must supply an answer to the question, How ought one to live? It is more likely merely to presuppose some answer. I mean rather that we cannot be clear about the project of moral education without some view of what a well-lived life includes. But if we gain clarity on what a well-lived life includes, then we shall certainly recognize that in the conduct of such a life there must enter ethical considerations only some of which would be recognized as moral in the narrow modern sense of 'moral' that Bernard Williams identifies.

Aquinas, following Aristotle, regarded prudence as supreme among the moral or nontheological virtues. And indeed, it seems inescapable that however we answer the question, How ought one to live? the answer will exclude imprudence or folly. We cannot describe a well-lived life without allowing prudential considerations to enter. Here then are ethical considerations that are not obviously moral in the modern sense. They may be excluded from the moral by our moral philosophy, but they cannot be excluded from the domain of a philosophy of moral education. Once again it seems apparent that between moral philosophy and a philosophy of moral education whatever relation may exist, if any at all, is by no means transparent.

Moreover, if we fix our sight upon the necessities of a philosophy of moral education, then we shall see that such ethical considerations are probably, perhaps even necessarily, rooted in particularity, that is to say, in one's peculiar station or role, even in one's job, for example. Moral considerations are not considerations simply to some generalized or abstract self. It is not mankind in general that we are enjoined to love as we love ourselves, but our quite specific and particular neighbor. Nor do actual educational chances ever occur in relation to generalized or abstract persons. They only occur in relation to this or that person in these or those particular circumstances. Such ethical considerations may even be rooted in self-imposed standards that a person might invoke as representing the limits of allowable action to himself or herself alone. That a contemplated course of action, for instance, would be viewed by members of one's family as unworthy is, though not decisive, nonetheless a possible ethical consideration in deciding to refrain from doing it. Only from within the special moral system that Williams describes could such considerations be viewed as nonmoral. And only from within a system of moral development, like Kohlberg's, which rests upon the moral theory of that special system, could such considerations be viewed as belonging simply to an early stage in the development of moral judgment.

Related to this point is the familiar fact that in the classical vocabulary of ethics, none of the central terms are recognizably moral in the modern sense. They have to do with 'hitting the mark', 'not over-reaching', 'finding the mean', and the like. These are all images belonging to a vocabulary rich in terms of skill and craft, all having to do with matters of conduct that would be regarded as nonmoral within what Williams calls that modern system of morality. It is also important to note that if a view like that of the Greeks is allowed into a philosophy of moral education, as surely it must, then the resulting language of instruction will inevitably contain less talk of reprimand and sanction, of rule and obedience, and more talk of practice. Such a view of moral education is likely to contain a large component of dealing with the skills of living. And along with this notion of practicing such skills will come the notion that there are tools for living.[6] In short, if it be asked, How ought one to live? a large part of the answer will come back—Skillfully! Prudentially!

The different placement of prudence in these two philosophical perspectives—the classical and the modern—is powerful evidence that we need to distinguish a broad range of ethical considerations from the narrower range of moral reasons that belong within what Williams calls the modern moral system. Moral education, in the limited and special sense required by the moral system, can perhaps do without instruction in prudence. But if moral education is to capture the range of our ordinary interests, then it cannot do without instruction in prudence. In short, if we rightly construe the domain of this project to develop a philosophy of moral education, then prudence will stand, if not at center stage, then very near it. It will take a leading role, and in that respect, a philosophy of moral education will have to be marked off as having a domain that differs substantially from certain versions of moral philosophy. The connection between the two is by no means obvious.

Thus, to the rather traditional question of moral philosophy, What is my duty? and to the Socratic question, How ought I to live? one needs to add the question, How does anyone get that way? This is the central question of a philosophy of moral education. The matter of crucial importance is not so much What is courage?, for example, nor even the next most general question, What is the nature of virtue? but rather, How is virtue spread about? What is an education in virtue?

V. The Idea of Conscience

It is partly to avoid these narrow limits of the modern conception of 'the moral' that I choose to speak of moral education as the formation of conscience. Speaking in this way locates the subject in a different way and gives it a larger domain. The project at hand deals not with moral education in the narrow modern sense of 'moral' in which 'the moral' and 'the nonmoral' are contrasted. The concern here is rather with the formation of conscience in *all* its voices, including excellence in the crafts and judgments of skill as well as folly. In order to avoid the need to constantly enter these caveats, however, I shall continue to speak of moral education, but shall always mean by it the formation of conscience.

But why 'conscience'? The selection of the term has advantages and disadvantages. It is hardly ever used in contemporary speech. Nor do any of the currently contending views of moral education employ the term. It does not enter at all, for example, into the theory or practice of values clarification. Nor would anyone think of describing the Kohlbergian stages in the development of moral judgment as stages of conscience. 'Conscience' is a term discarded partly, I suppose, because it is thought by many to represent a long-rejected view of faculty psychology. It is, in short, a quaint term to be classed perhaps with other quaint terms, like 'naughty' and 'wicked', and perhaps even 'duty' and 'honor', these latter being terms used nowadays mostly in the context of military conduct. This lack of common usage may seem a disadvantage in focusing upon moral education as the formation of conscience. But if that is so, it is a disadvantage with another side. The very absence of the term from current speech may allow it the more easily to receive whatever meaning can be constructed for it, either ostensively or by usage.

There may, however, be disadvantages of another sort in making the idea of conscience central to our grasp of moral education. The term is not *entirely* without contemporary usage. But the meaning discovered there tends to be misleading. To many, 'conscience' refers apparently to that dour, forbidding, internal voice that knows only how to say "No" to every pleasure and "Yes" to the performance of every hard duty. The term, to many an ear, rings with overtones associated entirely with a limited Kantian or Puritan conscience that sees the whole of the moral life as cast within those narrow limits that I have said already we do well to avoid imposing, limits that tend to cast the term entirely as the voice of duty.

By 'conscience', as shall become abundantly clear, I mean something much simpler. I mean simply *reflexive judgment about things that matter.* Each of us from time to time renders judgment on our actions and even on our own character. This is a fact known to everyone, a fact beyond question. Equally beyond doubt is the fact that we can render such judgments both in prospect and in retrospect, both in presenting to ourselves what we are about to do as well as in evaluating things already done.[7] The point I want to stress about this experience is not that it involves judgment of moral approval or disapproval, but rather that it is judgment that each of us makes in our own case. It is reflexive judgment. This reflexive judgment of approval and disapproval is what I mean by 'conscience'. Thus, conscience, in the sense intended here, is not represented by the

judgment of others on ourselves because that kind of judgment is not reflexive. And for the same reason, neither is conscience represented primarily by our own judgment on the conduct of others. That is not reflexive judgment either.

This focus upon the reflexive character of conscience is meant to preserve two features of common experience. The first is that conscience,
however conceived, is something imminent. Judgments of conscience
are self-given. That is their imminent feature. They also have authority,
however, and authority, it seems, comes always as though from a distant,
impartial, disinterested perspective. Thus, in most matters of social interest, we would not be permitted to stand as judges in our own case. To do
so would be to risk bias. The authority of conscience demands the distance of judgment as afforded by the perspective of a third party. This
means that the judgments of conscience must be understood as both imminent and distant, both self-given and authoritative.

The second point preserved by this focus upon conscience as reflexive
judgment is that conscience, so understood, is capable of commenting
upon matters that lie far beyond the boundaries of morality narrowly
conceived. There is self-appraisal even in such things as washing the car,
planting the garden, getting dressed, or crafting a good sentence. Although these are not normally viewed as matters of morality, they are
without exception things that can be done well or badly in our own eyes.
They are activities subject to the reflexive commentary of conscience.
That it allows the extension of reflexive judgment on things that matter
to activities of ordinary life is a considerable advantage of the term 'conscience'. Not only is it capable of taking on what meaning may be useful
to give it, but that meaning can be extended to create a domain sufficiently enlarged to encompass our ordinary nonphilosophical interests in
the conduct of moral education. It can incorporate self-judgment not
only in relation to moral conduct in the modern narrow sense of 'moral',
but also to personal ideals, social memberships, and standards of craft, including even the exercise of intellectual skills.

Nonetheless, to suppose that the character of moral education can be
captured by relying on so simple and old-fashioned a concept as conscience will be thought by many, even in their most charitable moments,
to be simple-minded. Conscience, they will think, is too variable, too
subjective, too prone to bias and error to be of any use in understanding
moral education. The very notion of conscience will be thought to have
been supplanted long ago by psychological, developmental, and philo-

sophical studies of sophistication and scientific validity. They will suggest that the notion of conscience survives only as an artifact of intellectual history, a relic to be deposited in the attic along with other detritus of our primitive (read "Puritan" or "Victorian") origins. And the idea that moral education might be understood as the inculcation of norms will be instinctively rejected by most students of philosophy and education on the grounds that it constitutes a hopeless endorsement of the status quo, provides no basis for social and moral criticism, and lacks any fundamental understanding of moral change or growth. Nonetheless, I propose to show that out of such archaic ideas, rightly understood, can be fashioned a fresh and more powerful view of the nature of moral education and its conduct than we now have available to us. Moral education is the formation of conscience. Conscience is reflexive judgment on things that matter and is formed by the acquisition of norms, norms that take on the role of governance. These three claims constitute the rough outlines of all that follows.

There are considerable advantages to any view that places the formation of conscience at the heart of moral education. Such a view accords with common experience of both the imminence and authority of the judgments of conscience, at the same time that it enlarges the scope of moral education to include an education in a variety of prudential skills. But to these may now be added the further advantage that such a view of conscience fits well with judgments of considerable standing in the philosophical tradition. For example, Aquinas's view is that conscience is reason commenting on conduct.[8] Conscience, he says, is reflexive judgment exercised in specific cases. Of the two principal elements in this formula, namely, reflexivity and particularity, he emphasizes the particularity of judgment, whereas Kant emphasizes its reflexivity. The term *conscientia*, writes Aquinas, "may be resolved into *cum alio scientia* (knowledge applied to an individual case)."[9] "Conscience," Kant says, "is an instinct to pass judgment upon ourselves" in accord with moral laws,[10] and he goes on to contrast this judgment of the self measured against moral laws with another kind of reflexive judgment measuring the self against rules of prudence. He says, "Prudence reproaches; conscience accuses."[11] Instead of focusing upon this difference between the moral and the prudential, however, I wish to focus upon their likeness, which is to say, the reflexivity that Kant and Aquinas find in both kinds of judgment. It is the reflexive character of judgment that I have argued is essential to conscience. Each of us has the capacity to be judge of our own conduct and of our own affections. This is *judgment that each of us makes in our own case*. Conscience is often described, in fact, as an interior voice of the self speaking to the self, offering advice, counsel, judgment, and reproach.

In addition to particularity and reflexivity, John Stuart Mill remarks upon a third aspect of conscience, namely, its associated feelings, a feature present already in this formula of reflexivity and particularity, but not explicit. Mill says of the "internal sanction of duty" that its "binding force . . . consists in the existence of a mass of feeling which must be broken through in order to do what violates our standard of right, and which, if we do nevertheless violate that standard, will probably have to be encountered afterwards in the form of remorse. Whatever theory we have of the nature or origin of conscience, *this is what essentially constitutes it*."[12]

In these three features—particularity, reflexivity, and the associated moral emotions—we have a characterization of conscience which, if not complete, is nevertheless complete enough to allow for a full account of the elements of moral education. The formation of conscience, when understood in this way, is a central educational task. In the chapters that follow, I shall advance certain claims about that task of formation. I intend to remark, in short, not upon conscience formed, but upon conscience being formed, and not upon the rational foundations of what judgments conscience may or may not deliver, but how those judgments come to be shaped and take up residence in conscience, what it means, in short, to say that they *govern* conduct.[13] The first and most basic claim is that the formation of conscience can be described as the acquisition of norms, a process that, for convenience, I shall refer to simply as 'normation'.[14] Normation, when viewed from another perspective, is the process by which governance, that is, the effective regulation of conduct, is made possible.

This focus upon the acquisition of norms rather than their validity, their logical status, or their justification, is the distinctive feature of these essays. This shift of focus illustrates in an interesting way how standard versions of philosophical questions often receive fresh formulations when cast as questions in the philosophy of education. It needs only a little reflection to see that it is not, first of all, in the validation of norms or in their criticism, but in their acquisition that we shall find the rudiments of moral education, perhaps the rudiments of any education. Norm acquisition is the central phenomenon of moral education, the matter that most needs elaboration and understanding. Issues in epistemology, for example, when viewed from the perspective of a philosophy of education, tend to become focused less upon problems of knowledge and truth and more upon problems of learning. 'Learning', however, is a concept seldom granted a role center stage in the history of philosophy. It was admittedly a question much favored by Wittgenstein to ask how the use of a certain term could be learned. Answering such a question is nearly always illuminating. To pursue it, however, is merely to employ a useful tool of philosophical method. It is not meant to open a central topic of investigation.

This claim of general philosophical neglect might be countered by showing that 'learning' is not as neglected by philosophers as it may seem. It is, after all, a concept of central importance in the Platonic corpus. In truth, however, it figures there primarily as a vehicle to carry the burden of the so-called doctrine of recollection. 'Learning' is a notion that for some reason philosophers have been content to leave to psychologists to study.[15] Whatever may be the truth about this historical claim, attention here is riveted upon the acquisition of norms, not their justification or their logical status in inquiry. The first claim of these essays is that the formation of conscience is to be found in the acquisition of norms.

The second claim is that normation, contrary to what Aquinas seems to hold, is not a special instance of the acquisition of knowledge, although it implies possession of various kinds of knowledge. My meaning is analogous to what Aristotle intends when he suggests that friendship, though not a virtue, nevertheless implies the possession of virtue. Friendship is a relation, but virtues are traits of character or settled dispositions of choice. Friendship, however, assumes the possession of virtue because, in its paramount form, it is a relation among persons requiring an approximate equality of virtue. And it implies a certain kind of knowledge only because the exercise of virtue requires the exercise of practical judgment, which requires, in turn, a kind of knowledge. Yet friendship cannot be described as a kind of knowledge any more than it can be described as among the virtues. Normation is just as distant from being a special kind of knowledge acquisition as friendship is. Friendship is related to the possession of knowledge only because it presupposes the possession of virtue. But friendship cannot be described as virtue, nor can normation be described as a kind of knowledge.

There is only such a distant connection between the acquisition of norms and knowledge, learning, or coming to know. Yet, if normation is not a kind of coming to know or even coming to believe but remains nevertheless the central business of moral education, it follows that such education cannot be understood primarily as a matter of inculcating or stimulating right belief, or even right reason. Moreover, because of the intimate conceptual connection between 'teaching' and 'learning', and between 'learning' and 'coming to know', it remains problematic in what sense, if any, we can speak of normation as an aim of teaching or even of learning, even though there remains no question at all that it is a central task, perhaps the very core, of education. It is admittedly odd that anything so central to education should have so little strong and direct connection to knowing, to learning, to teaching, or to coming to know.

As a third claim, I wish to defend Mill's view of "a mass of feeling" as what *essentially* constitutes conscience. The central role of feeling in the formation of conscience is implicit in the fact that normation necessarily structures the emotions of self-assessment. Normation is what gives specific content to the emotions of guilt, shame, pride, regret, and, as Mill suggests, remorse, among others, and thus makes it possible for self-deception to have its risks. These emotions stand in a peculiarly strong relation to the formation of conscience because, like the judgments of conscience, these are essentially reflexive emotions. They are emotions of self-assessment, emotions in which the self stands in judgment on the self.[16] In that respect they differ from other emotions, such as fear and hope, which must assume a prominent position in any full exposition of moral education, but which are not essentially reflexive and therefore are not essentially structured by normation.[17] These are difficult claims. They require and will receive extensive explication.

VI. Voices

Why now this talk of the voices of conscience? There are several answers. The first is found in the familiar fact that conscience speaks. When reference to conscience occurs at all, it is likely to include references to conscience having voice. When someone says, "Listen to what your conscience says," we have no difficulty grasping in a general way what is meant. That conscience speaks is a deeply entrenched idea.

Moreover, it is a matter accepted virtually without argument that conscience speaks in various ways. Reflexive judgment plays a role in a large variety of human activities, and therefore the province of moral education, conceived as the formation of conscience, extends far beyond the boundaries of what is usually assumed to be its proper domain. Think, for example, of standards of excellence in the practice of any craft in the light of which the self may reflexively comment on its performance, and consider not simply those standards themselves, their rational justification and critique, but their acquisition, their coming to assume the task of governance. Call this *the conscience of craft*.

Think also of the critical reflexive voice remarking on our behavior in retrospect and prospect when viewed in the light of our attachments, our relations to one another, in short, our membership in a group, more or less inclusive, ranging from family to neighborhood to region and beyond. Call this the voice of *conscience as membership*. With the conscience of membership come also the possibilities of loyalty and citizenship or the standards of public life. This voice of conscience asks us to consider the centrality and the limits of what fidelity to various groups requires.

Reflexive judgment speaks also in a voice that stands against the inclinations of self-interest. Call this *the conscience of sacrifice*. When the conscience of membership speaks, as it often will, in partisan ways, even in ways so narrowly partisan as to invoke the accusation of being prejudicial, then the conscience of sacrifice is likely to speak against it, advancing the claims of impartiality. When that happens, the conscience of membership and the conscience of sacrifice may enter into an awkward quarrel.

Then too, conscience speaks in *the voice of memory*, out of a body of recollection, reminding us of ancestral promises and the like. In this and other ways, it brings objects of the past into the present to take their place in forming standards of reflexive judgment. And finally, *conscience addresses us out of imagination*, asking that we measure the present against what imagination proclaims would be the character of our community if our community were all that it ought to be. The angels of our better nature speak, when they speak to us at all, in the tones of such a heightened moral imagination and memory of attachment.

Learning and Knowing as Hearing

So conscience speaks, and it speaks in different voices. But there are other reasons for this focus on voice. In Western philosophy knowing is presented largely (though by no means entirely) as a species of seeing. In biblical texts and other bodies of reflective moral literature, knowing is often a matter of hearing. There we find a closer conceptual connection between hearing and doing than we are accustomed to.[18] Remnants of this thoughtful union remain in English when, for example, parent says to errant child, "You heard me!" implying that if there really is hearing, then doing must follow. Hearing without doing can only be disobedience.

Also, of course, there is the naval version "Now hear this! Now hear this!" meaning "Now do this!" So a second answer to the question, Why this talk of voices? is that I seek not merely to preserve, but to highlight the role of speech and hearing in the formation of conscience and its pedagogy and the close union that is sometimes forged between hearing and doing. This link of hearing and doing, together with its connection to the idea of conscience as voice, is extended in an interesting way to include education when Vicki Hearne reminds us,

> 'Obedience' comes from an old French word that means 'to hear' or 'to heed', 'to pay attention to'. The great trainers of every kind of animal, from parakeet to dog to elephant, have said for millennia that you cannot get an animal to heed you unless you heed the animal; obedience in this sense is a symmetrical relationship.[19]

There is also, of course, a grammatical sense of voice—active and passive[20]—as well as a musical meaning, suggesting treble, bass, harmony, and counterpoint, to which we might add dissonance, discord, and even clash. This allusion to dissonance and clash merits comment. It often seems (to me, at least) that a major project of moral philosophy—less nowadays than twenty years ago—can be framed as the effort to demonstrate which among competing moral theories—deontic, consequentialist, intuitionist, for instance—is logically the more fundamental or morally the more satisfying. It often seems a project aimed, therefore, at uncovering which among them, or which combination of them, constitutes the one to which the others can be reduced without remainder and thus truly offers the foundations of morality. This reductionist project will be rightly rejected in a philosophy of moral education that attends to the formation of conscience, keeping in mind the variety and possible dissonance of its voices. There is no need to suppose that those voices ever speak in unison or in tight harmony or ever reach repose in some kind of tonic resolution. To speak of the formation of conscience is to lay aside this reductionist or foundational project of moral theory. This is still another reason to frame our educational thought in terms of voice.

If, for example, we hanker to advance the educational formation of conscience by introducing dilemmas for discussion, then we ought to perceive that the dilemmas that count are those that arise from the conversation, even the quarrels among the voices of conscience. The reductionist or foundationalist project of moral theory would quiet those quarrels; the project at hand would elaborate them. As I have already argued, a life without ties is barren, but when human bonds deconstruct to human biases and hence to prejudices, then pleadings for impartiality and duty may find their voice and speak up. And when a resistance to all prejudices takes shape as a lack of firm moral ideals, then pleadings of attachments and ideals may have their play. A developed conscience must be one in which such quarrels continue and are even cultivated, deepened, and elaborated. A mature conscience does not need to be one in which these quarrels and disputes are necessarily resolved.

Development

We may think of conscience as having voices, the voices of craft, membership, sacrifice, memory, and imagination. But if we aim to stir the conversation among these voices, then we ought not think of them as coming into existence in some developmental sequence. Rather, we ought to think of these different voices as standing side by side. None come first, none come later, and certainly none should be conceived as lost or superseded in the formation of conscience. I do not suppose there is any definable and invariable sequence by which these voices emerge through several stages; no single story can be told of their formation. There is development, of course, but it may be that all these voices are present at the beginning; certainly, all must be present at the end. Development is simply their elaboration and composition, perhaps even a kind of cultivated quarrel that each voice may find a fitting place in the four- or five- or eight-part chorus of conscience. Development need not require the death of any one of these voices in order that another may be born, nor should our understanding of development require it.

This, of course, is a controversial position. It amounts to a rejection of the now widely accepted stage theory of cognitive moral development as embodied in the work of Lawrence Kohlberg and his followers. But three points should be kept clearly in mind. The first is that Kohlberg's work was concerned mostly with the cognitive development of moral judgment, and moral judgment is only a small part of what a philosophy of moral education must include. How small a part must remain an open question. Secondly, Kohlberg's approach, in addition to its grounding in

genetic epistemology, borrows heavily from a quite particular version of
modern moral theory, variously described as a neo-Kantian or 'right reasons' approach. But as I have noted already, an adequate moral philosophy may omit much that is needed for an adequate philosophy of moral
education. It is not obvious, for example, that judgments of skill are
moral judgments by any view of moral philosophy. Still, as I have argued,
their development must be explicated by and incorporated into any satisfactory philosophy of moral education, not because such judgments are
moral judgments but because they are reflexive judgments, and because
the exercise of reflexive judgment is what testifies to the acquisition of
norms and to the presence of conscience. Their development must be attended to because they are of the representative sort that enters into, indeed constitutes, the formation of conscience. So a stage theory of moral
education is here rejected partly out of a concern with the formation of
conscience rather than the more narrow matter of moral judgment. It is
rejected also out of a desire to be more inclusive in drawing upon the literature of moral reflection and particularly upon its history. It stems finally from a concern to focus upon the problems of educational practice
rather than upon the concerns of moral philosophy.

To this outline of the project to follow must be added one further caution. The central problem is governance, self-governance primarily, but
also civil governance. It follows that this project offers no newly minted
fundamental moral doctrine as the central content of moral education,
no doctrine that moral education must be at heart an education in caring
or in respect or in honoring the dignity of individuals. A philosophy of
moral education is not an evangelical project. It contains no missionary
moral message that just has to be spread about. Nor can it be expected to
still the voice of moral skepticism and offer any solid proof, for example,
that murder is wrong, that gossip is not a good thing, and that we ought
to love one another. The project is neither evangelical nor foundational.
It is concerned simply with unwrapping the ordinary moral life of human
communities. A philosophy of moral education, like moral philosophy itself, can only be addressed to those of an already formed and serious
moral conscience. It can only be addressed to members of an already
formed moral community concerned with the task of improving that life
and preserving it in the next generation. In short, the view adopted here
is that central to a philosophy of moral education there lie not moral
questions, but questions of moral learning, not What is virtue? or What is
the standard of duty? but How does anybody 'get that way'? The central

question is not a question of ethics but of education, not a problem of moral philosophy but of the philosophy of education.

This perspective flows from the view that philosophy is essentially engaged in what I have described elsewhere as unwrapping the ordinary, namely, revealing for understanding what we already know to be so in the moral experience of an existing moral community. It seeks simply to expose those truths and restore to them the power of truth. The *aim* is that at the end of each step the reader will say, "I knew that." The *hope* is that to such a test the reader might be disposed to add, "But now I understand and see better how to educate."

Chapter 2

Moral Education as Norm Acquisition

By 'moral education' I mean the formation of conscience, and by 'conscience', the exercise of reflexive judgment about things that matter. The argument is that this formation occurs through the acquisition of norms. Thus, the agenda for analysis is set. What is a norm? What is meant by norm acquisition? What is meant by saying that norms govern conduct?

I. Norm and Normation: The Analysis

By 'norm' I mean 'social norm,' not 'statistical norm'. Nor, by 'social norm', do I refer simply to 'the done thing'. Norm acquisition is not to be confused with anything popularly meant by 'socialization', namely, a dumb acquiescence in custom. A social norm is not simply the modal tendency of behavior within some social group. On the contrary, we may take as *a kind of paradigm* that a social norm is a rule of conduct, not the formulation of a modal pattern of behavior. It does not describe how persons behave; rather, it prescribes how they think they ought to behave. It is not merely a statement of what people do, but a rule formulating what they think they ought to do. Social norms thus are paradigmatically rules of 'ought' and 'should'. If persons within some social group conduct themselves in ways that comport with norms significant to them, then there will be observable regularities in their conduct. Yet, merely from that regularity of behavior, we cannot infer the presence (or absence) of any definite social norm, as we might if 'social norm' were a statistical concept.

I describe this formulation as presenting a *kind* of paradigm because, as will become apparent later, I believe neither that social norms can always be described as rules nor that a moral life consists simply in following rules. Ideals and exemplars also have standing as models and thus provide standards of a sort. However, I do believe that what I say here about the acquisition of norms as rules will apply equally to the acquisition of ideals and to the ways by which exemplars receive their status as models. One connection, for example, between norms as rules on the one hand and as ideals and exemplars on the other is provided by the fact that, in both cases, some standard is presented for governance, for the guidance of reflexive judgment; and it is, after all, this acquisition of reflexive judgment that I aim to describe as normation and as constituting the heart of moral education.

Compliance, Obedience, and Observance

It is easy to imagine a social group the behavior of whose members is at odds with its norms. Suppose the observable behavior of twenty percent accords with a long-standing situational rule of conduct (say, a norm praising cooperation under certain conditions), but the behavior of the remaining eighty percent regularly does not accord with the norm. We cannot infer that in such a divided social group the norm of cooperation has changed or been abandoned. The distribution tells us very little. Beyond merely observing compliance or noncompliance, we need to know whether the miscreant majority feel guilty, ashamed, or remorseful about their noncooperation and whether the seeming cooperative behavior among the minority is genuine or only apparent. If persons present one face for public inspection and reserve another for their private moments, if they aim to shield their conduct, not alone for the sake of prudence, but to escape from shame, then in doing so, they advertise the existence of a norm and testify that it governs even as its demands are ignored. The noncompliant ones, merely by their noncompliance, no more establish the absence of the norm than the compliant ones, by their compliance, establish its presence.

If compliant behavior is insufficient to confirm the presence of a social norm, then what would be sufficient? Observant behavior comes to mind. But already the vocabulary becomes complex, unwieldy, and possibly confusing. How might observant and compliant behavior differ? We may say that behavior (B) 'accords with' some norm (N) if N describes B. Thus, to say, for example, that the behavior of the planets (their orbits) accords with the laws of motion is to say simply that such laws describe their orbits. It is not to suggest that such laws are being obeyed. Nothing resembling obedience occurs here. The planets do not obey nor do they disobey.

Beyond such talk of behavior that accords with a norm, as in the case of planetary orbits, there lies a vocabulary of 'compliance'. One might comply with a senseless bureaucratic rule or legal edict, for example. One might do whatever the rule directs under threat of harm, but without granting to such a rule or edict any authority. Such compliance may be driven by threat, but it need not be. Complying with a rule may simply be the most convenient thing to do, something done merely because non-compliance, though rationally and perhaps even morally more reasonable, is nevertheless a greater nuisance. To comply with such edicts is merely to 'take them into account' in the way one takes into account the weather by altering one's dress, or an aching back by altering one's stride. So behavior might either accord with a norm or comply with a norm. Considered as temporal and physical events, the difference will be indiscernible to witnesses, though experientially they are quite distinct.

To speak of behavior obedient to some norm is to invoke yet another vocabulary. A obeys N, or A's behavior is obedient to N, only when N is viewed as legitimately commanding. 'Obedience', in short, is a concept that applies only when a rule or norm is prescriptive rather than descriptive and when the behavior is compliant, but not *merely* compliant. Obedience requires an important addition to compliance, namely acceptance of the *authority* of the rule. When obedience to a norm within some social group deconstructs into mere compliance, then, as I shall try to establish, we have what has been called alienation.

Beyond this progression starting with 'accordance' moving to 'compliance' and thus to 'obedience', there lies yet a fourth vocabulary. We all know of conduct that is not in accord with some normative rule or standard, and which therefore cannot be described as either compliant or obedient to it, but which at the same time is undertaken in manifest admission of the norm's authority. Think, for example, of cases in which behavior is observant of a norm but nevertheless disobedient, cases in which the authority of a norm to command is granted, but the agent elects to disobey. By describing behavior as observant, in contrast to compliant or obedient, I mean to pick out just those features of conduct that display the agent's admission of the authority of a norm, leaving aside all questions of obedience or disobedience. Thus, behavior may be disobedient yet at the same time observant of a norm. By this convention, behavior obedient to a norm is necessarily observant, but observant behavior may be either obedient or disobedient.

One might, for example, lie and then feel guilty about doing so, thus disobeying a moral rule and at the same time acknowledging its authority.

We cannot describe such behavior as being in accord with a norm or compliant with it and certainly not as obedient to it. But we can describe it as observant of the rule. Behavior observant in this way, but disobedient, will often be concealed. In fact, the reach for concealment on the part of an agent, as I have noted, is one thing that counts (though not decisively) in favor of the view that such behavior is undertaken in observance of the norm. Concealment suggests that such conduct is undertaken by an agent who acknowledges the authority of the norm to command, otherwise concealment would not matter. Establishing that conduct is observant in this sense is sufficient to establish also the presence of a social norm, whereas compliance or noncompliance, with whatever frequency either occurs, is insufficient. As an empirical matter, the demeanor of an agent acting in departure from a standard of conduct, and the response of others to that deviance, will carry more weight in establishing the operable presence of a social norm or even of an entire moral order than will evidence of compliance. We learn very little from the fact that behavior corresponds to what a social norm would prescribe. Such conduct might fit any one of these four drastically different descriptions. However, the response of an agent and of observers to *departures* from the norm tells us a great deal as to which of these four descriptions is appropriate.

Given this array of distinctions, the interesting cases to study turn out not to be those of obedience or disobedience, but those of defiance. Refusing to sit in the back of the bus in the days of Jim Crow is not so much an act of disobedience as it is an act of defiance, a certain *kind* of noncompliance. The point of such action is not simply to violate the rule, but to reveal that the rule or norm lacked authority to begin with and that what had appeared as obedience to it was not that at all. It was only compliance, the sort of behavior often produced in the face of threat, the only kind, perhaps, that threat *can* produce. Such defiance, however, can be and often is undertaken in obedience to (and therefore observant of) some *other* norm to which one *is* being obedient. One disobeys a Jim Crow law in order to affirm some standard of dignity and integrity to which one *is* being observant. 'Civil disobedience' is too simple a phrase to describe an action undertaken not simply to disobey, but to repudiate one practiced rule of behavior in order to affirm another. It involves not merely disobedience, but the repudiation of one expression of moral authority and its replacement by another. And therein lies its threat. If such behavior were not an act of repudiation, it would have no moral point. It would be merely another case of disobedience, that is to say, a matter of an entirely different order.

Norm Acquisition—Criteria

These conceptual points about the acquisition of social norms can be elaborated in another way. Let us ask by what criteria we deliver third-person judgments identifying observant behavior. By what criteria do we judge that the behavior of some third person is observant of a social norm? Under what conditions would we say of someone that he or she has learned or acquired a social norm? It will be helpful to study this matter through an example as distant as possible from any moral rule and perhaps even from anything that we would typically think of as a social norm. How about a rule of grammar? We might ask what would have to be satisfied in order that we might say of someone that he or she has learned or acquired a rule of grammar as a norm of speech or writing.

I start at so remote a point partly in search of clarifying simplicity. Even at the risk of triviality, I seek a case in which the essentials of norm acquisition can be examined directly without having to peer through any thick cloud of surrounding moral sentiment. But in addition to this matter of simplicity is also the matter of scope. I hope to show, without need of further comment, that norm acquisition, though central to anything we might call moral education, nevertheless extends far beyond the domain of moral rules and principles, moral dilemmas, or moral problems. It extends, for example, even to learning rules of craft and decorum or rules of courtesy and 'getting along' at work, in hospitals, or within schools and other institutions. But even beyond this large domain, I want to establish that the criteria we employ in third-person claims of norm acquisition apply also to third-person judgments on the acquisition of ideals and exemplars. The process of norm acquisition, in short, like the business of moral education itself, covers a domain that includes both the moral and the prudential and even much in addition to that.

Such a remote and apparently distant case through which to explore these points can be found by considering the simple rule of grammar that subject and verb should agree in person and number. By what criterion can we say confidently that another person has learned to observe this rule of grammar, that is, has come to speak in observance of it? One test might be that the person can state the rule on demand. But this is plainly inadequate. One's speech, quite likely, will have been guided by this rule long before any encounter with its formulation. Being able to state the rule is neither necessary nor sufficient. Nor is it necessary or sufficient that one be able to identify a correct formulation of the rule as might be requested in a typical paper and pencil test. A second possibility would be to record the degree to which a person's speech accords with the rule as revealed in a performance test of some kind. But this too is clearly insufficient for saying that the person is observant of the rule. One's speech might accord with it yet not be governed by it.

Suppose we note, however, that A corrects his or her own speech and that of others in the face of departures from the rule. In that case, we will be justified in saying that the rule actually governs A's speech, that A actually applies the rule appropriately first to himself or to herself and then to others. Only under this third condition could we say that A has acquired the rule *as a norm*, that is, has become observant of it. Indeed, to say that A has acquired the rule as a norm, is to say precisely that *it is the norm that governs*.

In short, the criterion that norm acquisition has occurred, that someone has acquired a norm, even in so simple and remote a case as a rule of grammar, is *not* that his or her behavior accords with it, or that he or she can state the rule when asked or even pick it out from a list. Learning to repeat the rule on demand or learning that or knowing that the words "subject and verb should agree in person and number" state a rule of grammar—these kinds of 'learning to x' or 'knowing that p' are not the kinds of learning and knowing that we have in mind when we think and speak of acquiring or learning norms. If there is learning or knowing at all in normation, it is certainly not learning or knowing of this kind. If there is learning at all here, but not learning to, or learning that, or knowing that, then what kind of learning is it? The linguistic expression closest to capturing the phenomena being described here—if we aim to characterize it as learning at all—would be some form of the expression 'learning to be', as in "Anderson is learning to be more tolerant."

The Essential Presence of a Critical Attitude

If a person corrects his or her own speech and that of others in the face of error or irregularity, then something in addition to mere compliance or obedience is going on. This step requires the adoption of a certain critical attitude toward departures from the rule, the attitude that in some sense these departures are wrong, that these errors are indeed errors and not simply artful innovations or merely optional ways of doing things. The presence of this critical attitude—apparently a part of our very criterion for saying someone has acquired a norm—is the attitude that such departures call out for correction. With this step the notion is invoked that the rule does more than merely state a social expectation. The rule, *in the composition of the person who acquires it*, must receive the status of a rule of rectitude, a statement of what is correct. That this has occurred is precisely what is signaled by the adoption of a certain critical attitude toward error, a propensity to offer amendment, criticism, or correction in the face of departures from the rule. This is what signals, *in the make-up of the learner*, that the rule is binding not only upon his or her own self, but upon others as well. It has become a kind of public rule, a rule of right.

The vital matter to discern in this step is that in the acquisition of a norm, we do not start out with a 'rule of right' at all. Still, in my acquisition of any norm, if the norm makes no reference beyond me and my conscience to the conduct of others and its appraisal, then it will have no standing as a norm of my own conscience. In other words, *the rule cannot have the status of a rule of rectitude for me unless for me it has the status of a rule of rectitude for others*. To say that such a rule governs in my case is to say that *for me* it has the status of a rule of speech for anyone who cares to speak English. Only with this additional step, only with the adoption of this critical attitude in the face of error, does the rule become the expression of an 'ought'. Only then can I be said to have acquired a rule that can be said to govern in any sense at all.

With the appearance of this critical attitude, there emerge the ideas of 'correct' and 'incorrect', 'right' and 'wrong', 'propriety', 'impropriety', 'social gaffe', and possibly even 'moral breach'. An enormous range of norms and rules and departures from them is covered in that range from 'incorrect' to 'moral breach'. Which it will be depends upon the setting and the weight attached to the norm in question. To get into a cab in Paris on one's way to the railroad station and to pronounce "gare" as "guerre," especially in a time of civil violence, may produce embarrassment, even momentary damage to one's self-esteem, but none would count it as a moral breach. At worst, it will lead the driver to ask nervously, "Where's the battle?"

These notions of 'correct', 'incorrect', and so forth are not *produced* by the adoption of this critical attitude in learning. Their presence is a *part* of that critical attitude, not a consequence of it. Between the acquisition of a social norm and assuming the critical attitude that departures from the norm add up to error, we have not a causal relation, nor even a sequential relation, but a part-whole relation, a structural feature, in other words, of what we mean by norm acquisition. The acquisition of norms includes the acquisition of critical standards for judgment. To ask how we get from the acquisition of a social norm to the adoption of this critical attitude, is like asking how we get from Boston to New England. We have arrived already, but not because the travel is swift or the distance slight.

. . . And Caring to Be Correct

This critical attitude encompasses also a kind of caring. One would not allow the rule that subject and verb should agree in person and number to be the measure of one's own speech, let alone a standard by which to judge and correct the speech of others (even sotto voce), and therefore adopt it as a standard *of* speech, unless one *cared* to speak and write correctly and unless one supposed that others cared, that is, unless it has come to matter. Conscience is reflexive judgment about things that matter. The reflexive announcement of the self must be that rectitude matters, in craft and speech no less than in morality and propriety. What are we to imagine if called upon to picture a person who, when confronted with departures from the rule, makes corrections, but apparently does not care to be correct or care that others are correct? This is an odd conjecture, but it is precisely its oddity that reveals the tight logical connection between norm acquisition and this attitude of caring, that is, the attitude that rectitude matters.

We discover in this 'correcting, but not caring to be correct' one mark (there are others) of a kind of lethargy, a kind of indolent indifference toward the rule, perhaps even toward rectitude or propriety in general. If such lassitude were to become the dominant feature of our relation to social norms generally, then our behavior could no longer be described as either obedient or observant. Such behavior would be compliant at best. In short, when we imagine such caring to be missing from the critical attitude, as I have called it, then what we imagine is exactly what is meant by alienation and anomie, or normlessness. If this attitude of correcting, but not caring to be correct, were ever extended to the whole of one's social life, then we would be confronted with the life of an individual whose social surroundings are transformed into mere objects for manipulation, but which do not constitute a setting of anything to be engaged in. Without the caring aspect of that critical attitude—the view that rectitude matters—we would simply endure a kind of Kafkaesque world where conduct is prescribed, where prescriptions gain compliance, but where social norms lack any semblance of authority, legitimacy, or even sense. The internal speech of the self would be: "It doesn't really matter, but this is the way they like it. I know what they want, so I'll go along with this senseless charade even though nothing vital is at stake." Such a posture of detachment is the perspective of the uninvolved, the apathetic. It is the condition of anomie.[1]

The key to this interior speech is found in that indefinite, obscure, omnipresent, and distant 'they'. How remote, how disguised, 'they' always are! How senseless; yet, at the same time, how pervasive are the norms of everyday life when viewed simply as the edicts that 'they' deliver, and how thoroughly, under like circumstances, do those edicts lack even the most minute measure of moral authority! This condition, as nearly as I can describe it, is closely related to a kindred state that the medievals described as *acedia*, i.e., a kind of spiritual torpor or sickness that nowadays is often expressed as *ennui* or boredom.[2] The ancient idea extended, however, to something more fundamental even than mere boredom. It included the notion of a certain rebellion, a condition of being asleep to life, a resolute rejection of any possible contentment with being what one is, namely, a human being and thus essentially a creature.

When normation occurs in the sense I have described, that is, when norms are present, then concepts of 'right', 'wrong', and the like are also present, and with them the attitude that being right is a good thing, that it matters. Imagine a school in which a youngster is, say, suspended for some breach of conduct. What attitude should the youngster adopt toward the school in order to cope with the discipline? I suggest that the most immediate, the most likely, and most decisive strategy would be to withdraw moral authority from the norms of the school and from the institution. Come to view the institution with disrespect, even contempt! That is the tactic to pursue. The school will get the apparent compliance it seeks, but only by losing at the same time any semblance of moral authority. It will appear empirically that all is well, that order is restored, that whatever breach may have occurred in the moral authority of the school has been repaired. But when we grasp the nature of normation, we grasp also that these appearances are misleading. Compliance is confused with observance. To adopt as a general rule such a distant attitude of compliance with what 'they' desire, would be to adopt the posture of the alienated. That this posture of distance is anomic, is all the proof one needs in order to see that the critical attitude I have been trying to describe is what transforms the rule, or norm in question, into a public rule of right. The attitude that rectitude matters is a necessary condition for the acquisition of the norm to occur, which is to say, for the very existence of the norm *as a norm*. In its absence, instead of its acquisition as a norm we get merely the acknowledgment of a rule as a mere circumstance of life. By withholding this caring endorsement we deny the norm's very existence. We get anomie.[3]

This critical attitude has still another aspect. Depending upon the location of the norm in that expansive continuum from 'incorrect' to 'social gaffe' and thence to 'moral breach', we know that a norm has been acquired if, and only if, confronting violations of it or even anticipating one's own violations of it provokes some degree of shame, guilt, embarrassment, and the like in one's self and provokes disapproval, anger, censure, moral rejection, or even abhorrence on the part of others. The central point is not that there is an emotional or affective *side* to normation. The point is rather that normation just *is* this structuring of the emotions of self-assessment—shame, guilt, embarrassment, pride, and the like—both in our self-assessment and in our judgments of others.[4] It follows, of course, that it structures also the positive emotions companion to these that I have called the emotions of self-assessment. That is to say, normation structures also the appearance of elation, pride, self-assurance, and the joy and hope that accompany these. By saying that normation structures these emotions, I mean to refer not to the logic of their composition, whether they presuppose some propositional content, as in one or another version of a cognitive theory of the emotions. I mean to refer rather to their focus or object. Normation gives content to these emotions inasmuch as it provides their object. It tells us *what* things are going to provoke such emotions. In short, normation makes these emotions specific. Structuring them in this way is precisely what mere compliance is powerless to accomplish. Again, absent these emotions and the norms themselves will vanish. Observance will deconstruct into mere compliance, governance into mere behavior.

The relation of these emotions to norm acquisition is just as essential as the presence of the critical attitude and the 'caring to be correct' that I have discussed. A common conviction among students of education is that the acquisition of knowledge of all sorts is a matter quite independent of the emotions; cognition and affect are independent domains of learning. This view, I believe, is seriously mistaken when extended to such matters as the governance of norms. The empirical evidence offered in support of this misconception is simply that it is possible to teach things that don't matter and that children will learn them, things that don't matter at least *to them* but quite possibly just plain don't matter. So cognition and affect, it is supposed, must be discrete phenomena. Such a view amounts to the claim that persons can be brought to employ standards and rules of conduct without allowing them to govern. But our concern is with what it means to say that norms govern. The mere employment of rules and standards is not at all what occurs when behavior is norm observant. Once again, it becomes apparent that these are the conditions under which observance deconstructs into mere compliance.

II. Norms and Knowledge

Clearly, there is something peculiar about speaking of the acquisition of norms, that is, their presence in observant behavior, as a kind of knowing or even learning. If norm acquisition is to be viewed at all as some variety of knowing, it certainly cannot be propositional knowing. Knowing that Q, where Q is some norm, would be at best a kind of knowing that produces compliant instead of observant behavior, but it wouldn't necessarily produce even that. The expression closer to our educational meaning would be not that we learn norms, in the sense of learning, say, that Springfield is the capitol of Illinois, nor even that we come to know them, in the way we come to know that the square root of four is two, but that we come to *acquire* norms. The point is not that we come to know the standards of speech—to preserve the example—in some sense of 'know', but that we come to *have* such standards. We acquire them. We do not learn them, but they are impressed upon us. In the seventeenth century it was a common locution that we do not so much possess the virtues as they possess us. There is a similar point to the suggestion that we do not possess the norms of speech so much as they come to possess us.

The point is peculiar enough to require extension. It is often noted, as more than a mere etymological aside, that 'education' is a term derived from the Latin *educare*, meaning 'to lead out'. But the etymology is weak. *The Oxford Latin Dictionary*[5] suggests that the root is *educo*, the primary meaning of which is the kind of leading out that occurs when the sergeant leads the troops out from camp on patrol and not the kind of leading out that is aimed at drawing out from the child what is already there, and which needs only the assistance of an educator to be born. Leading out, in the sense of *educo*, is not midwifery. The *Dictionary* offers a secondary weak meaning of *educo*: 'to tend and support the growth of (offspring)', primarily those of animals and plants. This is not a meaning offering much support to the conventional educator's graduation speech appeal to *educare*.

Actually, when the Romans wished to speak of education, instead of using one or another idea derived from *educo*, they more commonly used *instruere*, which being derived from *struere*, means 'to build in' or, literally, to 'insert.' This is the word from which we get 'instruct' and 'instrument' in the sense of 'tool.' The same point is found in a related Latin term also more commonly used by the Romans than *educo* in discussions of what we would call 'education'. The word is *instituere*, from which we get 'institute'. It is derived from *statuo*, meaning 'to place in order to remain upright', or 'to put up', or 'erect'. Thus, the root idea of this term also is 'to place in' or 'upon' or, in short, 'to establish'. *Constituere*, from the same stem, together with its descendants, 'constitute', 'constitution', 'constitutive', carries the same meaning.

By this brief etymological excursus, I do not intend to prove anything. I aim only to establish that there is an ancient, still viable, and quite literal point in saying that norms are not so much learned as they are inserted or built into us or constituted in us or stamped upon us. Clearly, they are constitutive of our emotional lives. It is easy to say that we acquire norms; harder to say that we learn them; and a yet more remote possibility that we come to know them. This lack of any but a quite remote association between norm acquisition, on the one hand, and knowing and learning, on the other, is admittedly an odd result. I am concerned that it not be viewed as a mere intellectual contrivance created in order to gloss over some error. To that end, it is worth noting how agreeable it is to English usage that we refer to the developing powers of speech in infants as 'language acquisition', and reserve talk of 'learning' a language to the acquisition of a second or third one. So it seems a first language is acquired; a second or third is learned. What we should say of social norms is not that we learn them or come to know them, but simply that we *come to be normed*. This process by which we become normed is

what I mean by 'normation'. Normation is clearly not what is often referred to as socialization. It is this process of normation that I have urged
is the constitutive activity of moral education.

III. The Situational Location of Norms

I have already argued in some detail that a social norm does not describe
how members of a group behave. Rather, *for them* it prescribes how they
ought to or should behave. As I have also admitted, such norms are always situationally specific and subject to revision through time. That is
to say, the norms or rules expressing a certain value will differ in detail
from one institution to another, from one setting to another, and from
one time to another. The norms that give shape to relations of cooperation, for example, may be more restricted in the school than in the family. Behavior called cooperative in the family and therefore endorsed may
be described as collusion or cheating in the context of the school. The
same behavior endorsed in one setting will be forbidden in another.[6] This
undoubted fact that norms are always 'situated' is often interpreted as
though to endorse the claim that norms are hopelessly relative to group,
to situation, to time, and the like, and for that reason it is presumed that
normation cannot provide any firm basis for moral education. In consequence of the claim that norms are always situational, it is supposed to
follow that we must give up any rational foundations for the critical examination of norms and, therefore, any rational defense for their change
and improvement.

This objection—really a family of objections—rests on a number of
misconceptions, most of which arise from a tendency to overlook the
fact, barely stated here, that *no tradition is without its critical resources, and
no rational criticism is without its tradition.* This is a point that will be pursued somewhat later,[7] but for the moment it will be better to turn to a different cluster of misunderstandings, namely, those embodying misconceptions of the fact that norms are situationally specific. Just what does
this phrase 'situationally specific' mean?

Norms, Judgment, and the Foundationalist Project

Everyone learns some form of the dictum that situations alter things, but
nobody can anticipate all the situations likely to alter things so that suit-

able provisions covering all contingencies can be incorporated into norms. Furthermore, even if such a norm of action could be framed, its complexity would exceed what anyone could learn propositionally.[8] Fortunately, however, there is no need to introduce such complexity. To have acquired the norms of home and school and their separate but overlapping norms of collusion and cooperation is already to have acquired some judgment as to how circumstances alter things. Part of what we mean when we say that norms are situationally specific is that among those things acquired in the very acquisition of norms is a developed sense of propriety, a grasp of the fittingness of conduct to setting, the developed judgment, for example, that school is a place different from home and in what respects. Indeed, it is difficult to imagine how any sense of judgment or propriety in such matters could be acquired *except* through some such process of normation. It is partly this fittingness of conduct to setting, the demand for a sense of propriety and judgment, and not the so-called relativity of the norm, that we refer to by saying that norms are situationally specific.

There are really four points here, each crucial to the claims that moral education is education in observing and elaborating the voices of conscience, and that normation is the process by which that aim is accomplished. The first is simply to note that norm acquisition is not habit acquisition, at least not if one views habits as unthinking, fixed responses to situations. As Frederick Will has noted, it is a serious mistake to think of norm acquisition

> as a process in which (persons) are equipped with a repertory of fixed, unthinking modes of response. A person who was so equipped, in whom the norms of his social environment had been absorbed as if they were such modes of response, would not pass for long as a person trained in a certain discipline, occupation, or craft, or as a responsible moral agent.[9]

Such is the person whom we recognize as engaged in formula philosophy and formula writing, the person who plays the score but not the music, who cooks without imagination, who only in some Pickwickian sense, as Will suggests, can be said to know and abide by the rules of practice, but who has either forgotten or has never grasped the point of the practice. Doing things always and only 'by the book' is all that can be expected when norm acquisition is grasped as something akin to blind conformity to, or habitual compliance with, social norms. Such a person may for a moment be regarded as competent in this or that activity, but such a judgment, as Will suggests, will not be sustained. The impression of competence will not endure simply because it is not competence that such a person displays.

Paramount among things missing in the portrait of a person who plays by the book is just that fittingness of action to setting, that exercise of judgment, to which we refer by pointing to the situational character of norms. When introducing judgment into the conduct of such a person, it is tempting to begin by trying to frame a set of rules dictating when the rule is to be followed and when it can be bent. Yielding to such temptation is a mistake. The additional rules will do nothing to add judgment to the picture. They will only add to the rulebook. Learning that cooperation is a good thing, yet not always, is not to learn still another rule, a kind of superordinate rule that one needs to apply requiring then still another rule to govern the application of that one, and then still another and another and so on. Anyone who has learned simply that one should tell the truth in all matters and all circumstances, and undertakes to do so 'by the book', will soon run afoul of the norms of courtesy, for example, when bidding farewell to the host of a dull and uncongenial party. The missing element in such cases is not familiarity with some added rule of conduct needed to referee all conflicts between the norms of honesty and those of courtesy. What is missing is no defect in the norms that govern either candor or courtesy.

The tendency to find some fault in the norm in this and like situations is one thing that leads to the foundationalist project. Having supposedly found a gap implicit in the norm, some apparently unstated conditions perhaps, one is tempted to try filling in the gap. If we yield to the temptation, then the resulting project will aim at making the norm complete either by providing the presumably missing details or by offering some additional norm of a higher order, a norm of rather extraordinary juridical capacities such as are needed to mediate any conflict and remove any uncertainty that might arise. Deduction will be just the thing, a rule from which the needed supplement can be deduced, as though deduction might replace judgment in the way that measurement is sometimes thought capable of replacing estimations. The very project thus presumes that such gaps are deficiencies in the norms. But the thesis here is that there are no such gaps, or that if we acknowledge them to exist—if only momentarily as an alternative *description* of things—they are not to be viewed as deficiencies in the norms of practice, but simply as further evidence that one aspect of any norm is that its acquisition calls for the acquisition of judgment. To recognize such settings and such boundaries as exist in the difference between school and home is to acquire a kind of judgment that is already a part of norm acquisition, a kind of judgment already implicit in that achievement. Frederick Will, again, has put the matter adroitly. He says,

> It is not, of course that a person learns norms as fixed paths of action, and learns also an independent, supervening craft, namely how to judge. Rather, one learns to judge in learning how to act, in being educated in norms of action; and learns to judge only in relation to patterns of action.[10]

Norms Resident in Practices

In this reference to patterns of action lies a third important point on the situational nature of norms. It is not merely circumstances that alter things. Norms are also specific to practices and to institutions. Recall the earlier observation that part of what we mean by saying norms are situationally specific is that their acquisition entails the exercise of judgment, a sense of the fittingness of conduct to setting. But this fittingness is often negotiated simply by recognizing the activity in which we are engaged. Recognizing the difference between norms of school and home is largely identical with learning what it means to say that this (the place where one is) just *is* the school, the family, or the church. It is pretty much identical with such things as being able to say that we are now not simply tossing the ball, but playing baseball, that we are not simply stacking stone, but laying a dry-wall. This is the sense of Will's reference to patterns of action. Norm acquisition is always embedded in activities and institutions. Acquisition occurs by engaging in conduct of whatever sort is called for by those activities and institutions and appropriate to them not in ways detached from or abstracted from human action and activities.

The norms of the school or college governing the activity that we call 'grading papers', for example, are not simply regulations for sorting as though this activity were on a par with sorting apples at the orchard or classifying grades of paper in the stock room. The norms of grading papers cannot be grasped and criticized as though there is some purely ideal and aerie thing that constitutes the rules of sorting or ranking, applicable to all situations and waiting only to be brought down from some high place and applied to various human settings, in this case to grading papers, in that case to grading apples, and in another case to rank-ordering cherry pies. The norms of grading papers are first and foremost the norms of an activity *of the school*. It is *from* that setting and only *in* that setting that a certain activity gains its identity as the thing that we call grading papers. That is where the norms of grading gain their sense. And so, recognizing that certain modes of behavior endorsed in the home are forbidden by the norms of the school is not a recognition easily distinguished from simply recognizing that one is engaged in the activities of the school and what those activities are. The conscience engaged and formed in this way is the conscience of membership and participation, a voice recognizable in a large and varied assortment of memberships—a school, a church, a team, a polity, a profession, a scholarly guild, or a family.

The Illusion of Norm Application

Implicit in this idea that norms are situationally specific is a fourth point present in what has been noted already, but nowhere emphasized. In the fittingness of conduct to setting, the exercise of judgment is an essential feature of the acquisition of norms, not a tool of some kind needed for their application. But to this familiar point must now be added the further observation that behavior observant of norms is not applicative at all in any straightforward sense of 'application'. That is to say, one does not learn the norms of cooperation and then apply them. Such a view of norm observance—first comes the rule, then its application—virtually never describes what occurs whenever normation has been achieved. It may approach a description of some reality in those cases where norm acquisition is under way, yet is incomplete or in circumstances of institutional flux. It is there, amid the struggles of acquisition, after all, that the standards and rules of conduct are most likely to become not simply guides to conduct or presumptions of rectitude, but the *objects* of discussion. "What does good practice say about *this* situation?" we might ask. In the midst of learning a new craft or practice or when settling into a new environment, the guidelines may need to be discussed and something like their application practiced.[11] But these are all circumstances in which normation is aborning, not situations in which normation has been achieved. Even then, this applicative view of norm-observant behavior is by no means universal. One need only recall the paradigmatic case of becoming observant of a rule of grammar to recognize that this applicative model of norm governance is almost never an accurate account even in situations of norm acquisition.

In a faculty workshop on curriculum reform that I once conducted at a well-known liberal arts college famed for its fine teaching, one of the participants, a teacher of biology, was clear in describing one of his aims in teaching to be leading his students to 'apply' their knowledge of biology when, for example, they looked at the huge maple in the middle of the quad and the richness and interdependence of life in its surroundings. We discussed what, in this context, might be meant by 'applying knowledge' and readily agreed that this expression has no clear univocal meaning. This is not the 'applying' of applying a coat of paint to the barn door, or applying the tape-rule to the floor, or applying oneself to the task at hand. I asked whether it would make any difference to his understanding of teaching were he to describe his aim instead as simply getting the students to 'see' things biologically, that is, see them as a biologist would. The idea that behavior observant of norms can be understood on the model of norm application is a notion about as obscure as the idea that one is applying one's knowledge of biology when seeing the ecology of the maple tree in the quad as a biologist would. The applicative picture of norm observance is misleading.

As I have suggested already, one does not learn the norms of cooperation and then apply them. To the question, "What are you doing?" one simply answers "Helping with the dishes" or "Preparing dinner" or "Planting the beans." One does not *apply* the norms of cooperation, one simply comes to *be* cooperative. One comes to *be* normed. The norms operable in any setting with respect to some activity native to that setting are nearly always sufficiently identified by simply identifying the activity and its setting. To say "I am grading papers" is already to say what norms govern my current behavior and in what institutional environment they have their natural residence. To engage in such an activity is already to be governed by the norms of that activity, by its setting and its residence in whatever is the relevant institution. But this is virtually never a matter of shaping behavior in ways that the applicative image of things would have us suppose.

These points are internally related. They arise from focusing attention not upon the nature of norms, their validity or their logical status, and certainly not from studying the problematic of their application, but solely from attending to the nature of their acquisition. Norm acquisition, unlike the formation of blind habit, entails the acquisition of judgment and a sense of propriety. It can take place only in the context of human activities and settings; and the applicative model is inappropriate as providing a way to understand the governance of norms. These are all features of norm acquisition that become evident when we seek to explicate what it means that norms are situationally specific.

IV. Strong and Weak Normation

The model of normation offered so far can be described as a model of strong normation, that is, the sort that necessarily invokes the moral emotions of self-assessment. We have been speaking of normation to 'things that matter'. Not all normation, however, is of this sort. There can be weak norms or weak normation. When norms, otherwise of considerable weight, come to be construed as mere technical directives—as with rules of craft or rules of thumb in the practice of some craft—or when they are viewed as weak rules of prudence—as when we try to grasp the situational rules of decorum in a society where our relevant social group shifts from time to time—then we may describe the result as weak normation. Other chances for weak normation have been noted already, but under a different description, namely the circumstances producing alienation or anomie. These also must now be seen, however, in another light, and to do that it will be helpful to retreat a few steps in order the better to advance.

Gemeinschaft and Gesellschaft

In the history of sociological thought is found an extensive exposition of a distinction parallel to the contrast I seek to mark between strong and weak norms. The distinction, in one of its forms, appears as a difference between societies in which essential norms are extensively governed by the boundaries of the sacred, in contrast to other systems of social order in which norms are essentially guides to conduct of a purely functional, technical, and prudential sort. Ferdinand Tönnies introduced into sociology a useful distinction between Gemeinschaft and Gesellschaft.[12] Relations of Gemeinschaft, as he developed the distinction, tend to be rooted in kinship, blood, a shared memory or tradition, and often a common religion. Those of Gesellschaft, however, tend to be rooted more in contractual agreements of utility, in transient interests, or even in something as simple as a mere coincidence of compatible functions, but not in kinship, memory, or any shared religion. Tönnies' deployment of the distinction was typological. That is to say, the distinction was meant to establish two ends of a continuum, two ideal types. Since actual human associations, at different times and in different respects, vary considerably, bearing sometimes a closer resemblance to Gesellschaft and sometimes to Gemeinschaft, the distinction provides a means of discerning order in the midst of that variation. Given the conceptual distinction, empirical instances can be appropriately placed in relation to one another on a scale, depending in each instance on whether it more nearly resembles the conditions of Gemeinschaft or those of Gesellschaft.

In Gesellschaft, persons are separated except when related by agreement or shared interest, whereas in Gemeinschaft persons remain united, or at least strongly related, despite deep discord or even enmity. According to the justly famous formulation of Tönnies,

> The theory of the Gesellschaft deals with the artificial construction of an aggregate of human beings which superficially resembles the Gemeinschaft insofar as the individuals live and dwell together peacefully. However, in Gemeinschaft they remain essentially united in spite of all separating factors, whereas in Gesellschaft they are essentially separated in spite of all uniting factors.[13]

We find exemplars of Gemeinschaft in relations of friendship and families. Friendship is not a relation of utility, contract, or agreement. It is useful to have friends, but use them and they will vanish. Nor can one forge friendships by seeking to secure whatever utility such ties provide. Cronyism differs from friendship precisely because it tends to be based in a kind of *quid pro quo*, a utilitarian reciprocity of a sort alien to the relation of friendship. In this respect, cronyism typifies Gesellschaft and friendship typifies Gemeinschaft. Tönnies tended to assign these types to particular historical epochs, attempting thus to describe the transformation involved in the emergence of modern European societies from their earlier origins. I seek no such application of the distinction. I seek only to exploit its heuristic value. Gemeinschaft-like relations, such as those of family and friends, require strong normation, whereas Gesellschaft-like relations of contractual and purely economic ties do not. These latter are relations of weak normation.

A familiar description of the modern world is that strong social norms have become fewer and weak ones more numerous. This description, in which strong normation is seen to be a limited possibility, can be seen as one side of secularization, the expression of the idea that in modern societies relations among persons are more akin to the model of *Gesellschaft* than to *Gemeinschaft*. Nevertheless, even in such a world, there remain certain relations—most clearly those of friendship and some forms of religious, political, and familial association—to which strong normation seems not merely propitious but essential. The norms of friendship, for example, cannot be construed as mere technical guides to conduct. That one causes pain to one's friend must be viewed within the institution of friendship itself as a major normative violation. If such conduct does not evoke strong feelings of shame, guilt, or the like, feelings of pain, then we can doubt that in that instance friendship itself is present.

"All of the cherished elemental states of mind of society—love, honor, friendship, and so on—are emanations of *Gemeinschaft*," thought Tönnies.[14] Yet common experience in the modern world suggests that most relations are emanations of *Gesellschaft*, relations of craft, convenience, and utility to which we are weakly normed. If it be asked, "Why should we teach history?" for example, the question, in the instrumental modern world, will be readily understood to require an account of the utility of historical studies—"so that we do not repeat the past," "so that we may be freed from unthinking submission to the past." But if you ask that question of a Jew and specifically about Jewish education, the question will be greeted with incredulity—"That is just what education *is*; how could you *not* teach history?" The question itself will be disallowed. The difference is the difference in the way that education is conceived within the context of *Gesellschaft* in contrast to the way it is conceived in the context of *Gemeinschaft*.

No doubt the increasing domain of weak normation is central to the expansion of human liberty in contemporary societies. If you are a Jew, then strict adherence to orthodox dietary rules may be difficult to fit into the protocols of lunch within the chambers of commerce, and if you are Japanese, then rituals of greeting are difficult to combine with telephone communication. How does one bow over the phone? Persons become lightly normed to such conventions because their observation, in any strong sense, imposes serious inconvenience. Fresh rules for dining and greeting will be introduced, and in the process the norms will become situationally excepted. People are likely to insist that such rules of conduct have not been abandoned. They still apply *except* not so strictly any longer in these circumstances or under those conditions. Cooperation is still viewed as a good thing, except not at school or under certain circumstances. Such a transition can be described, in an extended sense, as secularization, a decline in the domain of the sacred.

Organic and Mechanical Solidarity

A related distinction, exploited by Durkheim, provides added perspective on the nature of strong and weak normation. In *The Division of Labor in Society* Durkheim distinguished *organic* and *mechanical solidarity*, and related to this distinction, he introduced the idea of 'collective conscience'. By 'mechanical solidarity' he refers to social cohesion of a sort that has existed throughout most of social history. It is based upon moral and social homogeneity and supported, he thought, by a kind of repression. Following Henry Maine[15] in his famous *Ancient Law*, Durkheim associated mechanical solidarity with penal law. Where there is mechanical solidarity, tradition dominates, justice is mainly aimed at subordinating the individual to a collective conscience, property is communal, and religion tends to be identified with cult and ritual. Social ties are underwritten by the sacred.

Organic solidarity, on the other hand, is based primarily upon the division of labor. Out of the division of labor, and in consequence of it, there emerges individuality, and along with it a kind of distance from the restraints of collective repression and from submission to a collective conscience. It then becomes possible to see society not under the guise of a kind of mechanical solidarity, but as the organically coordinated efforts of free individuals pursuing different functions but united, insofar as they are united at all, by the complementarity, perhaps even mutuality, of their different roles. Thus justice, under conditions of organic solidarity, becomes less punitive, as in penal law, and becomes more focused upon problems of restitution, a feature more typical of civil law. Individuals thus become disengaged from the constraints of kinship, class, localism, and the settled and predetermined roles of an inflexible traditionalism. Or so Durkheim saw it.

This distinction, as Durkheim drew it, will strike nearly everyone as putting things exactly in reverse of their apparent order. The mechanical solidarity of which he speaks will be grasped nowadays precisely as a kind of organic social order, and the organic solidarity of which he speaks will be recognized more easily nowadays as a functional order. But never fear.

Both forms of social organization can be clearly grasped in the single case of Jack Sprat and his wife, that couple liberated from a limiting traditionalism into the comparative freedom of strictly functional relations. Recall that Jack Sprat could eat no fat and his wife no lean; and so, between the two of them, they licked the platter clean. This is a wonderful division of labor, though not a firm foundation for marriage. Because of their different but complementary disabilities, these two can be joined by an agreement to accomplish together what neither can accomplish alone. Yet, the fact remains that both can be replaced by a disposal or by a dog who has no need to be as discriminating. This couple, of course, do not constitute a society. Yet, if we imagine a society to be the Sprats writ large, then we imagine a society based exclusively upon the division of labor with no ties of any other sort. Between Jack Sprat and his wife, there is only a kind of functional relation, an order of the sort that Durkheim meant by 'organic solidarity', and that we typically describe as functional. By noting how inadequate such relations are as a basis for marriage and other like associations, I mean to call attention to the character of a different kind of relation, typical of what Durkheim meant by a 'mechanical' and what we would mean by an 'organic' association.

Such, according to Robert Nisbet,[16] was the original argument of *The Division of Labor*. Durkheim said, however, that any society based upon human relations of the sort typified by the Sprats can persist only in the presence of some continuity with the first form of solidarity. "The division of labor," wrote Durkheim,

> can be produced only in the midst of pre-existing society. There is a social life outside the whole division of labor, but which the [division of labor] presupposes. That is, indeed, what we have directly established in showing that there are societies whose cohesion is essentially due to a community of beliefs and sentiments, and it is from these societies that those whose unity is assured by the division of labor have emerged.[17]

In short, in a world where relations of utility, contract, and ties of interest provide the integuments of a kind of solidarity, much depends upon sustaining the shared norms that contracts should be honored, promises delivered on, and that the conditions of trust should be realized and jealously preserved—*none of which can be understood to emerge out of transient interests, willed agreements, and other ties of convenience or social function.* Expressed in Durkheim's terms, organic solidarity cannot persist except where some residue of mechanical solidarity remains. As Durkheim would see it, the world of weak normation depends for its persistence on the prior and continuing existence of some domain of strong normation.

As Talcott Parsons has noted in explicating Durkheim's views,

> Since the collective conscience stresses the commonness of beliefs and sentiments that constitute it, this seems to identify it with mechanical solidarity and suggests that organic solidarity, associated as it is with differentiation in the social structure, must develop at the expense of the *conscience collective.*[18]

The picture is thus, that with the growth of organic solidarity through the division of labor, the domain of the collective conscience diminishes. It has less and less scope, is less needed, and governs fewer and fewer sectors of life. Hence, there is less and less that can be viewed as demanding a shared conscience. This is the picture that allows us to understand in a deeper way the distinction between strong and weak normation.

In the contemporary world, the problem is not so much that there are no shared values or beliefs, no sentiments, and no precinct to which it is proper to be strongly normed. The problem is rather to spell out just what the domain of that collective conscience may be, and that is another way of asking just what duties, what rights, and what responsibilities ought to be a part of the collective conscience. To what norms, beyond contractual ties and functional agreements, should we expect persons to be strongly normed? As the collective conscience shrinks, shared duties and sentiments are likely to be more abstract, more general, less tied to status and role, and certainly more contextual. Despite all that, their formation and acquisition is more critical. It does not follow that we should be strongly normed to every standard of craft, morality, or civic life. Anyone of whom that can be said is likely to be viewed, quite rightly, as rigid, inflexible, without judgment. These are the conditions that describe the fanatic and the bigot.

V. Moral Education as Social Criticism

There are relations, even in the most secular surroundings, of which strong normation is an essential feature. This fact needs further discussion for at least two reasons. Firstly, it will help to clarify the role of ideals and exemplars in the conduct of moral education, and secondly, it will reveal in what ways norm acquisition is not a path of appeal to some orthodoxy, but is instead a way to place social and moral criticism on solid foundations. These matters can be considered in connection with (1) a contrast between the empirical and the normative communities, and (2) a valuable distinction between what I shall call the internal and the external voices of moral interpretation.

The Empirical and Normative Communities

The regularity of conduct within a human community, that is, the actual modal behavior that occurs there, the presence of which might be confirmed by an external observer, almost certainly will differ from the behavior that would be discoverable if the community were all that the members think it ought to be. Among the norms of any community there will be some that proscribe behavior in the strong sense, norms whose violation will, therefore, produce guilt, shame, or some kind of aversion. In their response to violations of such norms, members of the community reveal their acquired sense of what the ideal embodiment of the community would look like. What the community is in fact, that is, what is empirically found there, is almost never what members of the community think it would be if it were all that they think it ought to be. Hence, the normative and the empirical communities need to be distinguished, *and the distinction is itself empirically observable in the behavior of the members.*

Being naturalized to the normative community, that is, putting on *its* standards as one's 'second nature', is what normation in the strong sense is about.[19] Acquiring the norms of the empirical community, *without* the normative, is what mere compliance is about. It bears repeating that this latter form of normation—that producing mere compliance—is the form that converts the norms of any community into something like technical directives or rules of thumb. Instead of describing the conditions under which ideals are realized, such rules then describe only how things work, how the world operates, and thus, what one needs to grasp in order to 'get along'. Consider the fact that any person for whom honesty is merely the best policy, that is, a person who views the standards and rules of honesty merely as an aid in getting along, a kind of strategic rule for seeing that things go smoothly in human affairs—such a person ought not to be trusted very far or with matters of gravity. In the contrast between the normative and the empirical communities is found the proper parent to, perhaps, a thousand dualities that lie within the boundaries of many traditions—The Heavenly City and the Earthly City; the City of God and the City of Man; heaven and earth; value and fact; The Garden and The Fall; being "in the world, but not of it."

Normation to the empirical community is the kind of normation that is often understood both by the lay public and also among educators as socialization. To whatever extent that is so, then by saying that moral education is a process of normation, I do not mean that it is socialization. Normation to the empirical community is not what I intend by 'strong normation' nor is it what Durkheim meant. Nothing of importance depends upon the question whether this distinction between the empirical and the normative communities is one that Durkheim devised. It is a matter of some interest, however, to observe that he did deploy it. When Durkheim speaks of social facts in *The Rules of Sociological Method*, the facts he has in mind are just such norms as I have described in the full sense of the prescriptive rules of a social group expressed in observant behavior. Thus, the social facts presented in Durkheim's classic study, *Suicide*, are not the tabulated data but the norms reflected in those data. The norms are those social facts that he describes in *Rules* as being as objective and implacable as any facts of nature.[20] It is also this view of social facts as norms that allows us to mark the crucial distinction between the empirical and the normative communities, between the way things are and can be discovered to be and the way things would be were they all that the shared norms of a society suggest they ought to be. In this sense, the norms of a society are its ideals, not its empirical mores. Normation, for Durkheim, provides the standards against which the actual community is assessed *by its members*. To be normed in the strong sense is to be normed to these ideals.

Thus, almost at the height of the Dreyfus Affair, Durkheim in "L'Individualisme et les intellectuel" wrote staunchly against the anti-Dreyfusards.[21] They had argued that decisions already made by the Army effectively denying Dreyfus's rights could not be reversed, because to do so would threaten the very survival of a system of national security and authority and thus the very foundations of the French Republic. Durkheim argued, on the contrary that *not* to reaffirm and defend Dreyfus's rights would be to commit moral suicide. It would be as it would be with a religion that through repeated indifference toward its central practices slowly declines and disappears. To neglect a defense of Dreyfus's rights would be to exercise indifference to the very core of the only set of beliefs that hold the nation together, for the heart of the French Republic, its unity, lay not in preserving the institutions of security, but in securing the rights of individuals. Even if this meant the demise of the existing institutions of security and state, still, it would not mean the end of the Republic, the essentials of which lay not in these realities, but in the normative framework of the nation. In short, Durkheim appealed to the normative community, to its constitutive norms, against those whose arguments were rooted entirely in the empirical community. He appealed to what he could have called the collective conscience, a set of norms that are nonnegotiable and deontic, norms to which strong normation is a necessity. *Call this the appeal to the voice of duty, the conscience of sacrifice.*

This distinction between the empirical and normative communities is crucial. It constitutes a vital extension of the idea that moral education is the formation of conscience and the formation of conscience is normation. For in this distinction between the empirical and the normative, social criticism and moral critique are assured a lofty position in what might otherwise appear to be a view of education implacable in its defense of the status quo, devoted to the cultivation of mindless habit and conformity. In this distinction between the normative and the empirical community, moral education enlists the critical resources of a tradition. Moral education understood as an education in social criticism then emerges. It appears when the members of a community, normed already, insist upon measuring what the community is against what it claims to be, against, that is, its best portrait. This is the larger context for what I have already called *the conscience of memory and imagination. It presupposes the conscience of membership,* the reflexive consciousness of the self as member.

Internal and External Interpretation

This contrast between the empirical and the normative communities, though framed at a high level of social aggregation, has its expression also at the lowest level of aggregation. This contrast runs parallel to another between the internal and external voices of moral interpretation. When I hear a voice addressed to me from some distance saying, in effect, "You are not the generous" or "the honest" or "the sympathetic and sensitive person that you claim to be," then I feel the sting. It hurts. I am charged with being false, with being insincere or inauthentic, with a lack of integrity. This voice has a strong moral bite to it. It gets my attention quickly. I call this the internal voice of criticism because although it always comes, and must come, from a point away from me, as if from another person, it is always as if from another person like me, not from a God on high. It is a voice addressed to an internal condition of the self. It is a critical voice directed against what I am, not against what I believe. And not being addressed to belief, neither will it be quieted by a change of belief. It calls upon me not merely to think something different, or to believe something different, but to *be* something different, namely to be what I claim to be. This condition is called integrity.

There is another voice addressed to me, however, saying there is something wrong with what I claim to be, a voice saying, in effect, that the goods I seek are false, that my opinions about what has worth ought to be revised, that they cannot be justified, that they are groundless. To this latter voice, palms upward, I might shrug my shoulders and respond simply, "So? You have your views and I have mine." I call this the external voice of criticism because, though it too comes from a distant point, it is another kind of distance and another kind of point. This is a voice addressed to the need for an external foundation of moral belief, a foundation so distant and so devoid of context that it represents what Thomas Nagel has called 'the view from nowhere'. This is an Olympian, or if you prefer, a magisterial voice, a voice that demands foundations not merely in my reason, but in Reason itself or in the very nature of things. It is addressed to me only because it is addressed to any reasonable person. Because it is a voice from 'no-where', it purports to be a voice for 'any-one' and thus for everyone.

With this external voice from nowhere my quarrel can often seem not simply academic, but 'merely' academic. What really is the standard of duty? Is there any such? Is the rule of utility enough? Does an acceptable standard of honesty allow for no exceptions? What about this one? Can it count as an exception? How much of a dissembler am I allowed to be? Any quarrel I might have with this external voice of criticism is likely to draw heavily on such talk of rules and principles and cases. This is the voice of the philosophic quest in its justificatory practice. It is the Olympian voice of philosophy preparing us to embark upon yet another evangelical project to convince the world.

With the former, the interior voice, the struggle is serious and in no sense merely academic. This voice addresses my personal integrity, not my orthodoxy. With it, I shall have to wrestle. The external is, as it were, the voice of a public bar of judgment before which my beliefs must gain approval; but the other is the voice of an interior bar of judgment before which I myself, in all my particularity, all masks aside, must stand and seek approval. Is this the voice of conscience?

These voices both speak of 'true' and 'false', but they use these words with different meanings, and the difference is stark. The external voice speaks of truth as correspondence and thus of falsehood as mistake or error. The internal voice speaks of truth in the logic of coherence—the coherence of a self—and thus it speaks of truth not as the absence of error but as integrity; it speaks of error not as falsehood but as dissembling.

Chapter 3

The Voices of Conscience I:
Craft and Membership

The voices of conscience are various. There is no reason to believe either that they can be or that they ought to be always—or even very often—in agreement. When moral education is grasped as the formation of conscience, that is, as cultivating reflexive judgment on conduct and character, then we cannot expect it to aim at reconciling these different voices. Nor should we expect a philosophy of moral education to produce a demonstration as to which of these voices can lay rightful claim to that magisterial role. Framing a philosophy of moral education is not a project of foundationalism. The aim is not to calm the quarrels of conscience, but to encourage their enlargement and their elaboration. The aim must be to make those quarrels more incisive, more rational, more passionate, more perceptive, more discerning, and more expansive in their scope than is likely to result from any education by chance, drawing neither upon the voice of reason nor upon the practices of custom and tradition.

Such claims need elaboration and illustration, of course, if they are to be understood, much less evaluated. Therefore, let us consider the voices of conscience *ad seriatim*, beginning with the conscience of craft, turning then to membership and from there to the conscience of sacrifice and finally to the expansive topics of imagination and memory. These we may take to be the different voices of conscience.

I. The Conscience of Craft

We encounter the conscience of craft being formed whenever we observe the novice coming to adopt the standards of some craft as his or her own. We see it also whenever we witness the expert, already proficient in a practice, struggling to shape a new vision of the craft. The conscience of craft is displayed whenever the norms of that craft come to govern with all the force of the emotions of self-assessment, which is to say, when we become judge in our own case, saying that our performance is good or bad, skillful, fitting, and the like. Whether one is a writer, a cook, a gardener, a mechanic, or a teacher, there will be standards for the practice of one's craft. Becoming a musician is more than simply becoming able to perform on an instrument. It is becoming able to act as critic of one's own performance and that of others, employing standards of musical taste and judgment as to what is good, what might be better, and what is downright unacceptable. Thus, to possess a conscience of craft is to have acquired the capacity for self-congratulation or deep self-satisfaction at something well done, shame at slovenly work, and even embarrassment at carelessness. This is the sense of craft which, when expressed in reflexive judgment, underlies *all* our educational talk of excellence and standards. It is what impels us to lay aside slovenly and sloppy work simply because of what it is—slovenly and sloppy.

That I have just written a bad paragraph presents no moral crisis to me. But still, I know and everyone else who cares about it knows perfectly well the difference between the unease that accompanies that judgment and the satisfaction that comes with having written a good one. Having the capacity to make such judgments, with their accompanying unease or joy, is what I mean by having a conscience of craft. The feelings associated with such judgments are crucial because their presence is precisely the sign that craft has come to matter, that judgment has indeed become reflexive, and that standards have become one's own and no longer simply mirror the judgments of some external tutor.

Conscience of this sort is exercised not only in writing, but in music, carpentry, gardening, cooking, conducting an experiment, eating, dressing, and even in mowing the lawn. The conscience of craft may be *formed* in all of these contexts. Certainly it is *expressed* in them all. It is not obvious just how this capacity for self-assessment in such settings differs from the same capacity in other contexts more likely to be called moral or ethical. Nor would it matter to the educational point if the conscience of craft were never to appear in a moral context narrowly conceived. It remains a voice of conscience as I intend it, that is, a form of reflexive judgment.

Nonetheless, when the conscience of craft is extended to settings where some other form of reflexive judgment, more characteristically moral, is called for, then odd things can happen. Some years ago I was engaged for a short period in conversations on ethics with candidates for the Senior Executive Service of the United States Civil Service. Candidates were all senior experienced professionals, practicing attorneys, physicians, archival scientists, CPAs, and the like. What is one supposed to teach members of such a class? Certainly not the difference between right and wrong, or the principles of moral philosophy. I was content to explore with them some features of their own conscience already formed. Simply making such features explicit, I thought, might be helpful.

Sooner or later in those conversations, and always with the proviso that there are no synonyms in the English language, the question would arise, "Which would you rather be known as, honest or sincere?" And nearly always the answer, after cautious consideration, would come back, "Honest." Why? Because, at least in the context of public life, to say of someone, "He is a sincere person," is to imply "He is naive, inept, can be had." That was a judgment repeated again and again in those discussions. You may test the matter. You know, as well as I, that in framing a letter of reference, it is one thing to write, "He (or she) is a sincere teacher of undergraduates," and a much more favorable thing to write simply, "He is a skillful teacher" or "She is a taskmaster." By emphasizing that someone is sincere, we tend to imply ineptitude of a sort, an undesirable sort of naïveté. To say of someone, "Well, he is at *least* sincere," is to imply that that person is ineffective or perhaps misguided.

So the preference for honest over sincere is understandable, at least in the context of public bureaucratic life. But then comes another question: "Which would you most fear, being known as dishonest or being known as inept?" And in this case the answer always came back with remarkable speed—inept is worse. Being known as inept, at least to this audience, is more to be feared even than being known as dishonest. Here we can clearly see the structure of a conscience in which concepts of skill and craft, at least in certain settings, rank even higher than standards of honesty, which, in turn, weigh more heavily than standards of sincerity. We have here an opening wedge in understanding the structure of what may be aptly called a technical conscience. I do not endorse this kind of conscience. I wish only to illustrate how concepts of skill and craft might come to leave their stamp upon the kind of conscience we may have formed, and how the voice of craft figures in reflexive judgments of persons.

Developing a sense of craft, of course, is not all there is to the formation of conscience. It is a part, however, and an important part. My sense of trust is quickened, as I suspect is yours, when a mechanic who repairs my car to my satisfaction voices a certain discomfort at not meeting his own standards. His evident conscience of craft gives me extra assurance. We make a serious mistake if we fail to recognize the conscience of craft and to acknowledge that *it may be in its acquisition that the formation of conscience takes place most clearly and most directly*. Developing a conscience of craft is a major part of what we ought to think of routinely as moral education, yet it is a part that is almost universally ignored. Why? Perhaps because we have too narrow a view of what moral education is about, thinking, erroneously, that to care for doing things well is not a matter of sufficient gravity, sufficient *moral* gravity, that is, to matter in moral education.

Evaluation and the Conscience of Craft

Consider what goes on in learning to write an essay or to play a musical instrument, say, the cello, or to carry out a laboratory experiment. A large portion of what must take place is the acquisition of a sense of satisfaction in a paragraph well written or in a passage of music well performed or in the execution of an experiment that comes out 'just right'. Along with this satisfaction must come a corresponding unease at turning in a faulty performance, as well as the resolve to do better and a knowledge of what 'better' looks like. What else could education to excellence in the arts and crafts amount to if not normation to the standards of excellence implicit in each activity and the disposition to rejoice at meeting them?

The distinctions explicated already between acting in accord, in compliance, and in observance of norms will inform our understanding of how expertise is acquired in any craft and in the exercise of any of the academic disciplines. It will be especially important to note the increasing complexity of reflexive judgments offered in the face of error or mistake. Observing a student's critical attitude toward error will reveal more about his or her current standing in the progression from novice to intermediate to expert than will observing performance when taken by itself in ignorance of such reflexive estimates. How the student frames judgments of error or mistake lies at the heart of any evaluation of progress. What one wants to know, in short, is not simply the level of performance, but whether and in what measure a student's critical judgments are becoming more complex and more suited to the conscience of an expert in

whatever may be the relevant activity. Indeed, it is precisely such reflexive judgments that reveal to us what level of mastery has been reached.

When one begins to play the clarinet, for example, the initial task is
merely to produce a sound, and a sound, moreover, that is not that initial
squawk. Thus reflexive judgment appears immediately. But as that capacity for reflexive judgment develops, it becomes more complex. An early
step is to produce not merely a sound but a clear sound (What is that?),
then a sustained sound (What counts as failure here?). But these difficulties are soon submerged in the need to judge a good or bad legato or stac-
cato. And to these will be added other judgments stemming, say, from the
need to maintain pitch when moving from register to register on the instrument. Our grounds for claiming that the student is progressing rest in
our estimate that the student's reflexive judgment is becoming increasingly complex and increasingly concerned with the musicality of performance. In short, what is sought in the acquisition of a craft is not so
much knowledge or even skill, but normation, namely, a growing capacity for the kind of reflexive judgment which, being possessed, constitutes
a ticket of admission to whatever guild of masters is associated with that
craft. In this observation lies a clue for the conception of achievement
tests generally, that they should measure not the level of what is known,
but the complexity of the student's reflexive judgment that gets engaged
when things go wrong; they should provide a measure of the level and
complexity of practice at which a failure of performance is detected by
the student.

The Craft Analogy

Admittedly, the kind of 'correct' and 'incorrect' in question here, this
'right' and 'wrong', is not a moral right or wrong in some restricted and
philosophical sense of 'moral'. Still, it is a 'correct' or 'incorrect', a 'right' or
'wrong', of a sort that belongs to the acquisition of norms of craft. Furthermore, it has its moral connection. The assimilation of ethics to craft is central in the Greek lexicon of ethics. In that vocabulary, moral terms—in the
modern sense in which the 'moral' is contrasted with the 'nonmoral'—are
virtually absent. Instead, the vocabulary is rich in references to such things
as 'hitting the mark' and 'finding the mean'. In that wellspring of reflective
moral literature that presents and represents the Greek perspective
through the ages, the skills required for living well are often compared to
the skills of the archer or the artist, the sailor or the armourer. It matters

not at all that this sense of right and wrong, of error and mistake, is not a moral right and wrong, not a moral mistake. Whatever we imagine the best kind of life to be, it cannot be a life filled with repeated exclamations of "Ooops!" In short, a kind of technical competence or proficiency in living really *does* count and counts rather heavily in our ordinary evaluations.

In the early dialogues of Plato, Socrates is portrayed as assimilating ethics *entirely* to a matter of craft. Plato modified this view in the Middle Dialogues. That living well can be understood as kin to the conduct of craft was an important claim for Socrates because he apparently thought that if ethics is essentially a matter of craft then its conduct can be taught. The appeal of such an analogy stems no doubt in part from the fact that we do count a lack of skill in conduct as a fault and the possession of such skill as one sort of virtue, a kind of virtue valued sometimes even more than honesty. The craft analogy, in other words, is not a dead thing. It is merely a thing too often overlooked, an aspect of conscience ignored precisely where attention to it would be most desirable, namely in our grasp of moral education. If we are careful about where to look for educational chances and attentive to what is happening around us, then, in our efforts to guide the formation of conscience, we might look first at cultivating a sense of craft. It may be there, in normation to a craft or to craftlike tasks of everyday life, that the formation of conscience takes place most clearly and directly.

II. The Conscience of Membership

It may seem strange to speak of a conscience of membership, stranger even than to speak of the conscience of craft. We all know that our conscience is for each of us a private affair, and that membership is not. We tend to conceive of conscience, moreover, as something uniquely our own. Mine is unlike yours and yours unlike any other. Thus, conscience comes to be thought of not only as something private to each self, but also one of the respects in which each self is unique and discrete. To speak of membership, therefore, is apparently to speak *contra* conscience in as much as membership is something public and shared, neither private nor distinct among individuals. No wonder that for many, the phrase 'conscience of membership' has an odd ring to it. The very idea of conscience echoes of privacy, concealment, discreteness, even of separation, and the idea of membership rings of plurality, connection, and being a part of some public. The two—conscience and membership—seem inherently at odds.

There is, however, another side to this presumed opposition. The conscience of craft, to take but a single case, is clearly a public affair, and the excellence encouraged by adherence to such standards is a public good. Standards of excellence in any craft are framed from the experience of those who exercise that craft and others who have done so through the ages. Such standards are not invented in a moment nor for the sake of a moment. Neither are they framed by or for any single individual. No one simply makes them up. That such standards take up residence in this or that discrete and private conscience has not the slightest tendency to show that such norms are not public. They are public standards or they are not standards at all. Acquiring such norms and disposing them in reflexive judgment is precisely what I have pointed to already as the formation of a conscience of craft. It is a further fact that through such acquisition we become members of a kind of public, members of something like a guild. Think of the standards of historians, musicians, athletes, cooks, gardeners, scientists, and so forth, how their judgments of excellence are formed and arrayed in reflexive judgment. We become historians, musicians, athletes, and cooks, by acquiring the norms of those engagements, and in doing so, we join the company of those who practice that craft. In such acquisition the conscience of a membership emerges. In other words, such norms are public in the sense of being framed not merely for a moment nor for and by any single individual. They are public in the sense that they are the norms *of* a public. They are norms that govern the conduct of members.

What kind of membership is this? Clearly, it is no mere casual association or aggregation of persons. The word 'member' in its Latin sense means simply 'part'. In its use we, therefore, make oblique reference to some whole. There is *this* member, a part of *that* whole. Even in the logician's sense of 'logical class', we have, if not a whole, then at least an aggregation whose elements we call 'members'. Members of that kind, however, are members only in virtue of some similarity and not in virtue of any relationship among them. Fido, Phaido, and Phaideux are members of the class 'canine'. But to say as much is to say nothing about any relationship among them. They may remain without any relation whatsoever. They are perfectly discrete creatures for all that we can discern from the mere fact of their being members of a logical class.

Societies also are wholes with members, but membership in a society is not the sort of thing that logicians mean by 'class membership'. Any actual society will have its members. Thus, corresponding to any actual society, say S, there will be a class, call it S_I, consisting of all those who are members of S. Yet the phrase 'member of S_I', that is, member of a logical class, is not what anyone *means* by the phrase 'member of S', that is, member of a society. Membership in a society is a thing radically different from membership in a logical class.

Yet, these two, S and S_I, are constantly mistaken one for the other. It is a costly mistake, arising for the most part from uncritically or even unconsciously adopting one or another version of methodological individualism, namely, the view that statements about any society can be uniformly reduced without remainder to statements about individuals. From such a perspective it is possible to view the members of S simply under their guise as members of S_I, and to suppose that nothing is lost in the translation. The import of this mistake can be vividly framed by dwelling briefly on the so-called theorem of the goats and dogs as found in Joseph Townsend's *Dissertation on the Poor Laws*.[1] It begins with the island of Robinson Crusoe off the coast of Chile. Townsend writes,

> In this sequestered spot, John Fernando placed a colony of goats consisting of one male, attended by his female. This happy couple finding pasture in abundance, could readily obey the first commandment, to increase and multiply, till in process of time they had replenished their little island. . . . When the Spanish found that the English privateers resorted to this island for provisions, they resolved on total extirpation of the goats, and for this purpose they put on shore a greyhound dog and bitch. These in their turn increased and multiplied . . ., but in consequence, as the Spaniards had foreseen, the breed of goats diminished. Had they been totally destroyed, the dogs likewise must have perished. But as many of the goats retired to the craggy rocks, where the dogs could never follow them, descending only for short intervals to feed with fear and circumspection in the vallies, few of these, besides the careless and the rash, became a prey; and none but the most watchful, strong, and active of the dogs could get a sufficiency of food. Thus a new kind of balance was established. . . .[2]

Karl Polanyi, in his account of the rise of the market society, says about this passage, "No government was needed (according to Townsend) to maintain this balance; it was restored by the pangs of hunger on the one hand, the scarcity of food on the other. Hobbes had urged the need for a despot because men were *like* beasts; Townsend insisted that they were *actually* beasts."[3] This may not be an accurate account of Hobbes's intentions, though it is no doubt more accurate than appears at first blush. Still, its rhetorical force draws our attention to the raw details of the path along which argument runs when social membership is understood under the guise of membership in a logical class and where social action is understood as governed by laws viewed simply as the summed result of individual activities. From such a perspective, we discover aggregate laws that prevail even though they do not emerge from any lawgiver, any government, or from any sense of moral imperatives or providential care, much less from the governance of social norms.

The parable of dogs and goats is substantially misleading if taken as a portrait of social life actually discovered in the experience of individuals. Much is omitted. To find the missing piece, we need only recall Thomas Huxley's observation that the minimum condition, even of the wolf pack, is that the wolves refrain from eating of one another in order that they may eat of the hare.[4] Not even membership in the wolf pack, in other words, can be understood as class membership, that is, an association without governing norms. Cancel that minimal restraint, let wolf eat fellow wolf, and there may for a time continue to be wolves, but there will be no pack. What is missing in this picture is *the pack*. What it lacks is any robust notion of membership beyond the barren gathering of a simple aggregation, which is to say that it lacks any robust notion of norms.

'Membership' is inherently a normative term. Being a member entails being normed. So when we speak of a conscience of membership, the membership in question is not class membership, but neither is it merely a consequence of mutual presence, a meeting of people who just happen to be in each others' locale like objects in one another's neighborhood or as critters on a crowded sidewalk whose only mutual aim is to avoid colliding. It would have to be membership of a sort that makes reflexive judgment possible, a membership in the light of which one can critically judge one's own performance and that of others. In short, the membership we seek to understand is more than any simple effluence of human sociability flowing from the inclination of human beings to seek each other's company. What we seek are the terms of that membership, an account of the norms that constitute its coherence. So the membership we seek to understand is neither a coincidental gathering nor a group of persons brought together by a momentary spirit of conviviality.

It is instructive to ponder the fact that although friendships do not have members, nevertheless, families, fraternities, and sisterhoods do. The difference is worth noting because any membership sufficiently robust to allow for a conscience of membership would have to provide also for the existence of something far short of friendship, even short of affection, among its members. It would have to be sufficiently robust in its norms to allow for enmity. Being a member of a family, we may think, is entirely a matter of biology, yet families may have among their members some who share no common parentage and others who share a common parentage but strain whatever alliances or ties of affection we may ordinarily expect to emerge. This is proof enough that shared norms, not shared parentage, make a family. 'Family' is a social, not a biological, concept. This feature of membership, that is to say, shared norms, is present whether we have in mind a professional society, a family, a craft guild, a polity, or even a civic community. In each of these associations a conscience of membership can be recognized. Conscience is private only in the odd and impoverished sense in which pain is private, but conscience, nonetheless, is shaped only within some membership and for the sake of life within the membership so formed.

Public and Private

The concept of conscience as private, however erroneous, is reinforced in many ways. We think easily of conscience as something individual and of public life, a certain kind of membership, as necessarily corrupting it. The familiar contrast between private conscience and public life is often drawn as though there were no connection between the two, as though the health of our private lives is a matter entirely unrelated to the health of our neighbors' lives, our public lives. If this is our game, then all our efforts to gain a grasp of moral education—assuming they mention conscience at all—are likely to attend to the development of judgment and the acquisition of virtue only in the individual. The accustomed view is that only after attending to the formation of conscience in individuals do we need to understand how the formation of conscience is related or unrelated to conduct within some public office—even within that most ubiquitous office of all, the office of citizen.

This is a point of view and a path of pedagogy that we must overcome, a legacy that must be remedied in any adequate view of moral education. But how? What might be an alternative view? I propose just this, that *aiming to form a conscience for conduct in the skills of public life is more likely to produce a conscience suited to private life than seeking to form a conscience for private life is likely to produce a conscience suitable for public life.* This proposition I take to be fundamental. It declares simply that one path is educationally more likely than another. Gaining competence in the disciplines of public life is a path more likely to prepare one for the demands of private life, than a moral education aimed at acquiring the skills of private life is likely to provide a path toward mastering the disciplines of public life. There is in this claim no doctrine of logical foundations or temporal priority. There is here no claim that normation to the skills of membership in our more expansive associations, like a polity or a university, must be grasped first, much less that they are logically prior to normation for our more limited associations of family or professional society. I offer little by way of proof for this claim, but proof is not the immediate need. It will suffice, at least for the moment, to firmly grasp the meaning of this claim or, falling short even of that, then at least to grasp the intuition that drives it.

That presiding intuition has two sides. On the one hand is the conviction that moralists in public life are dangerous to us all, primarily because the certainty that they always bring to public life is only one side of that utopian impulse that, as I have argued already, it is well to explore but necessary to restrain. The other side of that presiding intuition is that a vigorous public life in a republic, particularly in a legislative role—even as citizens are routinely called upon to enact it—imposes demands that are morally more serious and more inclusive, certainly more problematic, than those engaged by any private life, however exemplary that life may be. It is a kind of life that most immediately and routinely forces a detached appraisal of one's convictions and a practical testing of one's judgment. Muster all the confidence you can that you know the path of rectitude, call up all your resolve to adhere to moral principle, still, if you enter into public life, and at day's end your confidence is neither shaken nor deepened and your principles neither bent nor clarified, then it may be fairly asked whether you have been listening. It is in public life that judgments, principles, and lessons drawn from one's own experience will be most severely tested in confronting the principles, judgments, and experiences of others. That is where certainty is most likely to be tempered with doubt, not the doubt that leads to vacillation, but the kind that forges the patience of a plodding, long-term visionary, the kind that contrasts with the impetuosity of some white knight, however brilliant, who bursts upon the scene knowing precisely what is right for all, what is wrong for everyone, and what at all costs must be done about it. As one experienced legislator, Alan Simpson, expressed it, "in politics there are no right answers, only a continuing flow of compromises between groups, resulting in a changing cloudy and ambiguous series of public decisions, where appetite and ambition compete openly with knowledge and wisdom."[5] The most important part of this summary statement lies in that phrase "compete openly." In the stillness and separateness of private life, appetite and ambition can most easily have their raucous way in moving the soul against the more quiet virtues of knowledge and wisdom. But when they are made to compete openly, the hot winds of appetite and ambition are most likely to be cooled and calmed. Cabals do not breathe well the public air.

About those who headed up things during the rule of twelve in the French Terror of 1793, R. R. Palmer wrote,

> Their ideal statesman was no tactician, no compromiser, no skillful organizer who could keep various factions and pressure groups together. He was a man of elevated character, who knew himself to be in the right, a towering monument in a world of calumny and misunderstanding, a man who would have no dealing with the partisans of error and who, like Brutus, would sacrifice his own children that a principle might prevail.[6]

It is partly such a portrait of public leadership that underwrites our image of public life as corrupting, as fraught with "calumny and misunderstanding" sufficient to endanger the soul of any upright and "elevated character," any person of principle, who would enter it and run the risks of dealing with the "partisans of error." In such a comparison, public life always comes off second best, moralistically speaking. Such a contrast between the moral probity of public in contrast to private life seems to render all the more outrageous the claim that forming a conscience for public life is more likely to produce a conscience suited to private life than forming a conscience for private life is likely to produce a conscience for public life. The stumbling block to understanding such a claim lies partly in the popular conviction, no less erroneous for all its popularity, that there is no conscience of public life beyond self-interest and the skills of dissembling, and that lacking firm adherence to moral principle, all is adjustment, compromise, bargaining, aimless mediation. If politics is all deception and its skills deceit, then by what alchemical magic are we to suppose that such skills, converted into rules of conduct and granted

moral status, will serve well a conscience of private life? Yet such thinking is a mistake and, moreover, a dangerous and corrupting one. Consider
the contrasting grasp of public life that William Miller poses between the
moralists of the French Reign of Terror and those, like Madison, who engaged in shaping the foundations of the American republic. Miller
writes,

> The Robespierres of this world do not realize that in the politics of an
> actual republican state being right is only half the battle—maybe much
> less than half. In the work of complex social ordering—politics—there
> are always considerations beyond the pure "right"—of the sort that es-
> cape the moralists' eyes but have some "moral" weight—some value
> nonetheless. Order is value, a deep need of human beings in society,
> even though a value dangerous to liberty and other values; tradition and
> custom and social habit are values, although dangerous to social ideals.
> Dealing humanely with those . . . who hold something other than the
> "right" views is a very important value. One learns in the legislature of a
> genuine republic exactly to have many and continuous "dealings with
> the partisans of error." For the Americans—and for the English who
> were their primary teachers—these tolerations and collaborations and
> acknowledgings of multiple values were not violations of republican
> ideals but part of the essence of those ideals. And one of the places that
> republican ethos would be built into one's spiritual formation was the
> legislature.[7]

Miller is cautious not to describe as 'moral' those considerations that he
says "have some 'moral' weight—some value nonetheless." He 'brackets'
the word 'moral'. Yet these matters of value, whether described as moral or
not, are precisely those matters that matter most to a conscience suitably
formed for public life. Such a conscience is one that yields nothing to the
moralist in the way of conviction and devotion to principle but which *adds*
to these a capacity for judicious judgment about when to rise above principle. A person of such conscience is likely to suffer unease at failing to acknowledge the humanity even of those partisans of error with whom one
must deal. Such a conscience is apt to cite the dictum that half a loaf is better than none and even to add that getting none at all can sometimes prove
in the course of time to have been better by far even than getting half. A
conscience framed for the conduct of public life will find no offense in the
certainty that sooner or later the failure even of our most cherished projects can appear to a long and experienced memory as fortunate. Neither
will such a conscience be disillusioned by the knowledge that the victory

of cherished aims may turn out to have consequences neither foreseen nor, as it turns out, desirable. In short, one of the reasons why participation in public affairs can be said to be morally more demanding and more inclusive is that uncertainty is not simply incidental to it, but essential. It is a kind of moral uncertainty, however, quite compatible with strong adherence to moral principle. Indeed, public life, at least within a republic, offers the superlative context where appetite and ambition compete openly with knowledge and wisdom.

The moral education of citizens (one kind of membership) must be a preparation to participate in forming public policy. That is so, at least in a democratic social order.[8] Any adequate philosophy of moral education must provide a serious account of preparation for this 'office'. It is in our lives as public agents that we are most directly compelled to face the ambiguities, the depths, the uncertainties of moral life. Instead of searching for the foundations of public conduct in the moral principles of private life, we are likely to do much better by seeking to confront the moral tenuousness of our private lives by exercising and acquiring the skills of conduct imposed upon us by our lives as public agents. By such a thesis, civic education is no mere addendum, a footnote to moral education, something that comes after the main business has been accomplished. On the contrary, education for public life would have to be viewed as the central problem which, being understood, will allow us better and more completely to understand the formation of conscience for the more limited, private, and personal associations of our lives.

It is worth recalling how the ancients expressed this view. In Greek the term for 'individual' is *idiotes*, and its etymological descendent, 'idiot', expresses well the classical evaluation of what it meant to be an individual. He who lives outside the *polis*, says Aristotle, must be either beast or God—a beast because beyond the laws (*nomoi*) or a God because self-sufficient; but in neither case can such a creature be a human being.[9] Human beings are neither self-sufficient nor are they creatures who can forsake the maternal and pedagogical service rendered by the law.

Though the conscience of each of us is uniquely our own, and in a sense private, nonetheless, conscience is never formed except in some public and for the sake of life within that public. So the important unit of consideration in a philosophy of moral education is not the individual but *the member*. The conscience of membership is a truly fundamental reality that any philosophy of moral education must take as its object. It is not the only reality that can lay claim to such importance, but no attempt to understand the conduct of moral education can be adequate that does not give salience to this public formation of conscience. Here then is a defense of the primacy of membership in grasping the conduct of moral education.

Durkheim held that the first step in moral education is discipline, that is, the setting of boundaries, the bringing of order to the child's behavior.[10] The second step, he thought, is attachment to a social group. He says this partly because except within a social group, there are no social norms, hence no normation. Part of what distinguishes a social *group* from a mere aggregation is that in a social group the behavior of individuals, that is, the behavior of members, is governed by authoritative social norms. From the perspective of these essays it can be said that social groups are distinguished from aggregations by the operable presence of a conscience of membership. These points, though argued extensively already, are so central as to merit a fresh perspective through an extended illustration.

Response to Error Illustrated

Norms are always situationally specific. Norm acquisition cannot be understood as the acquisition of blind habit. It entails the acquisition of judgment and a sense of propriety; it can take place only in the context of human activities and settings; and the applicative model of their presence in activities is an inappropriate way to grasp the imminence of norms in human activities. These are all features of norm acquisition that become evident when we seek to explicate what sense belongs to the notion that norms are situationally specific. These features, furthermore, become evident as a result of attending not to the nature of norms and their validation but to their acquisition. These features of normation can be illustrated in another way by a single elaborated example, showing once again how the acquisition of norms is revealed not by compliance with their prescriptions, but by the character of our response to departures from them.

Imagine two youngsters, Punctual and Nonchalant. Punctual always arrives at school on time. In fact, he goes to extremes to do so, hurrying whenever the prospect of being late presents itself and showing evident relief at making it on time, embarrassment on those extremely rare occasions when he misses, and anxiety at the prospect. Nonchalant, on the other hand, lingers on his way to school, never hastens to make it on time, and becomes distracted by the friendly puppy, the argument on the corner, or any number of other things that might occur along the way. He wanders in late with no hesitation, embarrassment, or other evidence that he sees anything out of the ordinary about his behavior. Under these conditions, we would not hesitate to say that Punctual had acquired the norms of punctuality, but that Nonchalant had not.

But let us imagine further that Punctual and Nonchalant are good friends, and that it bothers Punctual that his friend is always late, even though it does not bother his friend. Punctual says to him, "You know, you really ought to get there on time. When you don't, the teacher really explodes and that doesn't help, you know."

"Yes, I know," says Nonchalant. "But so what? I don't mind really. And besides, I don't miss anything important by being late."

"Anyway," says Punctual, "it hurts me to see what you have to go through every day just because you are late, especially when I know that you don't have to be late."

And in response to this last remark, Nonchalant mends his ways and thereafter arrives at school on time. And so, on those rare occasions when he is late, he apologizes to his friend, but not to his teacher.

Under the conditions I have described, we would not hesitate to say that Nonchalant had acquired the norms of friendship, but we still might doubt that he had acquired the norms of punctuality *even though he regularly arrives at school on time*. Here again we note that norm acquisition is not displayed merely in the fact that the behavior of persons conforms to a certain pattern. Rather, the existence or failure of norm acquisition is displayed in the presence or absence of certain reflexive judgments and accompanying *feelings* associated with *departure* from what the norm requires. These are typically the feelings of guilt, shame, anxiety, embarrassment—the emotions of self-assessment—and sometimes fear, sorrow, and even pain. These are moral emotions and they occur also in association with the conscience of craft. We know that normation has succeeded when the emotions of self-assessment take this role, and when departures from the rule have the capacity to evoke feelings of outrage, indignation, pain, and offense on the part of others. This is what I have referred to as strong normation. Such emotions offer evidence of attachments, though not always and exclusively so.

Nonchalant, quite apparently, has acquired the norms of friendship in the strong sense. In him they govern. They govern to such an extent that in their governance of friendship, they force a change in Nonchalant's behavior, a plain manifestation of the imminent governance of norms in the strong sense. Indeed, it seems true that friendship cannot exist at all except where there is strong normation. That is one of the reasons why friendship has figured in the minds of many as offering at least one fundamental model of *all* moral relations. It is hard to understand how anyone can be a friend without feeling shame at causing needless pain to one's friends. If there is such a person anywhere, then that person literally cannot be said to *know* what it is to be a friend. Such a person lacks not simply feeling, but moral knowledge. Normation at a certain point has failed. Here again, we note that the distinction between cognitive and affective education may have application somewhere in education, but it is not a distinction that can make any sense whatever in moral education understood as normation.

The Devolution of Norms to Technique

I have maintained that something like norm acquisition can fall short of the point at which guilt, shame, embarrassment, and so forth are roused by departures from the norm. Nonchalant, for example, acquired the norms of friendship which then led him to *comply* with the school's norms of punctuality, not to obey them or be observant of them. Recall also that on those rare occasions when he is late, he apologizes to his friend but not to his teacher. Tardiness, for him, is serious not because it departs from the norms of the school, but because it violates the norms of friendship. It causes pain to his friend. We have here the account of a person who relates to the norms of the school as a body of purely technical norms, rules simply for 'getting along'.

It makes no difference to the purposes of the school whether Nonchalant's promptness rests in his relation to his friends or in his relations to the school. The school gets the compliance it needs in either case; but if Nonchalant's compliance is embedded only in the norms of friendship and not in the norms of the school, then the school regains absolutely nothing in the way of moral authority. Nonchalant's best personal strategy is to assume a posture of detached cynicism or, at its extreme form, contempt for the institution of the school. He can then be in the school, but not of it. He can know what the norms of the school are, abide by them, and at the same time not permit them to assume any legitimate moral authority. This is the prototype of weak or purely instrumental normation.

Such normation does not constitute a posture in relation to social practices that can be extended to the whole of life. Yet there is abundant evidence that it is constantly extended to work places where the norms of behavior are learned and complied with but without the kind of full acceptance that would give them any moral authority. This is often justified because such rules in the work place frequently have no moral point. The argument extended, however, would ask us to entertain the further prospect that such norms with no strong position in the practice of any craft or skill and no saliency in any membership of importance have all the status accorded to mere tools of expediency. Such a purely instrumental approach to life is untenable. It would rule out any relations of friendship, love, and any really serious competence in human attachments.

Moral education, among other things, is education in strong normation. It is the education of a conscience cultivated by attachment, not merely presence, to a social group. It is, in other words, the education of the conscience of membership. But weak normation is possible, frequent, and perhaps even necessary for survival in the modern world. Understanding that fact provides the grounds for understanding *one* tendency in our society from which there may be emerging a truly radical separation between the public and the private spheres of life and a kind of privatization of morality that can have enormous and quite frightening consequences.

It may be true generally that in modern societies the number of really strong and central social norms and settings for their appropriate exercise declines and people perceive themselves as increasingly subject to irrational authority. Authority, in that case, is experienced more and more as an expression of will, which is to say, more and more as a manifestation of power. As a society becomes more sophisticated (more *Gesellschaft*-like), its social norms are likely to become fewer and more instrumental. Strong normation is likely to be confined increasingly to those relationships whose nature intrinsically requires it, and such relations are seldom found in the context of anything that we would call a public. Instead, they tend to be confined to the kind of privacy and intimacy found among friends, within families or ethnic and religious groups, or within religious-like associations, like athletic clubs, whose members have achieved a rare sense of their mutuality and joint identity. Such relations are seldom found anywhere else in modern societies.

This path of development poses a threat to the strong maintenance of a public; for a civic public is neither an association among friends nor can it be as limited to a family or a religious or ethnic group. However, it is clearly true that whatever poses a threat to the formation of a strong public also renders problematic the grounds for the legitimacy of public education, except insofar as it offers a path toward an improved private life or work life for the individual. In whatever measure such a development progresses, to that extent education will tend to become understood as a purely technical and instrumental affair.

Is there no way out of this dilemma? I propose that there is, but only in a weak and most problematic way. First of all, we might ask whether there can be strong normation within the context of a profession or a labor union. And secondly, we may ask whether there can be a kind of curriculum of moral skill rooted strongly in the moral necessity of a public or in the conscience of membership.

Profession as Public

Where there is strong normation, there is moral authority. Where there is not, then at best, there can exist only a kind of technical, instrumental, or economic authority of norms. If a profession can constitute a normative order having moral authority over its members, then the conscience of the professional will be subsumed under the conscience of membership. Entering the profession will be likened to entering a public, though to those served by the profession, membership in it is less likely to resemble membership in a public and more likely to resemble membership in something like a priesthood, with all the social distance that accompanies the possession of priestly arcane knowledge.

Professions are characterized by a collegial structure. They are allegedly governed by their members. But by what norms? Professions are also understood as gatherings of experts. But it cannot be from the 'knowledge base' of expertise that strong norms emerge within the collegial order. At best, expertise produces only technical norms of practice, and that, as I have argued already, is not enough to engage our sense of *moral* authority. If strong norms are generated within a profession, they must be derived rather from a third feature of professions, not from the knowledge base nor even from a collegial structure, but from the fact that professions are always practices in response to some fundamental human need or social good *whose advancement is already a moral aim*.

The traditional professions are the practices of the military, medicine, nursing, law, and the priesthood or ministry. These are practices that answer to the most basic human needs for security (the military), for a response to social and physical pathology (medicine and nursing), for justice and the regulation of the social order (law), and for meaning at the

major events of life (religion). They are rooted in those events that bring
life into the world, that sustain it, and that aim to make it fulfilling. The
very point of the professions is that they shape a human response to the
simple brute fact that pain demands to be noticed, whether it is the pain
of injustice, of sickness, or of meaninglessness. Because of these roots, the
professions are recognizable practices that already have a moral point.
They do not need to search for it. That is why we can speak so easily of
them as professions and not so easily of hoola-hooping and 'making book'
in the same way. These last may be ways of gaining a living and so, in a
loose way of speaking, they might produce careers. But they cannot be
professions, nor can any voice with a shred of historical consciousness
speak of them as vocations. They answer to no fundamental human need.

If there are strong norms with moral authority by which to govern
within the collegial order of a profession, they arise, therefore, not from
the existence of a knowledge base, but from a consciousness of the moral
enterprise already implicit in the profession. Thus, if we seek to induct
persons into a profession by giving them command of the relevant expertise, and at the same time neglect to teach them the point of the practice,
then surely it will become necessary to offer instruction in professional
ethics. But in that event, the need for such instruction will have arisen
from a failure to teach the point of the profession itself, that is, it will
stem from a failure of normation and not from our failure to teach ethics.

A Curriculum of Moral Skill

We can think of moral education or normation in the context of membership by means of a kind of curriculum of moral skill. The moral skills
in question are not derived from considering the good of any individual
moral agent. Nor will they be disclosed by examining the necessities of
private and individual moral choices. They are problems instead that define the skills needed to be competent in public life. Thus, the curriculum of moral skills takes as its subject questions of decision and choice
having to do with some collective—the school, the neighborhood, the
town, the profession, the family, or whatever. They have to do with questions not about what is good for *me* to do, but what is good for *us* to do.

First Lesson If it be asked whether x is a good thing for us to do, or a good
way for us to do y, then it is never sufficient merely to answer no. The first
discipline, that is, the first thing to be learned, is that one must be pre-

pared to go beyond and offer some proposal for improvement. One must always be prepared to entertain the prospect that though things are not as good as we can imagine, nevertheless, they may be as good as we can make them at the moment, or conversely, that no matter how bad things have gotten, they might quite possibly get worse. In the school, for example, when students offer only the judgment that a certain course of action or course of study is bad, they have not yet offered a judgment in the context of their collective life that is entitled to be taken seriously. One must confront the possibility that in order to improve things, one needs the skills to propose the improvement, not merely to voice complaint. That things are in bad shape when they can't be any better, is not by itself a serious criticism. When offered alone, it forges no ethical claim upon our attention.

I have come to believe, for example, that in university committee work aimed at curricular reform, it is well to invite criticism, but also well to accompany that invitation with the caveat that criticism will be more responsibly given and more favorably received when it arrives accompanied by specific hints at a better way. We begin by assuming that what has been accomplished is defective in some respects. No matter what our accustomed practice may be, it no doubt leaves room for improvement. To repeat the assumption that our ways of life are less than we desire does nothing to rebut the presumption that they ought to be preserved. That things are faulty is an observation of practical importance only if they can be better. That is the first lesson in the curriculum of moral skill.

Second Lesson The second is a lesson in empathy. Whenever it be asked whether x is a good thing for us to do or a good way for us to do y, whether you answer no and offer a better way, or answer yes, you are obliged in either case to confront three more questions: (1) Whose interests are you expressing? (2) Whose interests are you not expressing? and (3) How does your proposal balance the goods being sought? The point of this exercise should be obvious. No one can entertain these questions seriously in any collective setting without acknowledging the legitimacy of others' interests, the reality of their conflict, and the need for their adjustment.

I do not speak merely of a utilitarian, arithmetic, or intellectual calculation. It is not enough to simply think about or merely entertain the interests of others. We are called upon to actually enter into those interests or, better yet, permit them to enter into us. Indeed, the very act of *stating* the interests of others *as others see them*, and stating them aloud and, if possible, in the actual presence of those others, is often in itself a powerful exercise in empathy, an exercise by which the interests of others are allowed to actually enter into our own. But it is even more than that. Such a lesson requires the actual employment of empathy and at the same time promotes its acquisition. Such an exercise extends our sensibilities and tests our sympathies and our capacity for self-control.

This might be a point in the curriculum of moral skill when persons are called upon to act in ways approaching moral heroism. The effort to understand and to actually state and proclaim the view of the other can be a step of fundamental change because, among other things, it requires the emotional flavor of moral distinctions to enter into the formation of conscience. Without that entry we do not have moral knowledge. We have only moral speculation. Without this exercise, we do not truly have normation. Facing questions of our collective life places one inescapably, both imaginatively and emotionally, in a network of relations in which the limits of membership are tested, and perhaps enlarged, by seriously entertaining the reality of legitimate interests. Admittedly, learning to deal with such questions requires also a great deal of skill and information, a lot of knowing how and knowing that. This is the step in the curriculum of moral skill that simultaneously makes the formation of a public possible and offers a kind of anticipatory setting for practice in forming public policy.[11]

This second lesson in the curriculum of moral skill engages us in an effort to stretch the reaches of our sympathy. Here is a capacity for attachment easily admitted to be important for life within our relations among friends, family and like affiliations of relative intimacy. Such associations could hardly exist, much less flourish, without such apparently natural human capacities of sentiment roused by the presence or the mere prospect of the good or ill of others. These are the sentiments of association that Adam Smith explored in *The Theory of Moral Sentiments*. "To seem not to be affected with the joy of our companions," he says, "is but want of politeness; but not to wear a serious countenance when they tell us their afflictions, is real and gross inhumanity." "We are not half so anxious," he continues,

> that our friends should adopt our friendships, as that they should enter into our resentments. We can forgive them though they seem to be little affected with the favours which we may have received, but lose all patience if they seem indifferent about the injuries which may have been

done to us: nor are we half so angry with them for not entering into our gratitude as for not sympathizing with our resentment. They can easily avoid being friends to our friends, but can hardly avoid being enemies to those with whom we are at variance. We seldom resent their being at enmity with the first, though upon that account we may sometimes affect to make an awkward quarrel with them; but we quarrel with them in good earnest if they live in friendship with the last.[12]

This second lesson of moral skill calls us to exercise these sentiments of association, but on a more expansive stage, namely, in the conduct of public life. That, it seems to me, is the way that this second lesson might prove useful in forming a conscience capable of judgment in public life in ways that serve as well the precincts of private life. Such sentiments of affiliation quite likely are stirred initially in our more limited associations. That is not, however, where they are most severely tested and extended to form the conscience of membership.

The point sheds light upon a claim advanced earlier that a conscience formed for conduct in the skills of public life is more likely to produce a conscience well suited for private life, than is a conscience formed for private life likely to suit well the rigours of public life. The question may be faced by asking how the sentiments of our limited associations can be brought to bear upon public questions, especially in view of the fact that it is precisely the strongest of those limited affiliations of family, clan, and personal attachment that most often must be laid aside upon entering a public forum. It is, after all, in the public forum that the issues to be decided are always matters of what to do and almost never what is right, or good, or to be believed. What kind of public debate is it in which *the actual thing to be decided is not what to do but what to believe*?

Distinguish two kinds of public discourse. Typically, in a public forum where policy choices are actually made, such as a legislature, we are asked to choose from a set of actions some of which may be better than others, but all of which must either be morally indifferent or capable of evoking moral approval. Given this presumption, we assume that human beings may agree on what to do without having to agree in their beliefs about what is right or wrong, good or bad. In this kind of public forum what is to be decided is a course of action, not a moral principle. In such a forum, persons may start from different moral principles, provided they come to agree on a course of action. In this exercise of empathy, stating the interests of others as others see them can be a boon in arriving at any resolve that can be translated into action. Selecting from among the variety of contending moral principles is not at all what the debate aims to decide.

It can happen in such a forum, however, that a course of action is proposed that, for some members, can be viewed neither with moral approval nor with moral indifference. It follows that *for them* the proposed course of action cannot be included within the initial set of acceptable policy choices. When that happens—think of many aspects of the abortion debate—then necessarily there must ensue an extensive public discussion in which the point to be decided *is* a matter of moral principle and the means of encouraging that agreement can be and often is to effect an extension of the sentiments of association. That is a second form of public discourse.

There is no point in denying that a debate of this latter sort is a part of public discourse or that it is aimed at the resolution or the clarification of a moral dispute. Matters of moral right and wrong, in that respect, can and must be discussed in public debate to whatever extent they are implicated in decisions of public policy. There is, however, a point in denying that such a debate determines policy. On the contrary, it can at best only determine the range of acceptable choices from which policy must be framed. In the kind of public forum where policy is determined, the thing to be decided is a course of action, not a standard of moral belief. But in this second kind of public debate, what is being shaped is moral belief, not policy.

By way of illustration, consider the Lincoln-Douglas debates. They are a stunning example of public discourse on public issues conducted in a public forum. No one can doubt that those debates were deeply infused with moral argument. Nor can anyone doubt that they did much to inform the public consciousness. But we can certainly doubt that those debates set policy. They plainly did not. They were not conducted in the kind of forum where policy is set. Rather, they were conducted in the kind of forum that shapes the conscience that we carry with us when we enter into the actual determination of policy. Thus, these debates illustrate how and when public arguments of moral belief are admitted to public discourse and how and when they are not admitted. The nature of public discourse is different in these two contexts. But the extension of our sensibilities for moral empathy in this second step of the curriculum of moral skill is relevant to both kinds of settings since it occurs in the one kind of forum where the reach of sentiments are tested and it is exercised, as it were, in the other. It has its educative parentage in the one kind of forum and its enactment in another kind.

Third Lesson A third lesson in the curriculum of moral skill calls upon us to ask certain questions about those interests themselves. Are they good? Are they long-run or only short-run? How extensive are they? Are they limited to a small group or are they widely shared? This lesson is a necessary step in learning to make useful judgments about the weight to be attached to different interests. And that is a problem in addition to the exercise of empathy needed to acknowledge the reality of those interests and to search for their adjustment. Secondly, it is a useful lesson in learning that any adjustment of interests is likely to lead to fresh problems needing fresh solutions. Circumstances alter things; but so does time. The problem of building a world is continuous. Among other things, such a step requires us to employ the prudential skills of foresight, and to confront such moral difficulties as having to do now what is undesirable or perhaps even unjust in order later to do what is beneficial and fair.

A simple matrix for the assessment of interests is contained in this step of the curriculum of civic skill. Duration is one dimension. It asks whether these interests are short- or long-term, whether they are momentary or durable. Extent is another. Are these interests that extend widely throughout the community or are they limited to a small segment? Putting the matter in this way immediately suggests important features of Bentham's calculus of utility.[13] Bentham listed seven dimensions of pleasures and pains that he thought ought to be considered in measuring utility—intensity, duration, certainty, propinquity, fecundity, purity, and extent. These seven, I believe, exhaust the considerations that, for the most part, enter even now into the practice of policy evaluation. Duration and what he means by extent and fecundity are the only elements of these seven included in the matrix I have suggested. However, including foresight as a virtue to be formed in the conscience of membership would tend to incorporate the others.

Foresight is an essential virtue in the skills of conscience. It is needed if we are ever to contemplate the consequences of our own actions and thus to engage in any kind of planning in the arts of living, especially the civic arts. It is also required if we are ever to deliberate skillfully about our duties to future generations. The exercise of foresight belongs to the voice of prudence in the conscience of membership. Cicero claimed that among the parts of prudence as good judgment must be included memory (the past), understanding (the present), and foresight (the future),[14] and Aquinas writes, "Memory, understanding and foresight, as also caution and readiness to learn and the like, are not virtues distinct from prudence; they are, as it were, integral parts or components, inasmuch as they are all requisite for perfect prudence."[15]

It might be argued that the virtue of prudence, understood in this way, is beyond the reach of schools to cultivate because the memory of the young cannot be more extensive than their own brief life. Thus, asking them to deliberate on their duties to successive generations is to ask too much. From the perspective of youth, especially the very young, what is owed to future generations is unlikely to loom anywhere near as large as it will in later years. For them, in effect, there are no successive generations. Prudence of the sort intended by Cicero and Aquinas is really a kind of wisdom in practical affairs, and to develop such wisdom requires having already had a fairly long life, something necessarily impossible for the young. In this critical appraisal of what is educationally required for the acquisition of prudence is found a certain relevant caution, but even so, such caution needs to be severely abridged or supplemented. We ought to recall that when the public in question is the school and the conscience of membership is membership in it, then a generation, for example in the case of high school students, is seldom longer than four years. The exercise of foresight, even if not in its fullness, is nonetheless within the reach of education in the school, but only if the school can cultivate the attachment of membership, a matter increasingly difficult in a highly mobile society and in schools whose members are increasingly transient.

Three points are suggested by this sketchy account of what I have called the curriculum of moral skill. The first is that instead of looking for the roots of policy decision in moral theory or moral philosophy, as though to discover there another decalogue, we might find a model of moral thinking and thus of moral education generally in policy deliberation, that is, in the thinking of the person who is already excellent in his or her exercise of public life. That is one thing meant by saying that the proper unit of consideration in moral education is not the individual, not even the individual conscience, but *the member*. Secondly, if it is the conscience of membership that is cultivated in the curriculum of moral skill, then civic education and moral education become more nearly a single enterprise. It becomes more difficult to regard civic education as a mere addendum or extension of moral education. The empirical clue as to when such education has succeeded is provided by the rhetorical shift from talk framed in the first-person singular to talk in the first-person plural, the shift of discourse from 'I' and 'me' to 'us' and 'we'. This is the transformation telling us that the language of membership has successfully entered into the formation of conscience, and that attachment to a social group has occurred. The time and manner of this occurrence is a perfectly observable educational event. Taking note of how and when it happens will tell us much as to whether the conscience of membership is being shaped within the school, within the peer group, or within some membership completely outside the school.

And finally, the assembled steps of the curriculum of moral skill add up to a complex set of norms. These are the kinds of practical judgments needed for moral conduct or moral thinking within the context of some public. Indeed, if we study carefully the problems and skills outlined in the curriculum of moral competence, we shall discover, I believe, that jointly they constitute a definition of what we mean by 'responsibility' in the context of membership. And it is vital to note that the unit of membership need not be described as *communitas* or as *societas*. Neither does it have to be the legal order. It might be family or school, town or neighborhood, or possibly even the boundaries described by membership in a profession.

Chapter 4

The Voices of Conscience II:
Sacrifice, Memory, and Imagination

I. The Conscience of Sacrifice

Much is missing from the account so far. Clues to needed additions can be found in a single brute fact about human beings, namely that in the order of learning, prudence precedes morality. Prudence is the threshhold to morality and in that sense prior to morality. By prudence I now mean not merely the wisdom of foresight, but the wisdom of foresight turned to the preservation of self-interest. There is a sense of 'morality' according to which prudence, in this more limited sense, is prior to morality. People do not need teaching to become self-interested; though they often need to be taught to be moral. I admit, of course, that learning *how* to be prudent in this sense is something for which guidance is often helpful, since what is in one's own self-interest is not always perfectly evident and even when perfectly evident to some, may not be so evident to others. It is this natural primacy of prudence, perhaps, that makes the second lesson in the curriculum of moral skill, the development of empathy, so necessary. Because of the primacy of prudence, that is, its status as a natural impulse, the exercise of empathy must be transformed from the status of a natural presence into something like a moral project, a kind of educational drill. Still, we are creatures who need no urging to be prudent in the sense of self-interested. That, it seems, comes naturally.

The Primacy of Prudence

It may be argued that attachment among human beings is natural and evident early on, perhaps even immediately, in the life of human beings and thus, the exercise of prudence as tending to one's own self-interest is no more natural than attachment to the interests of others. There is natural bondedness between parent and child, for example, and children often and quite 'naturally' care for the young of other species. Perhaps it is in such natural bondedness that we find the basis for the conscience of membership. I do not deny that these are facts, but neither do I affirm them. I mean only to point to another kind of fact, namely that the primitive status of self-interest over morality is what produces the voice of conscience as sacrifice. The call of duty, in fact, often presents itself as a voice calling for sacrifice, and in proportion as the magnitude of the sacrifice grows, then just so much does the appeal of duty need a more substantial struggle on its behalf in order to prevail. Here then is the stuff of which a kind of moral heroism can be composed, a fact sufficient to prompt the limiting reminder that in a world where being moral demands that we be heroes, there won't be much morality around.

This observation about the priority of prudence I would now expand into the claim that if we were not first of all creatures of prudence, we could not later become moral beings. Rational attention to one's own well-being may be, in fact, the principal threshhold for entry into the moral institution of life. This, I believe, is a somewhat more controversial claim. Yet, consider the familiar dictum that honesty is the best policy. In this so-called moral precept we are not, in fact, presented with a moral guide at all. We are given only a guide to good policy, a rule of conduct that we are told will work, on the whole, to our advantage. We are told, in short, that honesty pays. That seems plain enough. As a counsel of prudence in pursuit of self-interest, the dictum has a certain motivational punch. If honesty really is the best policy, if it really does pay, then clearly I do have reason to do whatever honesty commends. And because of this motivational push (or pull), the dictum can provide a good point at which to start our moral education even though it cannot provide a point at which to end it. Here is a familiar saying, in other words, that points in the right direction and which, therefore, because of its motivational strength, might help in pointing *us* in the right direction. The appeal is to the priority of prudence. Where shall I even look for a similar motivational sanction to underwrite my honesty when it clearly *isn't* going to pay? Am I simply going to say, "Well, it pays then too?"

Asking the question, I hope, will make more transparent what I mean by saying that prudence is more primitive than morality and that if we were not first creatures of prudence, we could not later become moral beings. Indeed, it is precisely the brute fact of the primacy of prudence that we rely on when we use such a dictum, and many others like it, as guides in moral education. We appeal to prudence though our aim is morality. Were we not already creatures of prudence, we could make no such appeal, and moral education aimed at arousing the voice of duty could find no place upon which to gain a foothold in the formation of our conscience.

In a personal statement (rare among moral philosophers) reflecting on his own search for understanding, Henry Sidgwick stated the problem well. His study of the methods of ethics was launched in large degree by the conflict he saw between interest and duty. "In consequence of this perception," he wrote,

> moral choice of the general happiness or acquiescence in self-interest as ultimate, became practically necessary. But, on what ground? I put aside Mill's phrases that such sacrifice was "heroic"; that it was not "well" with me unless I was in a disposition to make it. I put to him in my mind the dilemma:—Either it is for my own happiness or it is not. If not, why [should I do it]? It was no use to say that if I was a moral hero I should have formed a habit of willing actions beneficial to others which would remain in force, even with my own pleasure in the other scale. I knew that at any rate I was not the kind of moral hero who does this without reason; from blind habit. Nor did I even wish to be that kind of hero: for it seemed to me that that kind of hero, however admirable, was certainly not a philosopher. I must somehow see that it was right for me to sacrifice my happiness for the good of the whole of which I am a part.[1]

At a certain point in his philosophical quest, Sidgwick took the view that even the *rational* egoist, as contrasted with the psychological egoist, might accept the Kantian principle and still remain an *egoist*.

> He might say, "I quite admit that when the painful necessity comes for another man to choose between his own happiness and the general happiness, he must as a reasonable being prefer his own. . . . No doubt as I probably do not sympathize with him in particular any more than with other persons, I as a disengaged spectator should like him to sacrifice himself to the general good; but I do not expect him to do it, any more than I should do it myself in his place."[2]

We often view morality in just this way, that is, in the light of the conflict between interest and duty, between the claims of self and other. And when we do, then morality is construed as entering the picture only when we are willing to sacrifice self-interest for the interests of others. Morality, in short, is viewed as a thing 'set-over-against'. By such lights, morality appears always in contrast to another thing already present. Moral reasons are 'other regarding'; prudential reasons (nonmoral) are 'self-regarding'. So goes the familiar contrast. According to that perspective, morality enters only when we find the voice of conscience as sacrifice and when *that* voice gains its own motivational strength. Is it enough for the aims of moral education then, to find and to teach the *reasons*, even sound *moral* reasons, for such a sacrifice? No. It is worth a reminder that we can be rational and still be wrong. We do not become moral by consulting the reasons that endorse our sacrifice, even though we are likely to become morally more mature for having explored those reasons. It is those reasons that philosophers like Sidgwick seek; and that is what any reflective person who is already moral would insist upon receiving. What we require from moral *education*, however, is the actual sacrifice of self-interest and not merely its rational defense. In short, for moral education what we seek is not moral cognition, but normation. What the philosopher seeks, in contrast, is the rational defense of what is already implanted in consequence of normation.

Now 'sacrifice' may seem a term too strong, too violent to describe what is involved in surmounting the tug of self-interest. It suggests that a certain violence against the self must be committed. And we all know that if that is done in excess then our sense of self-respect and dignity itself is sacrificed. If we sacrifice too often the attention that our own self-interest deserves, then we may end by having no self of our own to affirm. There are whole groups of people in our society who, by moral ideology, by social position, or by a confused conception of generosity have virtually defined their lives in deference to the interests or preferences of others, and have found it necessary, in consequence, to learn again what is needed to assert themselves, without at the same time confusing self-assertion with aggression. I have in mind the too frequent position of women and, oddly enough, alcoholics. By attempting to please everyone, we end up pleasing no one. By pursuing a due regard for our own prudential interests, at least we may end up pleasing ourselves, and that is important even to our moral health. As Bishop Butler was keen to point out, we have a positive duty to attend to our own happiness. "Self-love," he says,

in its due degree is as just and morally good as any affection whatever. . . . Upon the whole, if the generality of mankind were to cultivate
within themselves the principle of self-love . . . it would manifestly prevent numberless follies and vices.[3]

What Butler means by 'self-love' may include what I have called self-
interest, though they are not the same thing. In any case, neither Butler's
self-love nor what I have termed self-interest should be identified with
selfishness.[4]

The voice of conscience as sacrifice is necessary to any full understanding of moral education, but it is not the only voice we hear. There
are those who, discerning its necessity, would assign to it a dominant position among the voices of conscience, and who insist that we must do
our duty though the heavens fall. To them, however, the proper response
is simply that if the heavens are likely to fall, then perhaps we should reconsider. The voice of duty is not the only voice of conscience; yet to
speak of it as a voice of sacrifice is to speak exactly of the kind of reversal,
the kind of turning from pure self-interest, that is called for in this one
among the many voices of conscience.

We recoil from such language. Perhaps—we are inclined to say *sotto
voce*—what *looks* like sacrifice is not that really. Perhaps we need to be
taught that our interests, if we truly understand them, will turn out really
to be the interests of others, that we shall find our true self-interest, our
deepest contentment—if we have but the courage to seek it—in the very
advancement of the good for others. But am I to suppose that that is what
I need to be taught, even when that teaching appears to be a transparent
lie? All such arguments, it seems to me, eventually reduce to a kind of
Panglossian appeal to prudence: in the long run, whatever you think to
the contrary, it really will pay to be honest. Perhaps instead, I am to say,
as Dewey did, that what appears to me now as self-sacrifice is not really a
sacrifice of the self in me. It is merely me acting now to advance the interests of the self in me that is now being formed.[5] But this again, it seems
to me, is a disguised appeal to prudence. The self in me that is being
framed, however future and however good, is still *my* self. To act in *its* interests is still to act in my own interest. Anything to fend off the sacrificial claims of conscience!

It is amazing what evasive and defensive creatures we can be. We will
apparently try all manner of devices to escape altogether or, failing that,
then at least to soften the sacrificial tone of this voice of conscience. But

if we are to be clear about the problems of moral education and discerning about our educational chances for its advancement, then we shall have to face the sacrificial character of this voice head on. To the *merely* prudential man or woman this voice of conscience speaks harshly. It says, in effect, "You must have other desires than you have. You must have the desire to serve the good of others even at the cost of what you desire now as your own good." And it will not do in reply to say merely that I *desire* to have other desires than I have. To desire to have other desires than I have is merely to harbor a wish, the wish that I were other than I am. Nothing will satisfy that voice, nothing will quiet it, except to actually *have* those other desires.

From Principle to Practice

If you grant the primacy of prudence as brute fact, then you must also grant as brute fact the claim that among the voices with which conscience speaks there is the voice of sacrifice. We may grasp this point in principle, but how shall we understand it in practice, and especially in the practice of moral education? It argues, I believe, for the educational necessity of performing acts that fall beyond the limits of mere duty. Any perfectly gratuitous act of caring or kindness aimed at the good of another has this characteristic. Such acts are required for moral education not because they follow the dictates of duty, but precisely because they exceed such demands. They are not acts of *in*justice, but neither are they acts of justice. They are not acts of self-sacrifice so much as they are acts of self-indifference and at the same time, oddly enough, of self-fulfillment. Just as dicta of prudence may point us in the direction of our moral duties and therefore serve well for moral education, so also such actions of self-indifference, though beyond the demands of duty, may point us in the direction of conscience as sacrifice. Such actions are perhaps most easily discovered in the context of friendship or membership. But they may also be found, for example, in the care of pets. Both experience and sympathy inform us, however, that it is difficult even to imagine such acts being performed toward total strangers, that is, outside *any* context of membership whatsoever.

The self-fulfilling, though not self-regarding, character of such sacrificial acts is most clearly revealed in the context of friendship. Whether there are duties of friendship can be doubted. It cannot be doubted, however, that acts of friendship fall outside the domain of justice according to merit. You do not receive the kindness of friends because you deserve it. It is vastly more likely that you receive such kindness despite the fact that you deserve no such thing at all. These are gifts that come to one only because those are friends. Any act of friendship, when viewed from the vantage of the observer, will be seen as gratuitous in the sense of not being dictated by merit. So when I say that the performance of some such acts is required for the *formation* of conscience, I do not mean that we must all be moral heroes. I mean only that we need the experience of performing such acts of grace. Such acts are sacrificial, not in the sense of being self-denying, but in the sense of being self-indifferent and other-regarding.

Friendship is that kind of relationship. It is a relation requiring (1) a certain reciprocity, (2) a certain equality of virtue, and (3) a certain kind of self-love together with a measured indifference to justice. The first point—the need for reciprocity—is made plain by the fact that unrequited love, provided it continues, turns quickly into mere adoration or adulation, both one-way relations that negate the notion of friendship. So reciprocity is essential to friendship. The second point—the need for an approximate equality of virtue—is apparent in the simple fact that, although it is easy to adore a saint, it is impossible to be friends with one. The third—the indifference to justice—is the point of paradox.

How is this so-called indifference to be described? Try this. There are several windows on the self. Some, for example, reveal aspects of myself known to me, but shielded from others. There are other aspects known to others, but shielded from me; just as there are aspects of others known to me, but shielded from them. In a good friendship, one thing that each discovers in the other, or perhaps through the other, is one's own self reflected. The only relation, outside of therapy, in which I come anywhere near knowing myself as others know me, is in this relation of friendship. It is there that the self of each is most honestly revealed, and revealed to each by the other. I am best known to myself, in short, when I come to know how it is that others know me. When the issue of that knowledge is good, I gain self-love. Self-love can come when I find that what I really am—all sham aside—is valued by another. And the self-indifference comes when I accept the ever present risk in making myself known to another, the risk that, after all, I might be rejected. And it matures, I think, when making myself known to another comes finally to contain no risk at all. When the risk falls away, the relation can take on the form of trust and finally love. No wonder that in such a relationship there is so much joy and at the same time so much freedom, such ease, along with vulnerability and release. It is as though this is the relation for which we are made; the kind that we are meant to enter. It is not a relation of justice, but it points us to the possibility of justice by encouraging us in actions that transcend it. It is a relation that points in that direction and that is why it points *us* in that direction.

The voice of conscience as duty may be shaped within the practices of friendship. That, if true, is educationally significant. It is equally significant, however, that there are certain moral practices of daily life quite beyond the limits of friendship within which the voice of conscience as duty also speaks clearly. Consider the keeping of promises, as well as the keeping of contracts and confidences, which are like promises. When I say, "I promise," I undertake to firmly fix the future. By pronouncing those words, I declare that whatever may be my prudential interests at some future time, I shall lay them aside. Instead, I shall perform the promised act. Anyone who says, "I promise to return your book by next Tuesday," meaning by that "I shall return it provided it is expedient, convenient, or in my own interest to do so at the time," simply does not understand what the words "I promise" mean. Fortunately, keeping promises, however inconvenient from time to time, does not often conflict deeply with our own self-interest. But the point is that by entering into such a moral practice we learn that there are times when in principle we must lay aside self-interest as irrelevant. And what is more important, we actually come to do it.

That promises should be kept is typically offered as a model of conscience speaking in this voice of duty, partly, I suppose, because the rule seems to offer the clearest cases in which interest and personal desire must be laid aside or sacrificed in the face of moral duty. If that is so, then here is a rule, a set of cases, of peculiar pedagogical power. Another general rule, of equal clarity, is the duty to tell the truth. For the most part, speaking truthfully, like keeping promises, presents no moral difficulties in our daily lives. We simply do it and expect others to do it. If someone stops me by the road to ask directions, I do not have to deliberate (nor do you) and remind myself of some presumed duty to tell the truth. I simply give directions as best I can.

Sometimes, however, it may appear that we will benefit greatly, even in the long term, by offering up a credible lie or by withholding some portion of the truth. Such are the times, perhaps the only times, when truth telling appears to us as a duty. Perhaps the only reason we come to think of truth telling as a duty at all is that temptation, expediency, and self-interest sometimes intervene and make it difficult to do.[6] That is when the English expression "because it is your duty" seems to find a natural usage. Someone asks, "Why should I be truthful (keep agreements, and the like) in *this* case?" (not in general). If the question is genuine, then the person asking is genuinely troubled about the matter. And if that is the case, then the answer may come back quite naturally, "because it is your duty." That response is an argument-stopper. It is meant to be. It is the last possible response at the end of a long line of thought. The voice of duty is a magisterial voice. When it speaks, and speaks truly, there is no appeal beyond it. That is something that cannot be said of any other voice of conscience.

There are, however, quite definite preconditions to satisfy if this kind of voice is to deliver such an appeal and have it heard, circumstances that go together to create the 'teachable moment' for such an appeal. First and most apparent among them is this condition of being genuinely troubled, that is, confronted with a real conflict between duty and interest or desire, and thus confronted not as some abstract possibility, but in some quite specific case. This combination of a conscience (a) being confronted by a specific case and (b) being genuinely troubled—this combination is what creates the 'teachable moment' in which the command of duty can be heard. Indeed, it is *only* when faced with specific cases that we speak at all of being 'confronted'. One might 'entertain' a general rule or abstract case, but we do not speak of confronting one except when faced with a genuine and quite specific case. That, moreover, is when we normally use the language of duty to describe some action.

Pedagogy and Serious Moral Language

Here then is a point at which context is crucial. We began by noting that the voice of conscience as duty, that is, the voice of sacrifice, must come to have its own moral strength, and that this must be accomplished in a certain world and in the soul of certain creatures for whom prudence, in the sense of self-interest, is more primitive than morality. Next, we began to see that there are contexts, like the care of pets, and relations like friendship, which though not defined by rules of duty, nonetheless, point us in the direction of becoming creatures for whom the voice of duty gains a chance to speak with some authority.

So much for attachments and practices that point us toward the care of others, and through concern with others to the voice of conscience as sacrifice. But now we come to see that the actual language of duty and the situations in which such language can be used with pedagogical force are remarkably limited. Suppose a person goes beyond the normal context for asking "Why should I tell the truth *in this case?*" and asks generally why truth telling is one's duty. The moment that this move occurs, we know that something has changed. We are transported beyond the serious speech of a moral conscience troubled in specific circumstances, and have entered instead into a different kind of discourse. We have passed from a moral argument to an academic one.[7] We have left the context of moral education in order to enter into a philosophical debate. The topic has shifted. Now a proof is sought, a general proof. This request for proof is not a request that arises from a conscience troubled by some specific case, nor is the response to it likely to offer such a conscience much in the way of guidance. It is to this troubled conscience that we say "because it is your duty." And this response has finality precisely because there is no subsequent moral question, only an academic one, only a question of academic philosophy.

By this observation, I wish to point in two directions. The first is to our need to understand what is meant by morally serious speech, so that we can grasp how and when our language signals entry into moral discussions as opposed to merely academic ones. Duty language comes into play when a troubled conscience confronts a specific case. The language used in philosophical discussion generally is not of that sort. In this respect it is not morally serious language. Philosophy does not provide the language needed for the formation of conscience. I think I understand how one learns to talk philosophy. But if we are to understand the educational formation of conscience, then the relevant need is for an account of how the serious language of the troubled conscience is acquired and the conditions under which it is used. It is when that kind of language is signaled, but of course not only then, that we have educational opportunities for the formation of conscience.

As noted already, however, I don't really believe that the words "because it is your duty" can readily find a use in contemporary speech, even in the context I have described. The word 'duty' may have joined a rather long list of terms likely to be viewed as simply quaint, outdated, or passé. In addition to 'duty' the list might include such words as 'honor', 'evil', 'naughty', and 'wicked'.[8] I am sure there are others. If 'duty' falls among these disused terms, then the argument-stopping expression "because it is your duty" is lost to pedagogy. It will have to yield instead to a mere "because you ought to," which is not an argument-stopper at all. This expression seems more easily to allow a subsequent question of a moral sort to arise. The question will be, "But why ought I?" "Because you ought to," in short, is a weaker claim, a claim of less finality than "because it is your duty." This contrast, together with the magisterial voice of duty, is captured beautifully by Arthur Murphy, who writes,

> "Good", in spite of its analytic corruptions, is essentially a reasonable word—it invites us to consider together what we "really" prefer and to act accordingly. But "right" and "requirement" are demanding words, and in their morally admonitory use particularly so. They are associated in our minds with claims, commands, laws, obligations and sanctions and those who use them often speak in a peremptory tone. Duty, "stern daughter of the voice of God," "whispers, 'lo, thou must'" and this is not a "must" with which it seems appropriate to argue. The councils of prudence have an "if" in them—"if you want this, do that"—but the moral law is presented as an unconditional command or categorical imperative which leaves us with no moral ground on which to ask "why should I?" Its dictates are obligations, not incentives, and to be obligated is to be obliged, bound, morally constrained to do not what we should ourselves prefer but what, as thus bound, we *must*.[9]

What are the pedagogical consequences if this stronger expression, this expression of duty fails to receive a use in ordinary speech? Merely to ask the question is to perceive one dimension of the problems in shaping a philosophy on the formation of conscience.

Let us return to the argument, however, and to the second direction in which I wanted to point. I have already said that truth telling and promise keeping are among the paradigm cases of the voice of conscience as sacrifice. They are often referred to as moral practices. One is tempted even to say that they are moral institutions. How does one enter these moral institutions? It cannot happen that merely saying the words "I promise" come to be the words of actually making a promise unless those words are uttered with moral seriousness within a whole system of pleadings, counter pleadings, excuses, and commitments included in such practices. As I have noted already, saying the words "I promise," when addressed to some A with respect to doing some y at some time t, involves, among other things, giving up being a utilitarian at time t. How does one come to learn this, and more than that, come to do it? That is the problem for the formation of conscience. I think it is just such an account of moral learning and the acquisition and use of morally serious language that we need for a philosophy of moral education and which, on the whole, we do not have and will not gain from moral theory.

The Pedagogical Uses of Ethical Theories

The appeal to duty is a special and fairly rare appeal within the domain of ethical considerations, and it is likely to become a dominant voice of conscience only within that narrow moral system to which Bernard Williams points. Of course, there are arguments aimed at demonstrating that truth telling and promise keeping are duties quite independently of distracting temptations. There is, for example, the familiar generalization argument that these practices can be universalized, whereas lying and reneging on our promises cannot be universalized and hence cannot become moral practices. There are also utilitarian arguments affirming that such moral practices are socially useful, that on the whole, like the conventions of language, they serve society well.

These and similar arguments implicit in a broad range of moral theories have, it seems to me, two educational functions. In the first place, such moral theories commend such duties for our rational assent. They are, in that respect, reassuring. They give us reasons, even justifying reasons. We could call this their justificatory function.[10] But such justificatory reasons can have moral force only to a conscience already formed. However much they may serve well in the continued guidance of a conscience already formed, they cannot function as justificatory in *originating* or *forming* conscience. But secondly, they help to make evident to a reflective person, a person who is already moral, what kinds of rational paths we typically follow in reasoning about some matters of choice. They help explain how we often think. They reveal to us the structure of our rationality, and making that structure explicit can be a substantial aid to clear thinking.

However, in neither case do such arguments account for or advance the moral learning we aim to encourage, and they have little, if any, motivational strength. No one ever makes promises, speaks truthfully, or holds to agreements in consequence of knowing that these moral practices, in the long run, are socially useful or because the maxims of such actions can be generalized. Once again, what is educationally required by this voice of conscience is not that we be given the reasons that endorse the sacrifice of interest, not even good moral reasons. What we seek from moral education is the actual sacrifice of self-interest, not merely its rational defense.

Back to the Conscience of Membership

Once again, consider a person genuinely troubled, asking "Why should I speak the truth *in this case?*" Being genuinely troubled, of course, implies on the part of the questioner the present knowledge or presumption that one *should* be truthful. The questioner already knows one kind of answer to the question or the question could not arise. Such a person is likely to be influenced by "because it is your duty" much less than by a host of other questions: Would lying, *in this case*, be a disloyal, dishonorable, cruel, foolish thing to do? In lying would you dishonor yourself? Would being untruthful (disloyal) in this case be a step in *becoming* an untruthful (disloyal) person? Do you think dissembling is a good thing?

These are questions of quite a different sort. They are questions not about rules, duties, and their rational foundations. They are not justificatory. They are appeals to virtue and association. It does not matter to my point whether virtues can be reduced to rules, though I think they cannot be. The point bears not upon the logical status of these questions as much as upon their rhetorical force in speech aimed at the formation of conscience. These questions call upon a person to exercise, and thus to further cultivate, the capacity for reflexive judgment or self-assessment so central to the formation of conscience, and they do so, moreover, in a way that appeals to duty do not. But such questions point also to a set of quite specific virtues that are cultivated within the context of membership or not at all. They point therefore to a different voice of conscience.

The syntax of 'loyal', for example, is such that one cannot be loyal or disloyal *simpliciter*. If we are loyal, then we are loyal *to* something or other. We can be loyal to communities, to institutions, to persons within institutions, and to ideals. Here is a moral virtue, in short, that can only be a virtue of persons *in situ*.[11] Apart from membership in some community, some institution, some profession perhaps, one cannot be loyal. Loyalty thus points to the voice of conscience as membership, and once again to the primacy of conscience as membership. Without membership we cannot speak of being loyal, because we would be without any object of loyalty. We might claim even that membership mandates loyalty. Can one be a disloyal member? Can one be disloyal to friends and remain a friend?

Can one be disloyal to a profession and yet retain any semblance of a credible claim to have grasped the point of the profession?

Only in consequence of membership is it possible for us to speak of such things as shaping the virtue of loyalty. With membership, recalling now the curriculum of moral skill, it becomes possible to appeal to what 'we' should do or what is good for 'us'. So the capacity for reflexive judgment that I have called 'conscience' speaks with a different voice in the context of membership. This is not, however, simply the voice of craft or sacrifice extended, as though the group were merely the individual multiplied. It is a distinctive voice altogether, a voice that arises *with* membership and speaks to us about virtues that seem to be uniquely those of membership. Not every kind of family or civic order, moreover, is capable of producing this language of membership. As the Greeks noted, quite rightly, tyrannies and kingdoms may have their subjects, but they do not have members. They do not have citizens.

II. The Conscience of Memory and Imagination

Central to the formation of conscience is a feature, present throughout this discussion, hinted at here and there, but nowhere made explicit. I have in mind what I have termed the conscience of memory and imagination. It is a tangled affair. Before turning to the details, however, it is well to situate memory and imagination in relation to aspects of conscience already considered. The central claim is that *the voices of memory and imagination are orthogonal to the other voices of conscience*. That is to say, the other voices of conscience—craft, membership, and sacrifice—have been considered distinct voices, distinct enough from one another even to engage in quarrel. The voice of conscience as craft, for example, is set aside from others by its propensity to speak of the moral life entirely under various vocabularies of skill. It tends to adopt the language of moral learning as though it were entirely a matter of skill, a problem of training. The voice of duty does not frame things in that way at all. Speaking in the vocabulary of craft, conscience may announce to us, "Do not act the fool!" "Don't be naive." But in the tradition of New Testament ethics—to take but one example from our inheritance of moral reflection—we are enjoined by the voice of duty to do precisely that which to the world will be adjudged the behavior of fools. "The Gospel," says

Paul, is "scandal to the Jews and foolishness to the Gentiles." If further
testimony be needed to reveal the contrasts among these voices, then
consider the fact that the conscience of membership has a voice distinctive precisely because it speaks in a vocabulary of certain virtues that
only exist in the context of membership, virtues such as loyalty and
honor. Craft, membership, and the voice of duty, as I have suggested,
might be understood as standing side by side. But the conscience of memory and imagination does not stand simply as another voice beside these
others. Memory and imagination are situated as cutting through the others, as being included within them, or as running at right angles to them.
Memory and imagination provide a distinctive voice *within* the domains
of craft, membership, and sacrifice.

The essentials of what I have called this tangled affair may be gathered in three large chunks. The first flows from the fact that human beings are creatures of roots, and a second from the first, namely that those
roots are ordered in traditions. Understood simply as reflexive judgment,
the exercise of conscience is evident everywhere in the exercise of craft,
as well as in the arts or the sciences, and in life within the myriad memberships of family, profession, party, or polity. Yet, no such membership is
even conceivable without its history nor any craft without some tradition. None of these come to us *de novo*. Each becomes present to us
largely through an inheritance reconstituted as memory. In every exercise of reflexive judgment in which the self is judged in the light of origins, or ancestors, or founders, or exemplars, there is manifest the conscience of memory and imagination. To assess the moral weight attached
to memory and imagination, one need only picture a father speaking to
his adult children, and saying, "It concerns me what stories you will tell
your children about their grandfather and, even more, what stories they
will tell their children about *their* grandparents." This is a profoundly important concern to express. It is the kind of concern that makes possible
the appeal to exemplars and predecessors as the self engages reflexively in
estimation. Such an appeal is impossible apart from the memory of predecessors and the imaginative presence of exemplars. To give any but the
most serious weight to the formation of conscience made possible
through memory and imagination or to casually reject such appeals as the
expression of an immature conscience would be a serious error. The second proposition, namely, that roots are generally ordered in some tradition, issues in a third claim parallel to it, a claim that I have advanced
from time to time as a kind of promissory note but must now make pay-

ment on. It is that *no enduring tradition is altogether without its resources for rational self-criticism nor does any rational criticism draw its strength except from within some tradition.*

Attached to this third proposition is at least one normative guide to the practice of any who aim to play the role of moral critic. Whatever critique one cares to offer must add up not only to a position that virtually anyone can argue for, but also to a position that persons of flesh and blood can actually occupy. It may be rationally impossible, for example, to decisively rebut the claim that whatever moral system prevails among human beings, it will be without any foundation whatsoever, except as an expression of mere preference or naked will or power, and thus that no one can justifiably advance his or her moral judgments as standards to guide the conduct of others. If we take such a position seriously, we shall be powerless to determine on any independent, rational grounds just what moral teachings ought to be transmitted to the next generation.

This, of course, is a crude rendering of an equally crude kind of relativism, a rendering encountered, however, with amazing regularity in discussions of moral education. The salient feature of such a view, the feature that cries out to be noticed, is the stark absence of memory in grasping the nature of norm acquisition. I offer both this crude formulation and this appraisal of it only to illustrate what might be meant by a position that anyone can argue for—if only as a kind of adolescent classroom exercise in feigned sophistication—but that no one can actually occupy. Any person undertaking to live by such a perspective will be bereft of family and friends and eventually of any civic existence and professional life, none of which can exist at all except when embodied in some tradition, modeled by exemplars, and recovered through memory and imagination. These three claims can be gathered under the headings of rootedness, memory as reception, and imagination as critique.

The force of these claims is that normation, that is, the formation of conscience, is largely a project in the reconstitution of memory. The formation of conscience is normation to histories of different sorts—to social histories and family stories, to biographies, and to the traditions of various practices, guilds of craft, and the like. The formation of conscience is also and at the same time normation to various ways of criticizing those different and often partisan histories and practices. Social criticism, to consider a single case of critical reflection, is more powerful—perhaps only powerful—when it comes from members, is addressed to members, and is offered from within the bounds of what members in some association can

recognize as their common ground. Michael Walzer, with his usual ele-
gance and directness, has put the point exactly. In an effort to make sense
not of the foundations of critique but of the critic himself, Walzer writes,

> The critic need not feel kindly toward the people he criticizes. But he
> ought to acknowledge his connections to those people: if he were a
> stranger, really disinterested, it is hard to see why he would involve him-
> self in their affairs. The passion for truth will not be a sufficient reason
> unless it is matched by a passion to tell the truth to *these* men and
> women (rather than to discover it for oneself or record it for posterity).[12]

Again, he writes of the social critic in words that call to mind the curriculum of civic skill:

> Though he [the critic] starts with himself, he speaks in the first person
> plural. This is what we value and want, he says, and don't yet have. This
> is how we mean to live and don't yet live. We criticize our society just as
> we criticize our friends, on the assumption that the terms of the critique,
> the moral references, are common.[13]

Rootedness

The human need for rootedness is a profound and difficult problem. Any
attempt to explore the topic runs heavy risks of falling either into loose
sentimentalism or into a kind of uncritical authoritarianism. The idea
suggests, of course, a biological metaphor, the image of a system of life in
which sustenance is drawn from sources by means that however hidden
are nonetheless real and tangible. It suggests also a certain necessity. Cut
the roots and the source of life itself is cut. The visible living thing will
die. The metaphor suggests also the idea of fixedness. Roots are put down
like an anchor. They constitute a fixed point. If there is movement or
growth away from them, they remain nonetheless the central point of an
orbit that can be dug up and discovered.
John F. A. Taylor writes,

> There is a species of mushroom, *Marasimius oreades*, which behaves in a
> fashion very satisfactory to geometers. It propagates itself in circles. On
> green turf, in an open pasture land, it will enclose a grassy space with a
> ring of yellow buds. You will run upon it of a morning, a whole bed of
> tiny globes sprung up over night, distributed with prophylactic regular-

ity about a common ideal center, each at the end of a radius, busily engaged in regimented but open array in setting spores astride the wind. . . .
They are in fact, as the curious have come to know, the organs of a single spawn, all connected with that center by subterranean filaments—
by the *mycelium*, as the botanist calls it, so that their center is not in fact
ideal, but material enough, simply, like the loves of geometers, not visible on the surface. A little digging will discover it, nor does it deserve
less to be celebrated that its geometry is realized, like yours and mine,
out of clay. It is nevertheless, that *mycelium*, the tangible emblem of
what in reflection men call a principle, that connection which, being
known, gives understanding and which buried, requires in the interest
of understanding to be dug up.[14]

It may be true that talk of human roots is metaphor, but that is not a
defect. The image of roots has its connection with concrete reality in
many ways. How else are we to comprehend the often celebrated efforts
of adults reared as adopted children to search the world over for their natural parents? What are we to make of the insistence of Afro-Americans
that we understand their various histories, indeed, that *they* be permitted
to understand them? How, in an age of apparently waning national sentiment among some and its virulent resurrection among others, are we to
understand the widespread pathos that people still feel in response to the
image of a man or woman without a country or without a place of peace,
and to the plight of refugees in a world that offers no refuge? How are we
to appreciate the Native Americans' recitation of their various histories
and their protest at the disappearance of their culture and its definition,
absorption, and subordination to the history of invaders? How indeed are
we to understand the surviving pride of the Vermonter in his town and
the earthy imagery of the Plainsman's speech if not as giving voice to the
significance of human roots needing to be dug up and thus understood?

And on the same order as these realities, how are we to comprehend
the cry of the oppressed of every race and every age, "You may rob me of
my money or my family or my land or my friends. You may rob me even of
my life. But do not take from me my good name"? What's in a name, if
not roots? Merely by noting these facts, this apparently inerradicable
human demand for roots is revealed. By our taking note we unwrap these
facts in order the better to see them for what they are. It cannot be
doubted that perhaps the most fundamental and, at the same time, most
general function of education, if not schooling, is to form an identity by
promulgating in each person some social memory that extends beyond

the literal lifetime of those in whom it is shaped. Human beings are mobile, but they are not rootless. Even the tumbleweed requires roots. It is wrenched loose from them only in one final wild excursion to recapitulate itself, drawn and pushed across the prairie by the wind. But it is dead already when it tumbles.

What I am here calling rootedness is sometimes, though mistakenly, called for as commitment. "If we cannot have roots, then let's have commitment." But the word 'commitment' is inadequate and misleading. It rings with overtones of will, as though we are free to choose just anything, free to choose what we are not free to choose. However much I may admire them and desire to be like them, I cannot choose to be French or Irish or Jew, or Indian or Black, or mountaineer or Cajun, or female. It is only within severe limits and even then, quite often, only by a difficult and enduring struggle, that we can decide to be anything that we are not already. This matter of roots is not a willful affair. It is not a matter of mere commitment, much less choice.

We all acknowledge that a person with skill and cleverness but without commitment is dangerous; and that a person with commitment but without skill is often useless. It must also be confessed, however, that persons with both commitment and skill but without roots can be among the most dangerous of all because they will be fanatics and at the same time clever. But the call for commitment, like the existentialist's call to choose, is one expression of an age when roots have been, if not abandoned, or forgotten or believed to be irrelevant, then allowed at least to go unnoticed or unacknowledged. There is something willful, grave, serious, final, and possibly even fanatic in the call for commitment. Roots are not like that. Roots are complex. They leave it open for us to choose what is within our reach to choose without giving in to the illusion that all is up for choice.

Both the circumstances and the time of birth and parentage as well as the terms of refuge are given to us and are thus beyond our making. It is merely circumstantial that, as human beings, we are creatures of this or that *particular* past. It is, however, essential to our nature and far from circumstantial that there be *some* such roots. Says Edward Shils,

> If we could imagine a society in which each generation created all that it used, contemplated, enjoyed, and suffered, we would be imagining a society unlike any which has ever existed. It would be a society formed from a state of nature. It would literally be a society without a past to draw on to guide its actions in the present.[15]

Such a possibility is more remote even than Shils imagines. Not only would it have to be a society formed entirely from a state of nature, but it would have to be one formed entirely from a state of nature in an instant. Its formation could not take time lest parents have some memory of their childhood and thus stand as legatees of a previous generation. There is no escaping it. We *are* creatures of roots.

Memory as Reception

To speak of such things in ways that engage the idea of education is to speak of education as the agency through which an inheritance is first transmitted, then received and finally, having been received, becomes a thing to be worked upon. There is a certain admirable tidiness to the lives of the social insects. No feature of their colonies is more apparent than the clear division of labor and the intricate devices for securing an optimal distribution of roles together with the orderly discharge of all the duties required to recapitulate the colony itself unchanged in any essentials. The fact has been a source of profound fascination for many who, observing such natural associations, have compared them with the disorder, ambiguity, and apparently endless contentiousness of human communities. All this has made it seem to some as though the design intended to be satisfied in the affairs of humankind is ordained to be fulfilled only in the lives of bees and termites.

There is this difference, however. It is the fate of the social insects to labor within a set of relations genetically transmitted, but not within their capacities, so far as we know, to make those relations the *object* of their labor. They suffer such relations, work within them, but not upon them. Human beings, too, may receive their social inheritance in as mute submission as the social insects receive theirs. This entailment, this handing down of property, is accomplished, of course, by means among humans other than among insects. In the one case its mediation is largely genetic, in the other it occurs by something that we variously call cultural transmission or socialization. Such transmission by itself, however, is not yet reception. Even so, we recognize in it the rudiments of education. The social inheritance of human beings is something handed over. It is, in that respect, tradition.

Like the bees, we too, are born into a set of relations. The human inheritance is always more extensive, but that should not cloud our minds to the likeness. We acquire the language; we do not invent it. Neither do we invent the law, the land and our relation to it, nor the arts, the family, nor our ways of worship. We are given these things, first of all. Like water to the fish, they are the medium that contains our lives. They come to us having the status of facts; that is, they come as things made, things already done. That is after all what we *mean* by 'facts', 'things made', from *facere*, 'to make'. This association of fact with things already made is what warrants the claim that there are no future facts. Facts are things already done. They are past. The future is a domain of things not yet done. It is not a domain of facts.

These things that come to us as fact are among the *traditum*, things 'handed over' from our predecessors. Their status as things already made and given is what produces our sense of their necessity. Along with this sense, however, comes also a sense of their utter contingency witnessed in the fact that things already made and handed down to others can be quite different from those handed down to us. They can seem strange to us. So we learn that our *traditum* could have been other than it is, and since it could have been other than it is we are prone to conclude, too quickly I believe, that its composition must be purely arbitrary, its alteration easy and its rejection essential. We may be inclined to view it as a 'dead hand' bearing down upon us. This last inference, however, that is, the move in thought from noting that our inheritance might have been other than it is to the claim that the *traditum* is arbitrary—this must surely appear near the top of anybody's list of huge *non sequiturs*. From the fact that the *traditum* could be other than it is, nothing follows to suggest that it is in any respect arbitrary.

From the certainty that the *traditum* we are given is presented as fact, neither does it follow that it cannot be altered. For humankind, unlike the social insects, there always lurks in what is given two further chances. First is the possibility that these things giving shape to our labors may themselves become objects of reflection. They are not things simply given, but self-consciously received, that is, remembered. By being made present in memory they also may become suitable objects of our work. We work, for example, within a structure of law already formed in its essentials, waiting only to be dug up and brought to the surface in order thus to be self-consciously received. But we may also make that gift and that possession the object of our work. We can and do reshape it. It is not recorded, however, that the social insects reflect much upon the given constraints of their lives which are contingent but not, for all that, arbitrary. Nor is it recorded that the social insects are much disposed to meet in constitutional conventions. We have no record of their having created large compilations of precedent to be consulted in their communal decisions. Memory, in short, does not figure at all in the orderliness of their so-called social existence, whereas it enters essentially in the various inheritances of human beings. The English language, for example, is for many of us at first the tongue that shapes our speech. We use it and play with it as though born to it, but we can become conscious of it and thus come to frame our speech to shape the tongue itself.

What should we say of this second stage, reception, and of the third, reconstitution? Are they equally the stuff of education or must we be content to describe the second as education and the third as something beyond, perhaps the unique work of genius? To this question I have no satisfactory answer. There can be no doubt, however, that the reception of some tradition is the aim and consequence of normation, even its very substance. Nor can it easily be doubted that the critical employment of the norms of a tradition, issuing either in its validation or in its alteration, remains the normative ideal of all education. It may be attained rarely or often, but it is always present as an educational ideal. And whenever it is realized, there is change. Humans labor, both in concert and in contention with one another, to alter the world they have received. In resisting their inheritance, by the intensity of the struggle itself, they reveal the power of its presence, and show how impossible it is simply to turn their backs upon it and walk away. We really *are* creatures of some tradition or other.

Imagination as Critique

Just as the conscience of memory is rooted in membership, so the conscience of imagination is rooted in memory. Persons who count themselves well educated because of their technical skill and their professional standing, but who lack vision, who do not dream, who assume that the world as it is, is as the world must be—such persons lack much in their moral education, however much we may count them good men and women. Lacking visions and dreams, however rooted they may be in other ways, they cannot lead. Where would they lead us?

For our moral education, and in addition to the voices of conscience as skill, membership, and sacrifice, we need the formation of conscience by prophets, that is to say, by poets and by the literary giants of our experience. *We need the conscience of imagination.* I have found no better formulation of the point than that provided by Walter Brueggemann when writing about the Old Testament prophets. "Prophetic speech," he says,

> is characteristically poetic speech. The importance of this cannot be overstated. The prophets are not political scientists with blueprints for a social order. They are not crusaders for a cause. They are not ethical teachers. They are speakers (not writers) who commit linguistic acts that assault the presumed world of the king, who expose the pretensions of the royal system, and who invite listening Israel to entertain new dimensions of social possibility which they had never before considered. The prophets (in much of Protestantism) have been mistakenly understood as social activists or as social reformers. But they have the more fundamental task of nurturing poetic imagination. By this capacity to draw new pictures, form new metaphors, and run bold risks of rhetoric, they create a new arena for Israel's imagination and derivatively for Israel's political actions. They seek to form an alternative context for humanness by creating a different presumptive world which is buoyed by different promises, served by different resources, sobered by different threats, and which permits different decisions. That is the visible result of this liberated imagination which goes public in Israel.
>
> The greatest threat to the prophetic canon, either in the ancient world or in our education, is to have poetic oracles from the prophets reduced to prose. It is like having great art diminished to technique or great music "explained." Prose is always the language . . . of the "managerial mentality." If the prophet can be reduced to prose, then the *message* can be translated into a *program*. And the program, predictably, will be administered by the same people who administer everything else.[16]

Part of Brueggemann's meaning is that present already in this conscience of imagination is the conscience of membership and memory. The voice of the Old Testament prophets comes from within a community shaped already by the Torah. It is always a voice of conscience that speaks as a member with all the accents, verbs, and metaphors that that implies. It is not and could not be an alien voice. Though the prophets speak often against the lived life of the community, nevertheless, they speak always from within it. That this voice of moral imagination comes always from within a community and is addressed always to the members of a community, is not a principle limited simply to a Hebrew tradition. It is an operable principle in many other contexts. For example, it is only those who are truly citizens of the world who can speak in credible ways of world affairs instead of mere foreign policy.

The conscience of membership is critical to the conscience of critical imagination. It is only imagination that allows us to speak to other members about the chasm that exists between the hopes and fair expectations of the society or community and the failure of our lived lives. The rootedness of that voice in membership gives the judgment its sting. That judgment hurts precisely because it comes to us as the voice of an insider, speaking out of a shared memory and turning it against us to reveal how great a distance there is between the ideals we espouse and the realities into which, willy-nilly, we seem always to lapse. It is unpleasant to see how blind and to hear how deaf we can be. It stings! And the reason it stings is revealing.

The central contrast between the empirical and the normative communities was initially framed as a contrast between the society as it is and can be known even to some external observer, and the society as it would be if it were all that its members think it ought to be. This difference was shown to be one source of social criticism the development of which is already *implicit in the process of normation itself.* That the acquisition of such critical capacities is implicit in norm acquisition is shown by the fact that norm acquisition is revealed not by compliance, but by the critical judgment and demeanor aroused in the face of departures from the norm. Normation, in the strong sense, was found to consist in taking up one's habitation as member of the normative in contrast to the empirical community. Parallel to this distinction between the empirical and the normative communities was another distinction between two voices of moral criticism, the one an internal voice calling upon persons to be whatever it is that they represent themselves as being and not something else. This was the interior voice of criticism in the individual, that prophetic voice as Brueggemann describes it: the interior call of conscience to the self to be what the self pretends to be, the voice of prophetic criticism that can come only from a member.

Social criticism nowadays is often conducted as though there could be some independent platform of criticism remote from any involvement as participant, drawing upon a standard of reason that rests in no particular tradition and stands apart from any membership. Whenever I think about such claims and ponder their sheer audacity, I am reminded of a lecture I once attended in which the speaker advocated a wholesale abandonment of philosophy and all its traditions on the grounds that its ceaseless attachment to the search for final and universalistic truths represented serious obstacles to human progress. We need a fresh beginning, so the argument ran. It took an enormous effort of forgetfulness to lay aside the problems of so narrow, misleading, and partial an understanding of the history of philosophy in order to actually entertain the thesis. "Well and good," I thought. "Let us start over. But how then shall we know that what we are starting over is philosophy?" What can "starting over" mean in such a thesis? Or is this merely a ruse, a thesis that anyone can advance but no one can actually interpret, much less pursue?

Social criticism, as with educational criticism, theological criticism, and architectural criticism, is an enterprise affording fresh beginnings only because there are paths of achievement already bearing their own standards of excellence and because that criticism is offered from within such a context. Any rational critique is an exercise of the conscience of imagination, that is, the reflexive voice of members standing somewhere. It is a critique of members governed by standards as to what matters and what makes 'mindful' sense. The criticism of norms is something that can be done well or badly. It is itself either norm-governed or it stands nowhere and touches no one. The fact is that "one cannot even be downcast, angry, grim, indignant, sullen or embittered *with reason* unless one inhabits some social setting and adopts, however tentatively, its codes and categories."[17]

The Sacred

At some point, however, this adoption must be more than tentative and this habitation more than temporary. In addition to the orthogonal voice of memory and imagination is yet another essential, not another voice of conscience, but a prerequisite for the conduct of moral education even to begin. I have argued that there is no enduring tradition without inherent resources for rational self-criticism nor any rational criticism except from within some tradition. I propose now an additional proposition of equal necessity. It is simply that *in a world where nothing is sacred, moral education is impossible*. In such a world it could not even get started.

It is not my aim to say what things are sacred and what things are not. Where the sacred may be found, I take to be an empirical matter of importance for the conduct of moral education in any society. Almost anything can be and at some time or other probably has been regarded as sacred. Almost anything can be viewed in that way. But what is 'that way'? What human response would we identify as a response to the sacred, *whatever its objects*? This claim that in a world where nothing is sacred, moral education is impossible, is not a religious claim. It is simply a claim about the necessary conditions for the conduct of moral education and moral learning to begin.

The sacred is usually described as provoking awe or reverence, or stirring a sense of mystery. The central thought is that of a boundary or barrier, hence the derivative idea of the sacred as something hidden, distant, and powerful. When I have discussed the sense of this idea with students, those who have children have often spoken of birth as a time of being in the presence of the sacred in this sense as provoking awe. Others have said the same of death. I have in mind holding the hand of a much loved friend at the moment of his death. What is one to say at such a moment? He was here and now he is not.

It is as though we stand on one side of a line and look across to the other side with a sense of awe and whispered respect. Substantial effort is needed to do so, but such a boundary can be ignored. We can become indifferent to it. It may be crossed. There is a quite detailed and explicit vocabulary which gives implicit acknowledgment of such a line, marking off the boundaries of the sacred, a vocabulary including words like 'transgression', 'desecration', 'breach', and 'violation'. 'Evil' is a kindred term powerfully associated with the sacred and with the forbidden, the untouchable, the boundary separating what is permitted from what is not. Words like these are used in circumstances where our response can reach even to expressions of horror. To think of the absence of the sacred, that is, its *total* absence, is to conceive a condition in which nothing excites horror. And in such a world, moral education cannot gain a foothold. The possibility of moral horror signals not only the presence of the sacred, but an essential prerequisite for moral education itself.[18]

To convey the force of these points, we need not invoke any overtly religious language or talk, for example, of heresy, irreverence, sacrilege, or impiety. We need not impose any creedal talk or essential rites. Yet consider what is happening when, in efforts to advance a kind of ecological sanity, it is argued that our attitudes toward nature must change. The argument often aims at pointing out, among other things, that we must come to view certain human acts in relation to nature as destructive and eventually as doing violence against nature, perhaps—dare we say it?— violating nature. In this progression of language from 'destruction' to 'violence', and finally to 'violation', we approach a point where nature is sacralized. When along that line of rhetorical escalation our vocabulary drives us to talk of desecration, then we know we have arrived in the presence of the sacred. Such pleadings for an 'ecological conscience' are usually offered as the fruits of a naturalistic inquiry needing only scientific persuasion to make us mend our ways. To advocate a more sane care of natural resources is one thing; to find in such judicious environmental management the grounds of an ethical perspective is quite another. It is not my aim to argue in support of one or the other of these two points of view, but only to point out that if we find in such concerns a matter for moral education and not simply for a more sophisiticated grasp of prudence, then we are likely to find ourselves sacralizing nature. Whenever language of the sacred comes into play, fresh chances of moral education are presented. Allowing such chances to emerge, and indeed, encouraging them, is the entire point of such pleadings for a so-called ecological ethic. It is both the aim and the content of those pleas.

Linked to such words as 'violation' is yet another cluster of terms offering clues to the presence of the sacred. What is the opposite of the sacred? I suspect it is not the secular, but the banal. You and I might find the boundaries and barriers of the sacred in different places and therefore use the vocabulary of the sacred in respect to different things. But how shall we describe the presence in the world of one who finds the sacred nowhere? Where some use the vocabulary of the sacred, such a person will see only banality. Where we might recoil in the neighborhood of the forbidden or the horrible, such a person will see only what is mundane and ordinary. For this he shall need a language expressing a sense of triviality, in which the presence of things excites no interest and stirs no one to attention, much less to awe or to a sense of mystery. Strong arguments can be advanced that to eradicate *every* boundary marking the presence of the sacred, we would need to trivialize death. Consider the case of those leaving instructions to eschew any religious ceremony in observance of their death. It is a request virtually impossible to observe unless we make a travesty of death, that is, dress it up in sentiment and pretend it is something it is not. Death is an event that forbids treating a corpse as corpse alone, reducing it simply to an object in our path needing only to be removed and prepared for compost. That would be the ultimate banality. Death, as the end of a life, is among those events of life that most demand interpretation, and its interpretation is likely to be an occasion when sheriffs write poetry and logicians weep. The opposite of the sacred is not the secular, but the banal. Those who live in a world of banality will confront the sacred nowhere.

Euthyphro, on his way to bring charges of impiety against his parents, was approached by Socrates and asked whether an act is pious because the gods approve it, or whether the gods approve it because it is pious. The answer worked through in the Socratic dialogue is sometimes interpreted as the declaration of independence of moral philosophy from religion. If the gods approve an act as pious because pious is what it is, then no act is pious simply because they approve it. Instead, they must have their reasons for approval. And if they have their reasons, and not merely their legislative will, then having Reason, we too may have their reasons. Thus, moral philosophy is born. This Socratic jolt of rational independence may suffice as an opening wedge granting human reason the liberty it needs for the conduct of moral philosophy, but it will not suffice for a philosophy of moral education. If the gods have their reasons, then, indeed, we may have their reasons too. But having good reasons for good conduct, even divine reasons, is not enough if our interest is moral education. The aim of moral education is that beyond good reasons we have good conduct and good character, that our conduct comes to be *governed* by moral norms. For that to occur, it must be possible at *some* point to arouse moral horror, excite awe, and provoke reverence.

By claiming that moral education is impossible in a world where absolutely nothing is sacred, I do not mean that religion is necessary for moral education, or that religion supplies the needed grounding for moral education because it provides the needed grounding for moral laws. No such foundational theory is intended here, and none is necessary. Instead, I mean only to point out the sort of thing around which religious responses invariably cluster, and to advance the claim that those conditions must be satisfied somewhere if moral education is even to get a start.

It is not that these things or those things are sacred which this or that religion proclaims, but rather that in finding ourselves in the presence of the sacred somewhere, we give a religious-like response. Wherever we find the sacred is where our religion is found, no matter how much we insist that it really is found elsewhere. So, for example, a piece of cloth, a symbol, the flag, say, can become sacralized. It can become a sacred symbol, even a sacred object, in which case we can and do describe certain uses of the flag as desecration. And when we do that, then we know where our religion lies. This is an expression of one kind of religion that the biblical texts describe as idolatry. Idolatry, after all, is religion too. It is a religious response and is inconceivable except in a world that includes some version of the sacred somewhere.

Does this in any way show that moral education is inextricably reli-gious? I think not. Yet it seems impossible to give this fact concerning the essential presence of the sacred any strictly secular, that is, strictly ratio-nal, interpretation. Suppose we say simply that what is needed for moral education is either the sacred *or its functional equivalent.* Can this make sense? John Kekes has given a slightly different twist to this view. He points out,

> All moral traditions have some lightly regarded conventions whose vio-lations incur only disapproving cluckings. But there are . . . others, and they go very deep indeed; they set limits not to be crossed, they are the moral equivalents of the sacred. I think some . . . are deep because they protect factual, hard, and inexorable conditions of human welfare. They provide morality with some objective content, and that is why their vio-lations are unreasonable.[19]

The claim that the presence of the sacred somewhere is essential for moral education to get a start, makes it appear that moral education is at heart religious. This claim, however, may amount only to the idea that there must be deep conventions in Kekes's sense. These, he says, are the "moral equivalents of the sacred."

I have doubts about this formulation. Aristotle remarks that however excellent it may already be, any life will be improved with the addition of friends. Friends are essential to any life if it is a good life. But suppose someone says, "Well perhaps it is not friends that are essential, but surely either friends or their functional (moral) equivalent." What can this pos-sibly mean? What would be the functional (moral) equivalent of a friend? Would a puppy do? There is, in fact, no such thing, no functional or moral equivalent of a friend. Any being that stands to us in a relation of mutuality, and equality of virtue, and with a certain kind of indifference to the claims of justice, such a being just *is* a friend, not the functional or moral equivalent of one. Neither is there any such thing as the functional or moral equivalent of the sacred, in the sense in which I have claimed that the presence of the sacred somewhere is an essential precondition for moral education.

I can hear an objector growling, "Well, in the meantime, deep con-ventions will suffice." They will not suffice, however, if we are to grasp the point at hand. It is nice to know that to treat a corpse merely as an object and nothing more, not as someone's sister or neighbor or friend, and to deal with death as needing no interpretation and provoking no awe is unreasonable because it violates "inexorable conditions of human welfare." To say this is to speak in the voice of a person already morally educated, but in the tones of a detached observer.

John Kekes has provided a description of the presence of the sacred and its place within the moral traditions of human communities by pointing to a moral equivalent. It is a detached description, however, of things as they must appear to an outsider. The proposition I aim to defend, however, is a claim offered from the vantage of the insider. In a world where nothing is sacred, moral education cannot get a start partly because in such a world there would be no moral horror. Nor is it true, I think, that anyone actually standing within a moral tradition and normed to its deep conventions could possibly regard those merely as conventions. To describe such deep conventions as "the moral equivalent of the sacred" is already to express what, to the insider, must appear to be a thorough alienation from the sacred. For a participant in such a moral order to describe such deep conventions in such a way is already to be far advanced along the path toward their desacralization. Finally, it seems to me apparent that such deep conventions could not possibly be derived from, much less acquired by, anyone out of the knowledge that, being grounded in "inexorable conditions of human welfare," their observance accords with reason. That such deep conventions accord with reason is to engage the language of moral philosophy in its office as explicator of the rational paths that we ordinarily follow in thinking about such matters. But anyone who stands within a moral tradition respects such boundaries marking off the domain of the sacred precisely *because* they mark off the boundaries of the sacred and not because they accord with reason. In short, such a description may provide an account of how deep conventions *function* in a moral community, but it cannot be the description that any participant could or would offer either as explanation or as rational defense. Neither can such a description, as far as I can see, provide grounds for rational acquiescence in such deep conventions sufficient to account for their acquisition as norms. One must hasten to add that neither could such deep conventions be made to arise by any path of intentional education. If they are taught or learned at all, they will be taught and learned by teaching and learning of the sort that we describe as acquisition. Finally, if it is true that the presence of the sacred is a necessary prerequisite for moral education, we should not suppose that such presence can be produced by moral education. The presence of the sacred cannot be an *outcome* of education.

Hope

Insofar as the argument to this point has concerned the education of
the emotions, it has been an education limited to the emotions of self-
assessment. The argument has been that normation necessarily structures the emotions of self-assessment, because it gives specific content to
the emotions of guilt, shame, pride, regret, remorse, and many others,
and these emotions are *essentially* reflexive, not incidentally so. In them
the self renders an estimate of the self. In that respect they differ from
other emotions, such as fear and hope, which are not essentially reflexive
and therefore are not essentially structured by normation. Nevertheless,
both fear and hope are of first importance in any robust philosophy of
moral education. Any life actually lived must at some point offer an
analysis as to how the twin questions What ought I fear? and For what
can I hope? are engaged in the formation of conscience.

I do not propose an analysis of fear, except to note that its rational
control and cultivation is precisely what has been identified, at least
since Homer, as basic to the virtue of courage. I propose to attend, however, to the nature of hope, not only because it has long been recognized
that a life without hope is among the most miserable of human conditions, but also because hope, though not among the reflexive emotions, is
nonetheless firmly rooted in memory. Thus it is fittingly considered in relation to the voice of memory and imagination.

If hope is reflexive at all, it is reflexive in time. Though forward-looking
in its object, hope is backward-looking in its formation. Its foundations
are found only in memory. This rootedness of hope in memory derives
partly from the fact that hope is rooted in fact and facts are things done.
Proof of this lies in the peculiar contrast of hoping and wishing. Hope is
always realistic. Wishful thinking is not. Hope is always grounded in the
past, that is to say, in fact and thus in memory. The point can hardly be
stated more clearly than by an extension of Aristotle's analysis when he
considers the domain of objects capable of choice. He says,

> There can be no choice where impossibilities are involved: a man who
> declared that he chose something incapable of realization would be con-
> sidered a half-wit. On the other hand it is just impossibilities for which
> we do tend to wish—for instance, to live forever. . . . Our wishes are di-
> rected more to ends than to means. For example, our *wish* is to be
> healthy, but what we choose are things that will make us healthy. We

'wish'—it is the regular word in this connection—to be happy, but it would be an incorrect expression to say we 'choose' to be happy.[20]

To this distinction of Aristotle's between things pertaining to wishes and things pertaining to choice, we may incorporate things pertaining to hope. The nature of hope can be discerned in the grammar of the term. We may wish for what we know or believe to be impossible; we may even wish for what we know or believe to be contrary to fact or in the past. We can hope, however, only for what still lies in the future and for what we believe to be possible. For example, we may wish to live forever, as Aristotle suggests, but we cannot hope to. We say "I wish he had not been elected" (past), but "I hope he will be elected" (future). From these observations, we learn also that 'wish' can take the subjunctive mood, which is to say that it extends to matters contrary to fact. But 'hope' has no such usage. We can say "I wish he were . . ." or "I wish I were . . ." or "I wish things were . . ."; but we say "I hope *to be* so and so," not "I hope I *were* such and such." Because wishing can extend to things contrary to fact and to things past, it follows that wishing can survive after all hope is lost. In fact, wishing, despairing, and yearning may be all that could survive the utter loss of hope. Yearning can be described as desire without hope, that is, without its foundation in fact. To yearn is like wishing, untethered to memory and thus to foundations in fact. To be without hope is partly to be of the opinion that what might have been the object of one's hope is incapable of realization; still, we can wish, even when we are without any hope that our wishes can be realized. Hope, in all of these ways, contrasts with wishing. Hope is always based in the belief that the object of hope is attainable and, unlike the object of a wish, is always in the future.[21] I cannot hope to do what I have already done, not because what I have already done is impossible to do, but because it is already done. It is past. Hope, being directed at the future, is an expression of confidence, whereas wishing is more closely related to apathy and *ennui*, conditions both kin to hopelessness.

This suggestion that hope and confidence are related deserves further reflection. It suggests the need to introduce into the mix yet another term, 'trust'. Hope is apparently related to confidence as trust is related to its grounds. I shall trust someone or the likelihood of some event to the extent that past behavior or events confirm that he or she is reliable. To trust, it seems, is like making a forecast. In that respect it is like expectation, which also seems to involve a forecast. The grounds of the forecast rest in memory. To hope, however, even though it is also grounded in memory, is not to advance a forecast. I can say, "I hope that such and such will happen, but I don't expect it." Hope can survive the passage of expectation. I may have confidence in my hopes and confidence in my forececasts, but confidence moves along logical paths where hope does not easily follow. These relationships may be graphically illustrated by the epistemic scale of hope (figure 1).

Figure 1.
The Epistemic Scale of Hope

wishfulness	expectance	confidence	certainty
apathy	hopefulness	greater hope	knowledge

The domain of hope, in respect to variable chances of fulfillment, seems to lie within the two central categories of this scale, somewhere between wishfulness and apathy on the one hand, and certainty or knowledge on the other. Outside this central region, hope does not sit well. Examining the ends of this continuum, we note that hope, at one end, does not belong in the midst of wishfulness, and, at the other end, is not at home when the object of hope is already fulfilled. As the grounds of hope are strengthened in fact and memory, one becomes expectant, and as those chances improve, hope is strengthened. Yet, as assurance is replaced with certainty, then this entire sequence is replaced by knowledge or, as we say, with fulfillment, and hope again is no longer the fitting term to use. Thus, to say "I hope the sun will rise tomorrow" is to speak as though there is either some uncertainty about celestial facts, or else some doubt that one may survive the night. Hope can survive neither the total absence of factual foundations nor the total assurance of fulfillment. When the future is firmly known, we are more likely to say something like "I hope that nothing untoward and unexpected will intervene." *That* kind of hope will be born when memory and experience provide some cause for uncertainty, and it will be transformed into joy when such doubts are stilled.

One last addition to this brief examination of hope is needed, this time concerning fear. Consider these questions:

i. What do you expect to happen?
ii. What do you fear will happen?
iii. What do you hope will happen?

These questions differ in just the ways that hope, fear, and expectation differ. I may expect what I hope for and expect what I fear. But I cannot hope for what I fear. So (i) and (ii) may receive the same answer, but (iii) and (ii) may not. Hope can take as its object only good things. We may hope for disasters only on condition that we find in them some good. Absent that expectation, hope vanishes. Even in such cases, however, the object of hope is not the disaster but whatever good we think likely to emerge from it. That the object of hope must be viewed as a good thing is the reason that I cannot hope for and fear the same thing.

The immediate import of these observations is that since hope is grounded in memory and is necessary to any livable life, the educational task is to ensure that memories of good things and of good things being possible are being formed so that hope can find a place in the moral world of the child. A second point is found in the fact that hope, being firmly founded in fact and not in wishes, cannot be encouraged by efforts to shape a 'good self-concept' unless those efforts are directed at actual achievement. The educational world that we create must be one in which achievement is possible, where struggles bear fruit, and where there are good things to do and we are endorsed for doing them well. If that occurs, then good memories of good things can be formed and hope itself is planted. With hope formed in such conditions will come also a sense of deep self-satisfaction. The worst conceivable educational mistake would be to suppose that we encourage achievement by creating a sense of self-satisfaction directly, without the intermediary of good things actually achieved.

Chapter 5

Teaching Values: The Grand Delusion

I. The Problem

Early in these essays it was claimed, but not argued, that reducing moral education to something called 'teaching values' or 'values education' is unlikely to add anything to our understanding. Instead, it is likely to present obstacles. The entire exposition of moral education as the formation of conscience, that is, as normation, has been conducted so far without any mention of values or of values education. Nothing that I can detect has been lost by this omission. Like a distinction without a difference, we have in this case, an omission without a loss.

Yet, this interpretation of moral education as 'teaching values' is widely accepted, so widely accepted, in fact, as to have become a kind of cultural assumption. In this idea we are presumed to have an entire way of understanding many things, not simply the education of children and youth, but the conduct of politics, the formulation of public policy, the conduct of family life, even standards of professional practice. If one attends at all to the range of such discourse about values, then the conclusion is unavoidable that there are religious values, family values, political values, economic values, and of course, moral values. In the use of this vocabulary any mention of educational or intellectual values is almost universally omitted. In short, this notion of values and 'the values we have' is not so much a single idea as it is an entire tool box of ideas and assumptions of such resplendent certainty and such luminous clarity as to constitute not the conclusions of anyone's thought, but simply a part of the environment in which any thought whatever about moral education must apparently be cast.

In what follows, I propose to examine this perspective through several

stages. First is the matter of origins. We must ask where this cultural artifact may have its roots. Especially urgent is the need to discern, if possible, what has produced the assumption that people have *values* (plural
noun) at all, and thus that moral education or values education could be
understood as an education by which persons come to have some values
rather than others. What is the conceptual content of such a notion?
Next is an attempt to construct an alternative approach to values once
the idea that persons *have* values is expunged from our vocabulary. The
notion that individuals can be said to have values at all is a snare and a
delusion—or so I shall argue—and if we wish to speak of values at all we
shall have to speak of institutions and the quite objective social arrangements of our common life. And finally, if indeed this perspective has become a kind of cultural artifact, then we need to explore what of fundamental human interest we seek to express by it. I aim to demonstrate that
the significant content of the modern view of values and of values education, its undoubted human import, can be expressed more precisely and
more clearly within the view of moral education as normation. The thesis is that by 'having values' we mean 'being strongly normed'.

Something Odd about That

To spot the meaning of a concept, ask how we would be disabled were it
simply stricken from our vocabulary altogether. What linguistic innovations would be needed in order to express whatever we mean to express
by that now discarded notion? I propose that we enter the experiment
and purge all talk that rests, however remotely, upon the claim that people have values. Oddly enough, this notion is virtually without any history. It appears nowhere in the classical literature on ethics, nor is it a
biblical idea, nor does it, or any conceptual equivalent of it, appear in the
Renaissance, the Reformation, or the Enlightenment. That people have
values is not a notion that appears in the thought of any major philosopher in the history of western thought. In fact, we may say with assurance, though also with apologies for what must initially seem little more
than rhetorical exaggeration, that until sometime in this century—
maybe around 1910—nobody 'had' values. This way of expressing the
point may seem odd, but I urge upon you that it is also true.

Instead of this vague, generalized abstract talk about having values,
we used to speak of a host of quite distinct but specific things, such as
virtues, beliefs, convictions, failings, hopes, commitments, loyalties, and

sometimes even a glimpse of happiness or good fortune. These are all things that human beings may have. Virtues, beliefs, and loyalties, however, are very different things. They are learned in different ways, expressed in different ways, established in different ways, and they require different things of the world that we inhabit. Until quite recently it would have made no sense at all to obscure these differences by subsuming them all under the general rubric of persons having values, as though in doing so we were describing something different from or in addition to having such things as loyalties, virtues, and beliefs. To fall into such a slovenly manner of speech and thought is to invite confusion, and we know that wherever confusion is invited, it quickly appears. This claim that the idea of 'having values' is a recent invention will seem so blatantly false, however, so outrageous, so counterintuitive, so strange, that its serious advancement as a truth requires some explanation.

This use of language is a distinctly modern one. The earliest citation in *The Oxford English Dictionary*[1] is from the *Times Literary Supplement*, November 1921:

> In the effort, again, to give his characters and scenes the vivid impression of reality, the novelist, whether voluntarily or not, cannot avoid revealing not merely his powers of mind and imagination, but his spiritual and philosophical bias, his views of society, of religion, *his values*.

The next citation is dated 1938: "You've got a completely lunatic set of values."

This talk of 'his values' and 'having a set of values' is a radical modern invention. A search of Eric Partridge's *Origins*[2] yields similar results. There one finds an extended family of terms etymologically related to 'value', ranging from value to valence, valetudinarian, validation, validity, convalesce, countervail, and prevail. Nowhere is there even a trace of the notion that people have values. And we get no closer to this modern idea when we consult Partridge on the origins of 'worth'. The adjectival origins translate as 'valuable' and 'desirable', not 'valued' and 'desired'. The notion was that things have value (a property) and persons value things (verb or activity), and persons might value things that lack worth. It is conceivable even that they might hanker after undesirable things.

We find the same state of affairs when we consult the article "Value and Evaluation" in the *Encyclopedia of Philosophy* (1967). William Frankena writes,

The terms 'value' and 'valuation' and their cognates and compounds are used in a confused and confusing but widespread way in our contemporary culture, not only in economics and philosophy but also and especially in other social sciences and humanities. Their meaning was once relatively clear and their use limited. 'Value' meant the worth of a thing, and 'valuation' meant an estimate of its worth.

In other words, the idea that some things have value (some more than others) and that persons value things (some persons some things and others other things) or that all persons value some things more than they value other things—these ideas of value and valuing have a long history. I am not disputing that. But in the idea that *things* or states of affairs have worth, value appears as a property, and in the idea that people *value* things, it appears as a verb. There is a long history of discourse and dispute concerning what things have worth and how that worth might be assessed. So we have 'value' and its cognates used as a predicate to refer to properties of things, as a noun (usually singular) to name that property, and then as a verb to refer to the human activities of valuing and evaluating. But in this new, evasive, and deservedly vacuous language in which we speak of persons having values, we use cognates of the term 'value' neither as predicate nor as verb. Instead, 'value' now appears as a noun, usually plural, and apparently to refer to something that persons have as a kind of possession. This is new.

The transformation in our vocabulary of value is not simply a different way of talking. It represents a different way of seeing things, a different way of being. It creates an entirely different kind of world. This change in discourse may, in fact, reflect the most fundamental cultural transformation in the West of the past one hundred years. No longer do we speak of the value that *things* have, that is to say, their worth. Instead, we speak only of the values that people have. We speak not of what is desirable, but of what is desired, not of what things have worth, but only of what people prefer—their values.

The Worldly Evacuation of Value

The very oddity of this new-speak needs first simply to be noted. But next, we need to consider what might be its roots. Part of the answer can be found, I think, in certain nineteenth-century movements of thought, especially in economic theory. The classical economists usually considered value to be a form of utility and regarded price and value as things conceptually distinct. Value was taken to be a property of goods and commodities that was inherent in them. On such a view, the value of anything cannot be the same as its market price, since its value is something inherent in it and price is nothing of the sort. That value and price are distinct is evident to every amateur economist who has ever been tempted to say "I paid more for this than it's worth." Among those of a conscience not yet seduced by the charms of modern economics, it is a widespread, though perhaps naive, assumption that the price demanded for anything on the market ought to stand in *some* relation to its actual value. That seems, even now, a reasonable demand, a demand the rationality of which rests upon the necessity that price and value be viewed as things conceptually distinct. This moral conviction is what produced the medieval problem of a 'just price', a notion whose logic is worth recovering.

That a price might be unjust (quaint idea) rests on nothing as personal or momentary as a mere complaint. To say, "I paid more for this than it's worth," is not simply another way of saying, "I paid more for this than I had to" or "more than I would have had I only gone somewhere else." That a price might be unjust is not simply a rueful complaint that I didn't luck out or another way of saying "Poor me! Had I only known." It is not as though I had just made a mistake, a kind of slip, in my market behavior. The idea of an 'unjust price' is a much more robust notion than that. With it comes an entirely different and extensive vocabulary invoking an entirely different set of distinctions. It is a vocabulary, for example, that bars taking unfair advantage of neighbor,[3] and thus makes room for such familiar phrases as 'excess profits' and 'price-gouging'. It includes the notion that simply because I can *get* a certain price is insufficient to justify either my asking such a price or my getting it. The claim underlying the notion of 'just price' is that no price is allowable simply on the grounds that a sale can occur at that price. This is only another way of saying that though there must be some relation between price and value, nevertheless, they remain different things and what occurs on the market is an insufficient account of that relation.

This problem of the relation between price and value—an idea that to contemporary economics has the ring of primitive pre-scientific lore—was examined, twisted, and wrung dry without notable advancement from the medieval philosophers to Adam Smith and on down to Karl Marx. But with the neoclassical economists of the nineteenth century, and especially with Jevons and Marshall, a revolutionary advance was made.[4] The problem was met by simply changing the subject, that is, by giving the problem a substantially different formulation in what Jevons called 'the final degree of utility'.[5] His formulation later came to be known as the theory of marginal utility. What is that formulation?

We may offer two logically equivalent versions. First, we are not surprised that a person who has a pantry filled with loaves of bread is unlikely to be much excited at the prospect of another. We are prepared to conjecture that such a person, for some time now, will have been less and less excited by the prospect of another loaf, counting the addition more a burden than a benefit. Neither are we surprised that a person who has none at all may exert great effort to get the first. The next loaf is likely to be valued highly by one and not at all by the other. To the one, it is the staff of life; to the other, merely a storage problem. Neither would we be surprised that a person who has none will value the first loaf highly, the twelfth less highly, and each successive loaf even less. So the value of a loaf of bread, or any other good, is a function of the stock of that good that one already has. The marginal utility of any good is always defined in our actual behavior as the value of the next unit (or the last one) in relation to the stock of that good that one already possesses. Marshall expressed the matter by saying, "the additional benefit which a person derives from a given increase of his stock of a thing, diminishes with every increase in the stock of it that he already has."[6] Its value, in short, resides in its marginal utility, not in any inherent utility or in its virtues or in the labor required for its production, which, presumably, would remain unchanged no matter how many loaves one already has.

We may define marginal utility in a second way. From the certainty that the value of the next loaf is slight for anyone who has a thousand, we may infer that such a person is unlikely to give up much of anything else in order to get one more; and from the fact that the next loaf has large marginal utility for someone, we may infer that that person is likely to risk a great deal to gain the next one. He may even risk his liberty by turning to theft. Thus, we may define the marginal utility of any good as the amount of some *other* good (it might be money) that one is willing and able to give up to secure the next increment. By this second version, marginal utility is the rate of exchange. The measure of marginal utility just *is* the price, not the price asked but the price actually paid, assuming that the exchange is not compelled. Thus, price becomes the measure of value. Use-value and exchange-value become united. Perhaps this is what makes it possible to replace speech about the value of a loaf of bread with speech about how much someone values a loaf of bread. The notion of marginal utility refers strictly to behavior, not to nature.[7] "Utility," says Jevons, "though a quality of things is *no inherent quality*. It is better described as a *circumstance of things* arising out of their relation to man's circumstances."[8]

The beauty and the power of this formulation will become self-evident if we take one further step and note that the concept of marginal utility is always defined as utility *to* someone or *to* some aggregate of persons. Utility is not a property *of* any good or commodity in itself. It turns out, by this analysis, that if value is utility and if utility is marginal utility, then there is no such thing as inherent value at all, at least not in the case of commodities in exchange. There is only value to someone, and that value will differ from person to person and also from time to time for the same person. Thus, we purchase a powerful view of consumer behavior in a market society[9] by giving up the view that *things* have value for talk of *persons having values*. This is the new-speak whose origins we set out to discover. When persons are said to have different values, what is meant is that they have different preference schedules. When they calculate their marginal utility, they arrive at different conclusions. In this way, value is reduced to preference as measured in actual exchanges. In what is called full-value assessment, for example, a method of evaluation used with increasing frequency in determining property taxes, the value of a piece of property is determined by the recent history of exchanges for adjacent pieces of comparable property. The estimate of value is determined by recent prices in actual exchanges.

One may be excused for suspecting that the logic of such a view is impregnably circular. Nothing in that suspicion, including its truth, however, can reduce the significance of this shift in the conception of value for the development of economics nor weaken the claim that this pattern of thought is indelibly stamped upon the culture of the modern world, and thus, upon the practice of education. In a world in which value is understood simply as marginal utility, value is always value *to* one person or another. Nothing in that kind of world has value except as it has value to this person or to that person. Nothing is presented to us as valuable in our experience or in and of itself. From such a world, it may be said, value as a predicate, as a property of things, has simply vanished.

This conceptual move, I believe, is one source of the modern concept of values and the idea that persons have values. The idea of value as a property, though abandoned in economics, persists in ordinary usage whenever people say such things as "This isn't worth the price." Such remarks express claims about the value of a certain thing, implying that the value of a thing is not to be confused with its price. Such claims, however, are inevitably understood by economists as expressions of individual utility, and interpreted by social scientists as expressions of individuals' values.[10] Similar intellectual moves have occurred in other fields of thought, though none with quite the logical power of the concept of marginal utility. In each case, the movement of thought has been to move from discourse about claims that X is valuable or that X has worth, to a concern with claims about the values possessed by individuals and groups.

Such a view, when extended to the whole of life, can be described quite literally as the evacuation of value from the world.[11] No longer is value in any sense 'out there'. It is simply 'in here'. The notion that things have worth is transformed into the view that people have values. Thus, we arrive at a distinctly twentieth-century world in which people have values but without any corresponding assumption that worth is actually present in the world or presented to us in experience. In place of value, we have valuational behavior.

It would be a gross exaggeration to suggest that the consumer ethic, right now endemic, the most fundamental proposition of which is, "I shop, therefore I am," was produced by this intellectual artifact. Perhaps it is even exaggeration to say that such a conceptual transformation was a necessary step in that moral evolution. But it is surely not an exaggeration to say that this movement of thought together with its conceptual companion, the theory of 'the values that we have', has been a powerful force in that direction. It used to be possible to frame the central questions of moral, civic, and aesthetic education by asking how we can educate persons so that they come to value those things that have worth. But in a world in which things no longer have worth, we can no longer frame the educational questions in that way.

If to this direction of thought we now add two further facts, we can begin to see how this language of 'values' functions in educational discourse. First is the fact that if we are to speak seriously about different perspectives on what things have worth, then we shall be speaking sometimes (but not always) of whole different ways of life. We shall be speaking not simply of loaves and fishes, but of tyrannies and liberty, of risks and security, of fairness and prejudice, of charity and greed, of different views of our destiny, and of different religious perspectives on life and death itself. These are controversial matters, sources not merely of dissent but of dissension. Differences of this kind can be the source of whatever is the present version of religious wars. The great achievement of the liberal tradition in political theory since Locke (possibly since Hobbes) has been the realization that differences of belief on such ultimate matters ought never impair one's capacities as a citizen. Tolerance of different ways of life is the taproot of the liberal understanding of things. It requires a public vocabulary that is essentially neutral, formal, vacuous, and noncommittal in respect to all competing claims of what has worth, especially when such claims are about matters of ultimate worth. To create an arena of relative neutrality as between such ultimate claims is a major achievement, one moreover, into which the modern vocabulary on 'the values people have' fits nicely.

We live in a pluralistic world in which whole different ways of life must coexist. The modern vocabulary of values allows us to avoid their clash. It helps preserve civil peace by allowing us to frame a kind of public vocabulary suited to escape the controversy. To afford this evasion is precisely the function of such language. To controversy aroused by religious differences, economic interests, and cultural perspectives, we can simply shrug our shoulders and say, "Well, we have our values and they have theirs," and promptly retreat into the cozy confines of our own community.

The victory of this kind of language in educational discourse also exacts its cost. It allows us to ignore the fact that some social goods, like liberty and justice, depend less upon any psychological condition of individuals than upon the creation of social institutions within which liberty and justice can flourish. Social goods such as these depend for their preservation and their nurture not upon what values persons have (whatever that may mean), but upon the quite objective social constitution of the moral world persons inhabit. These are not values people have (or fail to have). They are gifts, parts of a legacy, that persons may enjoy provided the institutions of their social world take on a shape that will contain such goods. The educational problem in a world from which value has been evacuated is not that we may lose our values, but that we may lose our legacy.

So, in addition to the mishmash we create by collapsing the differences between teaching beliefs, forming virtues, vindicating hope, and the like into the obscure language of 'having values', we must now add the dangerous collapse of political principles into the same shapeless discourse. Were we to strike all language of 'having values' from our vocabulary of value and worth, we would be forced to make distinctions where distinctions exist. Such radical surgery practiced upon our educational discourse might also restore to currency some discussions (never mind agreement) about what things have worth, and foremost among those new (old) questions might be the question as to what things have educational worth.

II. Social Values as Social Structure

This movement of thought permitting talk about values to assume a central place in our grasp of education, and especially in moral education, has also contributed to new and powerful ways of study elsewhere in the social sciences. I wish to sacrifice nothing that may have been gained for these fields of study through such movements of thought. Still, my central claim is that no clear and univocal sense can be attached either to the notion that people have values or that values change. The view I want to explore is (1) that such human goods as security, health, friendship, community, justice, liberty, privacy, and a host of others that we often call values, are not best understood as 'values that people have'; rather, they are present or absent quite objectively in the structure of our social lives; (2) that the nature of such goods does not change, although (3) their distribution, rank order, standards, and mode of appearance clearly do change. The second of these claims is a thesis about the stability of values; the third about their indicators.

A discerning reader will already have inferred what needs in any case to be made explicit, namely that in speaking of values as objectively present in the structure of our social lives, I refer to *social* values, not *personal* values or what are usually called virtues. It was a practical certainty, from the beginning of this inquiry, that the hopeless ambiguity in the idea of teaching values would force upon us some such distinction as the difference between social values and virtues. To any seeker for clarity it will be disquieting to note that by 'values' might be meant almost anything from beliefs, habits, and preferences, to virtues, personal commitments, and even traits of personality. Some modicum of clarity might be attained if we consider values under their guise as social and defer attention to others of this large assemblage.

Values as the Form of Social Relations

Values are the *form* that our relations assume in social life. Every social value is a social form of life, and the important thing to discern is its shape or structure. Friendship, for example, is sometimes said to be a value and friendliness a virtue. If we are to describe what friendship is, we would describe a relationship involving (1) a certain kind of equality, (2) a certain reciprocity, and (3) a certain indifference to justice. The adage that "birds of a feather flock together" is a summary formulation of the empirical observation that among friends, if friendship is to endure, huge differences of virtue are unlikely. They strain the relation. As noted already, it is hard to be friends with a saint. The second feature is revealed in the fact that unrequited love may be expressed in adoration or adulation, but not in friendship. The necessity for the third feature of friendship can be established by a simple thought experiment. Treat your friends with an imperious regard for justice, asking each, for example, to stand in line for your attention, and soon you will have no friends. The kind of relation that we describe as friendship is the same in these respects even when the friends are different persons. The relationship, that is, its 'shape', remains, though the occupants of the roles change. The form of friendship is the same everywhere and everywhen. That is the point in saying that a value, like friendship, is the form that our relations assume in social life.

Similarly, we speak of privacy and justice as social values, and also of freedom, community, and security. These are often described as social values because typically they are present or absent not in the character of individuals, but in their social life. In that respect they are values rather than virtues. But these also have their structure. When we speak of privacy as a value, for example, we have in mind two quite definite structural features of our world. First is the possibility of escape from surveillance, and second the achievement of anonymity. If the second can be attained, then the first is less important. Americans abroad, for example, having the anonymity that comes from being among strangers in a distant place, have been known to publicly behave in ways unthinkable at home where they are known. Anonymity can convert a public act into a private one. Conversely, where surveillance is blocked, privacy exists whether there is anonymity or not. Privacy, construed as a value, just is the existence and maintenance of a social structure affording either escape from surveillance or anonymity. Where these things exist, privacy exists. Where they are threatened, privacy is threatened. Thus, when we speak of the value, privacy, we speak of something objectively present or absent in the structure of our social lives. It is not a psychological preference or a commodity valuable only 'on the margin'.

With this understanding of values, we can easily understand also what it means to say that some institutions are ill-suited to contain, secure, or advance certain values. That would mean simply that the social roles comprising the institution either do not support or do not allow the social structure required by certain values. Values are themselves a kind of institution. In stressing this point, I mean to suggest that the only sense in which values exist, the only sense in which they can be said to be real, is the sense in which institutions exist as objective structural sets of relations among human beings. Consider these remarks of George P. Adams, when considering the very idea of civilization:

> If it makes anyone happy, as it apparently does, to reflect that everything, everywhere and everywhen, is organized in some fashion, so be it. That leaves us just where we were before, profoundly interested in discovering the objective differences between organization and disorganization, between order and chaos, and this difference is to be looked for, I think, in the fact that it takes a certain kind of structure and organization to house and embody certain kinds of significant contents. . . . A chaotic society is one with a type of organization which bars it from incorporating significant ideas and values, such as justice and freedom. The question whether you are confronted by order or disorder, civilization or barbarism has nothing to do with subjective preference. *It is the question of the adequacy of a container to its contents, or a body to its soul. In short, institutional organization of any society is not the totality of its civilization.* . . . It is not enough to say that the social structures perform certain functions in the sense in which the nerve ganglia of mollusks perform a function. No doubt they do; but that is not their distinctive trait. The new, utterly unique, and momentous thing about the functions performed by social structures is that the individuals belonging to these institutions can become aware both of the social machinery and of the ends which it may serve, the significant contents and meanings for which the social machinery is but the vehicle.[12]

What Adams refers to as the content of institutions is part of what we often refer to as social values. It illustrates what I have meant by advancing the claim that the significant feature of social values is their shape. They can be understood as having a certain organization or structure of their own and therefore, it is easy to understand why those values can only exist in certain kinds of institutions as their containers.

The point needs further illustration. If we must speak of values at all, we would surely agree that justice and freedom are among those things that we call values. But consider them in some of their more important aspects. Freedom, viewed as a value, includes freedom of information. But what is that? What does it require? What is its 'shape'? Its structure includes arrangements for access to information which, in turn, means a great many things about the ways that libraries are organized, about how publication is carried out, how archives are kept, how the instruments of communication are regulated, and how the institutions of law define the limits of what I must reveal or may refuse to disclose about myself.

First, as illustration, in the former Soviet Union telephone directories were conspicuously absent. So, according to accounts related to me, if one tried to phone a friend and called the operator for the proper number, the operator might ask, "Do you know this person?" "Yes." "Well, if you know this person and he (she) wanted you to call, he (she) would have provided you with the number." And that would be the end of it. Secondly, a colleague of mine, wanting to consult some standard American undergraduate textbooks in economics, inquired at the library of the State University of Moscow only to learn that his privileges as a foreign scholar, even of great distinction, did not include access at a level of security sufficient to allow for the inspection of such volumes. These are not institutional arrangements much suited to encouraging freedom of information or inquiry. Freedom of information, understood as a value, has a shape that these arrangements cannot contain. These are, however, arrangements admirably designed to secure and maintain surveillance. Freedom of inquiry itself, as a value, just *is* a certain set of arrangements. It is a social structure. The presence or absence of the value, freedom of inquiry, just is the presence or absence of such structural arrangements.

Consider once again that in one of its forms, justice requires that we treat like people in similar ways. If we treat similar persons in drastically different ways, we are required to give some account of how the different treatment can be justified. It seems a good thing that courts of justice should contain the value, justice, and that lawyers as a minimum standard of their practice should be encouraged in that conviction. And so we try to embody this feature of the value, justice, in the ways that we define pleadings and counter-pleadings and in the rules defining what is admissible as testimony in a civil case. On the other hand, justice also requires that when significant or relevant differences exist between people, then those differences should be taken into account and people should receive different treatment.

Justice, in this form, requires roles and relationships in which it is possible to take account of the relevant differences among people. If many differences are relevant, then justice requires many sources of information on individuals. For example, if a just distribution of educational resources requires that we distribute aid to those individuals who need it most, then we must be able to determine who those individuals are, and to do that not simply by identifying large groups whose members as a general rule tend to be needy. We must be able to determine need for each individual. That in turn means that we may need financial information, not simply on groups, trends, or categories of persons, but on each actual individual. So information that would otherwise have been irrelevant to justice may become highly relevant. What may have been private and unrecorded, such as family income, must now become public record in a manner suitable for use in allocational decisions. Doing so is required by the structure of justice for the practice of justice. So in the name of justice, individuals may have to record information that had been left unrecorded on grounds of privacy. Two values conflict. We extend justice, but in some measure diminish privacy. To secure a definable gain in one, we pay a definable cost in the other. Because of their respective forms or shapes, the values of justice and privacy may conflict—a point to which we must now turn.

Conflict of Values

To be adequate to our needs, the vocabulary of value must allow us to say that values conflict. We must be able to express what that means. If we understand values to be the forms that our relations take in social life, then conflicts among values can be precisely described, perhaps even measured. There will be conflict among values at a definable point where the social structure of one is either incompatible with or an obstacle to the advancement of some other value. In other words, conflicts among values occur when the roles required or allowed by two or more values are such that the enactment of one prohibits or hinders the enactment of another.

I have already suggested how the shape of justice may conflict with the shape of privacy. But there are other ways of illustrating conflicts of values in this sense. Keeping the extent of one's property a private matter may explicitly conflict with running for public office. There are more subtle cases. I have sometimes wondered, for example, why ecclesiastical bureaucracies (in my view) are typically so badly managed when measured against the standards of ordinary bureaucratic management. If we are permitted to regard pastoral care as a value or cluster of values, then the explanation may lie in the fact that pastoral care is a value in conflict with the values of efficiency and detached judgment. To a pastor every case is unique. Exceptions are ordinary. But to a bureaucrat, exceptions are extraordinary. That is why they are exceptions. A bureaucracy whose incumbents are self-selected by training and disposition for pastoral care is bound to be badly managed by bureaucratic standards. The values conflict. Bureaucracy is not a form of life that can easily contain, advance, or assure the presence of pastoral care. Bureaucratic management is not what pastors are typically good at.

Change and Permanence of Values

Our vocabulary of value must allow us to speak not only of how values conflict, but also of how they change. Yet, from the perspective I have been outlining, values don't change at all. Privacy, for example, always and everywhere consists of a social structure affording escape from surveillance and maintenance of anonymity. Freedom, likewise, is always and everywhere the same in the social structures that it demands. Often what seems to be a change in values is only the result of an adjustment sought when there is conflict among values. Strictly speaking, from within this perspective on the nature of values, it makes no sense to talk about values changing. That is something that simply cannot be said. The point is not that saying it would be saying something false. Rather, saying it would be saying nothing at all.

Still, there is something that we notice and *describe* as value change. What is it? The values justice, privacy, and freedom are always continuous and everywhere the same in the social structures that they demand. Still, those values, even within the perspective outlined here, can be construed to have certain indicators, certain public clues to their presence or absence or their relative rank in some ordered scale. Each value might be understood to have (1) some domain, (2) some distribution, (3) some context, (4) some standards, and (5) some position in the rank order of values. Given these indices of values, we can express a great deal of what persons mean, perhaps all that they mean, when they speak of values changing. Every alteration in these indices will imply that the society is somehow altered in the values that it contains.

Domain: We do not ordinarily think of values as social structures or as the forms that our relations assume in social life. It is a useful idea, however. It suggests, among other things, that the same values may be found in different institutions, though not always realized in the same way or in the same degree. Some institutions offer congenial settings for the exercise of personal initiative and others, as in military organizations, may be hierarchical in ways that purposely inhibit it. In a family, anonymity being impossible to secure, the social arrangements typical of privacy might call for times and places for concealment. In contrast, privacy for a person in government bureaus is likely to require anonymity; yet anonymity in such offices can be a means of escaping accountability and thus something to be discouraged. Thus, when we think of social values as the shape of our social relations, we think of values that can appear in different guises in different institutions of society, in some more easily than in others. This characteristic of values is what I mean to refer to as their *domain*. When we ask about the domain of a particular value, we are asking where among the institutions of society that value is likely to be found.

That the domain of a certain value has enlarged or contracted means simply that the social structures constituting that value appear in institutions where they did not used to appear, or that they appear less than before in institutions where they used to be readily found. It might be argued, for example, that the opportunity for private life on the part of public officials, especially elected officials, is much reduced compared to what it used to be. Escape from surveillance has never been easy for persons of fame. But the difficulty may be increasing for public officials. Fewer of their activities are acceptably screened from public knowledge. The domain of such privacy in that respect has changed.

Distribution: We might say that the *distribution* of certain values has changed, not as in the case of domain, when the structure of those values is appearing more or less frequently within the various institutions of society, but when the structure of such values falls within the experience of more or fewer people. The domain of a certain value can be very restricted provided it appears among few institutions. Yet those institutions may be so fundamental to the character of the society that virtually everyone has intense and intimate experience with the social relations of that value. In that case we have a value with a restricted domain, but with a very broad distribution. For example, when children in a particular school are drawn from a more diverse array of cultures than was true of the school when attended by another generation, and when the school takes cognizance of that fact, so that this fresh multiplicity is seized upon as an educational opportunity in the practices of the school, then it might be said that pluralism is being more widely experienced by children than it used to be.[13] Pluralism as a value—however construed—then receives a broader distribution.

Context: The Parable of the Good Samaritan was offered to illustrate our duties to neighbor. It is the story of a man robbed and beaten and left by the side of the road, and also of those who passed him with evasion in mind. Our duties to neighbor are illuminated by the parable. They remain clear enough. But when the road is a subway, our neighbors number in the millions. When the robbed, beaten, and unfortunate are evident everywhere, then we may ponder not whether our duties to neighbor have changed, but how we are to carry them out. How those duties are experienced may be altered by numbers, by proximity to need, by the visibility of the need, and by changed methods for meeting those needs. The context of our lives may influence not simply the goods that we seek to secure, but the manner and clarity of their enactment, the ways we make them visible, and how they are experienced.

The shirt, the blanket, the extended hand, the soothing touch, the dressings for wounds, the proverbial cup of cool water, all these may be called for. But providing them cannot become anyone's principal occupation. One must eventually come to ask why such extremities of need arise. Where are the police? Neighborly duties, seen and discharged as though to one another, simply between me and my neighbor, must now be seen and met through the mediating agency of public instruments of one sort or another. What was a relation of neighbor to neighbor is transformed by context into a relation of member to some collective. It is too much to say that in carrying out our duties to neighbor nowadays we have to become politicians. It is not too much, however, to suggest that the altered context of modern urban life calls for a renewed attention to our respective roles as citizens or as public agents. Context alters things and alters them enormously.

Standards: To suggest that the *standards* of certain values are changed, is to suggest that the acceptable level of their experience has changed. Crime may become so common that we will accept lower standards of personal security. In the search for clean air and water, we may aim to eliminate all pollutants, insisting on more purity even than nature provides, or we may simply settle upon a new acceptable level of pollution. It can happen that an acceptable level of air pollution in certain areas is so costly to attain (in both economic and social costs) that we shall change our notions of what is acceptable. And so it is with levels of crime, equality, competition, efficiency, quality of goods, and a thousand other things related to our experience of the goods that we value.

It may be argued that, in a strict sense, values do not change. Still, it must be admitted that we may apply altered standards to determine an acceptable level in securing any particular value or social good. This observation may seem a mere quibble. But it is not. In this matter of standards is found an important aspect of the very concept of public policy. We are seldom in a position to maximize values. The more normal problem is to discern how and when we shall have to secure less of one or another value considered separately in order to secure as much as we can of several different values when taken together. Formulating questions of policy in this way will inevitably lead to questions of standards, and changes in standards over time may appear to be changes in the values people have.

Rank Order: I have often wondered why *sophrosyne* was viewed among the Greeks as such a high virtue. I suspect it had something to do with the fact that they were a people strongly inclined toward extremes, even to the point of finding in extremes themselves the true goods of life. The Dionysian impulse was extremely fundamental to their religious life, which is to say, to their drama, poetry, and self-understanding.

This conjecture brings to mind two points about values generally. The first is that values, in addition to domain, range, context, and standards, may also stand in relation to one another in a scale of worth. We can be said to attach value to values. Some will be viewed as more important than others. Freedom might be worth more to us than justice, community more than competition, privacy more than equality. On the other hand, the rank order of values may be a reflection not of their relative worth, but simply of their relative and perhaps even temporary position in an agenda for public attention. In other contexts we refer to these rankings as priorities. A value might be more important than others for the moment without being regarded as more valuable.

If a change in rank is a kind of change in values, then it is worth asking under what conditions the rank order of values is likely to change. The answer, I believe, is that it is likely to change when the interests of some population appear to be threatened, that is, when the structural arrangements of life necessary to contain a certain value are threatened. In rural America, where anonymity is hard to come by, escape from surveillance is simple. Privacy can be found at the end of a short walk over the next hill. Securing and maintaining the social relations of privacy is not likely to appear high on the agenda of persons living under those conditions. Privacy is unthreatened. But if we lived in a world where anonymity requires a disguise and conversational privacy can be secured only by standing next to an operating jet engine, say, then maintaining the conditions of privacy might appear near the top of a public agenda. In such circumstances, privacy—the value—will have a very small range and domain, but assuming that persons see such a state of affairs as threatening to their interests, its rank order will rise. It will not follow that privacy would be of more worth, say, than community; it will follow, however, that it is viewed as more of a problem. Being more of a problem, it is likely to receive more attention; and its receiving more attention is likely to be seen as a change of values.

Values are social structures. They are like institutions inasmuch as they require certain worldly arrangements in order to appear. These are not to be described as 'the values persons have', but as the worldly conditions essential if persons anywhere are to enjoy certain social goods. From such a perspective it cannot be said that values change at all. Nonetheless, as I have argued, values, in this sense, have certain properties—domain, range, context, standards, and rank order. Given these indices of values, we can express a great deal of what is often meant by changes of values. To say that the domain of a certain value has enlarged, is to say that the social roles constituting that value have been extended. To say that the distribution of certain values is enlarged, is to say simply that they are experienced by more and more persons. To speak of the context of values, is to speak of the *ways* certain values are experienced. These may be altered though the value itself is unchanged in any particular. And the same with standards and rank order of values. These too, when altered, give the appearance of changes in values.

Values as a Public Affair

From this brief reconstruction of the language of values, it should be apparent that values are understood here as public in two senses. First, they are public because they are objective. Values are objective states of affairs, not subjective preferences. But they are public in another sense. The business of the public just is to advance or to secure certain values and to secure them not in the sense of 'getting', as in "Next week I shall secure (get) a new computer," but in the sense of 'tying down', as in "I have just secured the house against the coming storm." The business of the public, seen in this way, simply *is* the distribution and maintenance of values, that is, social goods.

We may see the point in another way. Policy, whether in private organizations or in the more comprehensive sphere of government, is typically concerned with conflicts of values in exactly the way that I have described them. Were there no conflicts of values (or we might say, goods), then there would be no problems of policy. Conflicts among values, in the sense just described, are precisely what public policy is about. The resolution, balancing, or adjustment of such conflicts of values is precisely what we seek to achieve, at least momentarily, through politics. We seek to achieve this, furthermore, within an already existing polity that reflects still another set of values or ideals in conflict. And this which I have said about values may also be said about our social ideals. They too are bound to conflict in the ways I have described.

The claim being advanced here is that values, goods, or ideals conflict, not that human interests conflict. No doubt there is conflict also among the different interests of different persons and between different groups of persons. But that is not what is being asserted here. If the unlikely were to occur and all differences of interest between different human beings vanished, it would remain the case that goods, values, and ideals conflict.[14]

III. Other Views of Values

So far, in attempting to reconstruct the vocabulary of values, I have entertained only talk about what are often called social values. But there is also something that we mean by individual values. Sometimes, in speaking of values in this sense, we have in mind beliefs or belief systems, sometimes virtues or entire sets of virtues, and sometimes we refer to what may be called an explanatory fiction. But beliefs, virtues, belief systems, and so forth are very different things. That we manage to subsume such diverse things under a single term is evidence of our philosophical and practical amnesia in such matters. These are things that ought to be distinguished.

Values as Beliefs

Persons do not *have* values, if by 'values' is meant the enduring social forms of our relations. Persons cannot be said to *have* social structures. Nonetheless, persons may have values if by this we mean to refer to beliefs. But in advancing such a view we do not typically have in mind just any kind of belief. We mean to refer to beliefs about the worth of things—of pleasure, honor, wealth, power, community, justice, skill, friendship, and the like, and beliefs about what constitutes excellence in many kinds of performance, in short, the conscience of craft. Such beliefs are, in effect, judgments. They are evaluative judgments about the relative worth of things. To change values, in this sense, is to change those evaluative judgments, and one way to do that is to examine our beliefs about the worth of things, clarify them, discuss them, and test them to discover their consonance with our experience.

We should note, however, how the view that values are beliefs leads inevitably to the classical, pre-nineteenth-century view that value is a property of things. If the values that we have are beliefs that we have, then they are beliefs about the worth of things. On such a view, value is a property or a predicate, and the idea that people have values at all is a way of talking that is perfectly dispensable. It serves no logical function except to endorse our slovenly inattention to important distinctions between beliefs, virtues, affections, and the principles of explanation.

If by 'values' we mean to refer to such evaluative beliefs, then we must be prepared to ask how such beliefs are formed and, therefore, what is required for them to change. Can such change be wrought by teaching? Such judgments or beliefs are typically framed on the basis of evidence either in the form of precepts and dicta, teachings, firsthand experience, or on other rational considerations rooted in beliefs that we already hold. No one of these sources is likely to be sufficient. But some kind of evidence for belief there surely must be. The evidence or grounds or reasons for belief may be found in memories of experiences and relationships, or in arguments, or in what one has been taught by a teacher, parent, or some other person in authority. It is difficult to fall in love with the violin if one never sees, hears, or touches one. It is difficult to believe that schooling can lead to a better life if all around one sees the failure of the schooled and the success of the unschooled. Evaluative beliefs, in short, must be supported by some kind of experience, memory, or teaching. It is difficult to reevaluate one's beliefs about competition, for example, unless one has experience of other ways of life that contain alternatives.

In short, if by 'values' we mean the evaluative beliefs that people hold, then changes in values involve changes also in the domain, the range, and perhaps the standards of values as social structures. It may mean more violins and more models of people who care for them. It is true that beliefs are not social structures; it is also true, however, that beliefs about the worth of things cannot be sustained except in social structures that verify those judgments of worth. To suppose otherwise would be to suppose that human beings are free to believe whatever they choose to believe no matter what may be confirmed in their experience or supported by their memories and reasoned conclusions. And that is just not the way that anyone comes to believe anything.

Thus, by 'values' we may sometimes refer to evaluational beliefs or judgments. But at other times we may be referring to valuational *acts*. A person may love an heirloom and at the same time acknowledge that it is worthless. "It is not that I *believe* grandmother's brooch is valuable. I simply treasure it. To me, it is beyond price." Such a person values the object highly. And in saying this, we refer not to a belief, but to a love. Valuational acts, for this reason, are sometimes described as acts of bestowal. They bestow worth on things that would otherwise be worthless.[15] Valuational acts, in contrast to evaluational beliefs or assessments, are acts of love or expressions of desire. We have here still another sense of 'values'. By referring to a person's values, we may mean to refer simply to his loves and desires, his affections; and so by a change of values, we may mean a change in one's loves and desires. If we take the view that this is what we mean by human values, then one may doubt that human values, even through enormous historical transformations, change very much.

Values as Explanatory Fictions

I have already considered one possible source of the concept of values in nineteenth-century economic thought. We are now in a position to consider quite another. Moderns are inclined to move conceptually from discourse of a rather traditional sort about valuations, evaluations, and claims about the worth of things to a quite different, supposedly more scientific vocabulary aimed at explaining human behavior. I have illustrated this intellectual move from economic theory focusing on the shift from a concern with economic value to a concern with consumer behavior. This shift of focus occurred also in other fields of thought in the nineteenth and early twentieth centuries. A similar shift transforms political theory into the study of political behavior, and moral theory into the theory of moral claims, and moral conduct into the psychology of valuational behavior or preferences. In each case, the movement of thought is away from the idea that value is a predicate to the idea that there is simply valuational behavior or the expression of preferences. Thus we arrive at that distinctly twentieth-century idea of values and persons' values without the assumption that worth is actually presented to us in experience.

This shift of interest from the worth of things to the explanation of human behavior permits, encourages, and perhaps even requires the invention of the concept of values as an explanatory principle.[16] We want some adequate explanation, for example, for the commonly observed fact that two persons, in the same situation, may nevertheless behave in quite different ways, all other things being the same. One may seek to deceive, the other tenaciously to avoid deception. In the midst of disorder, one may take steps to restore order; another may not. Why do they behave differently? A rough, but common answer is, "They have different values."

Viewed in this way, the concept of values is needed to provide the missing premise in an explanation of behavior. It functions as an explanatory fiction. Explanatory fictions are perfectly admissible in scientific explanations or, for that matter, in other fields of inquiry and professional practice, in psychology, in economics, and in law, for example.[17] But wherever they occur, two methodological demands are paramount. The first is the need to be quite precise, though not exhaustive, in the meaning attached to the explanatory fiction. The second is the need to demonstrate that the explanatory fiction is necessary. It should be shown that the explanatory role of the fiction cannot be satisfied without it. If the first problem is unmet, then it follows that we do not know what the explanatory fiction is supposed to account for, and thus, quite literally, we do not know what is explained by its use nor would we know what kinds of empirical data would be relevant to its use. If the second condition is not met, then it follows that the explanatory fiction is simply dispensable. Nothing is gained by its adoption.

Enough has been said already about this vocabulary of values and 'having values' to show that neither of these conditions is usually satisfied by the concept of values as it is typically used in discussions of moral education as education in values. I have already pointed abundantly to the vagueness and ambiguity of the idea that people have values. The first demand for clarity, in short, remains unsatisfied. But what of the second demand that the explanatory fiction be demonstrably necessary for purposes of explanation?

When we compare two individuals in the same setting (think of Presidents Nixon and Ford) and seek to explain why one wanted secrecy and another openness and candor, we do not explain anything by saying that their different behavior, or their recognizably different demeanor, stems from their having different values. At any rate, we do not explain anything that cannot be explained better by saying that they have different beliefs about the worth of things, power, for example, or that they have different evaluational beliefs; or that they have different beliefs about how things work, that is to say, they make different prudential judgments; or that they have different habits and dispositions, that is to say, they have different virtues. We gain nothing in the way of explanation by introducing the fiction that their different behavior is accounted for by their different values. On the contrary, we lose the clarity of thought and appraisal that result when we are forced to distinguish among habits, dispositions, and affections on the one hand, and beliefs, valuations, and evaluations, on the other. These are things formed in different ways, changed in different ways, explained in different ways, and playing different roles in the effort to describe social change. The notion that persons have values is not simply of doubtful explanatory value. It is a positive liability in achieving conceptual clarity.

In a constructive vocabulary of value, we ought simply to abandon altogether the idea that people have values. Doing so would clear the way for a more careful attention to advancing and securing in our social life the objective forms of decent political and human social values—such goods as freedom, charity, friendship, competence, and the like. Such an amendment of our philosophical speech would allow more clear-headed attention to educating all the voices of conscience, not only those concerned with the preservation of social values, but those reflexive voices of conscience closely related to the acquisition of many virtues—the conscience of craft and the advancement of the intellectual virtues, neither of which is often included in discussions of values education. Such an amendment in our very vocabulary for thinking about moral education might even make it possible once again to understand moral education as the effort to educate persons so that they value those things that considered judgment and long experience testify to having worth.

IV. Values as Strong Normation

Despite its coming to us without antecedents, despite the obscurity of its meaning, talk about the values people have is now so natural a part of our vocabulary as to have become simply a part of the cultural atmosphere we breathe. This is especially true whenever we turn to ponder the conduct of education. If all this is even nearly correct, then we need to ask what of fundamental human interest we express by this new-speak. Despite the confusions and evasions that such a way of thinking generates, substantial similarities exist between what analysis shows is involved in norm acquisition and what is struggling to be said when moral education is conceived simply as the formation of values. Between norm acquisition and values acquisition there are strong similarities. They are sufficiently strong, in fact, to warrant the claim that whatever of worth there may be in the notion of teaching values is already present in the notion of being strongly normed.

When we speak of persons' values, we point not simply to what they espouse, but also to what their conduct displays; not simply to what they intellectually assent to and verbally commend to others, but to what path of conduct they can be relied upon to follow. We refer not simply to what they *say* they value, but to what conduct *shows* they value. We point, that is, to what norms actually govern in their lives. By such talk of persons' values we attempt to reach also for what such persons find emotionally beyond the pale, because that is a clue as to where their sense of the sacred lies. In the more ordinary circumstances of life, far from any apparent presence of the sacred, we speak of the values persons have in order to discover and clarify what stirs in them the emotions of self-assessment, their sense of shame, guilt, pride, and embarrassment, including what conduct of their lives they regard as necessarily concealed. It is this combination of reason and emotion, of thought and conduct, that we seek to stress in our accustomed talk about 'having values'. Where is your agony? we ask. Your joy? Your shame? Questions such as these are the sort that reveal one's values, the standards that we observe, the boundaries of our failures and our evasions.

How much more vivid, however, is the question and how much more directly is one's gaze fixed upon the details of life if instead of asking, What values should we teach? we ask, What norms are we implementing and reinforcing by the design of our schools and the conduct of our daily lives? The question, What values ought to be taught in schools? remains terribly abstract, vague, amorphous and contentious. Such a question shrouds the relevant differences between virtues, duties, loyalties, habits, skills. It conceals the central importance of reflexive judgments rooted not only in rules of right, but also in the exercise of craft, in the moral courage of sacrifice, the care and generosity of membership, and judgments rooted also in what thanks we owe our predecessors and what care we owe our children. When the familiar and slovenly speech of teaching values is extended from virtues and beliefs to embrace the forms or structures of fundamental social goods, then such speech does more than obscure, it threatens. When we point to the social goods embedded in the 'forms' of our institutions and political principles and then refer to them as 'values that persons need to have', rather than the worldly conditions of a good life, then we not only misconstrue the nature of such goods, but, what is worse, we pose a threat to their maintenance. Such matters are sometimes captured by our concern with teaching or forming values. But mostly they are not. In any case, it seems a fair conclusion that attempts to express the nature of moral education by reducing it to something called 'teaching values' is not so much the solution to our problems as it is the source.

Chapter 6

Public Speech

I. Introduction

Once the notion is dispelled that moral education consists in 'teaching values', the way is cleared to explore the normative structure of practices vital to moral education in a republic. These essays began in an effort to frame an account of the origins and scope of governance, first by showing how reflexive self-governance makes its appearance both in the self-governance of individuals and also in the self-governance of a people through their institutions of republican government. The aim was to reveal a seamless progression from the reflexive self-governance of individuals to the activities of citizenship.

In these last two chapters, I aim to deliver on that promise. The final chapter will focus directly upon some normative features of the office of citizen, where being a citizen is understood as being a participant in the formation of public policy. Its emphasis is on normation to an office concerned with the formation of public policy. In the present chapter, however, attention falls upon a practice presupposed in the disciplines of that public office, namely, the practice of public speech. I mean to explore the normative disciplines that enter into the practice of public speech and the relation between those disciplines and the actual formation of a public. I aim to do so, moreover, out of a concern for what appears to me a stark deterioration of public speech in contemporary America.

We now have nearly a generation of students who in their entire lives have heard no major public leader speak to the nation powerfully about our ties to one another, much less with conviction about what gratitude we owe our predecessors and what we owe our children; no major public leader who has managed to speak to youth with captivating power about the dignity of public service, none apparently able to say that a life devoted to it might be challenging, might demand the best that anyone can offer, and might test our capacities at the highest level. This estimate of the contemporary scene can be contested, but I believe it to be accurate. If it is true, it is an awesome truth. I believe, moreover, that it is precisely this silence about the nature of our presence to one another and from generation to generation, silence about the nature of the political office that we share as citizens, that has permitted us to engage in a virtual deluge of deeply confused talk on educational reform. We live in the presence of a broad movement aimed directly at the revision of schooling, yet the movement remains virtually silent on the role of education in the formation of the public.

I offer in response a simple argument. Its generative premise is that public speech is constitutive. Were it not for public speech, there would be no public, only a babble of lamentations and complaints, pleadings, pronouncements, claims, and counter-claims. Without public speech, the public dies. Politics degenerates into polemics, becomes partisan in the worst sense, even venomous, and we are left with nothing we can reasonably speak of as public education, public service, or public life. That is why it matters that we understand *how* public speech is formative and *how* it does its work.

My first aim, therefore, is simply to offer reminders of some aspects of speech, especially the power of speech to create the world and thus to create a public. We are born and there is a company already there to greet us. With birth we enter a plurality, but it is not given that we thereby enter a public. We are thrust into a world of plurality; we must be nurtured to enter whatever public there be. The one is a consequence of birth, the other an achievement of life. It is, moreover, an *educational* achievement. In saying that the public is created by public speech, I do not offer a claim of causal or temporal precedence, a statement about which comes first, the public or public speech. Neither is this claim that the public is created by public speech a mere rhetorical trick. I mean rather to be asking an *educational* question: What needs to be done, what skills acquired, what practices employed so that a public may emerge from the plurality in which we begin and so that it may be sustained for all the years of our lives and of our children's lives? The answer, or at least a major part of it, will be found, I think, in the skills and practices of public speech. Public speech is formative; it is constitutive. That is the first premise. The public is created by speech or not at all. So my first aim is to persuade you that the quality of our public speech matters because that is what educationally forms the public.

My second aim is to construct a view of the nature of public speech and its fallacies, those habits of mind by which it is destroyed or its development aborted. I mean to ask, on the one hand, What makes public speech 'public'? and on the other hand, What slovenly yet winsome habits will suffice to undo its public face? In order to accomplish this task of describing the character of public speech and its fallacies, I intend, as my third aim, to persuade you that we speak of the public and of public life in two quite different ways. One view draws upon the notion of a forum a kind of public in which the speech typically required is the speech of inquiry, evidence, demonstration, argument, and claims and counter-claims of entitlement. Call this the forum view.

The other view stems from what I call umbilical stories, and its typical mode of speech is not argument, but narrative. In all portrayals in Western painting of the first man and the first woman being evicted from paradise, the figures are represented with anatomical accuracy except for one detail. Whether in the vision of Giotto, or Leonardo, or sweet Raphael, Adam and Eve are always pictured with navels. The first man and the first woman had belly buttons. The thought amuses.[1] I call it to your attention, however, not for its amusement, but in order to render another fact more memorable. We find it as difficult to conceive of any culture, or any public, without its antecedents as to conceive of the first man and the first woman without theirs. And with antecedents, of course, come stories, umbilical stories, stories of attachments. By this view, the public is a public of some memory. Argument, evidence, and claims of entitlement are less at issue than are simple reminders of umbilical connections. Identity is the problem, not inquiry. Call this the umbilical view. I hope to show, if not actually demonstrate, that the first of these, the forum view, depends for its existence upon the latter, the umbilical view, and that the principle of public speech I want to explore relates the two in just that way.

II. The Power of Speech

That the public is created by public speech is an idea thoroughly known to us. But, like the very end of our nose, it is constantly overlooked. Effort is needed even to notice. Yet, it must be noticed. The oddity of the idea must be detected. Only when the ordinary becomes strange do we see it in fresh ways. The constitutive character of public speech is an idea that has its roots in tradition and in familiar experiences. I cannot hope to cite all the sources. We can, however, conduct some forays into memory and tradition and in that way try, as best we can, to make the matter plain.

For the first of these forays, recall the ancient Roman concept of the *res publica*, by which was meant, and still is meant, in the language of law, the 'thing' of the public. The *res publica* is literally the affair of the public. And this affair is, or ought to be, and in healthy circumstances always is, a love affair. The 'thing' described is both a residence and a courtship, both a place of habitation and a project of our affections. The *res publica* is the republic, a word familiar to us. Yet here, as everywhere, familiarity breeds amnesia. We know it so well that we forget its meaning. The re-public is the affair of the people. We should not think of it as our system of government. We shall do better to think of our system of government as the structure, the machinery, or, in another metaphor, that hardy bar-rier to barbarism which, standing firm against the constant threat of chaos, gives us time to speak. The government is formed by law, but the public by public speech.

This first foray then, lies on the side of recalling what 'public' means. I offer a second to remind us what 'speech' is about. Often, speaking is it-self a form of acting. We are likely to look past this obvious truth because of an adjacent vocabulary by which speech is viewed not as action, but as inaction. "She is all talk and no deed." "Cut the gaff and let's get busy." In these expressions and others like them, speech is opposed to action. By this vocabulary, speech is made to reside with indolence. I admit there is that truth. Speech can be an instrument of evasion, but that is not the truth right now I mean to stress.

We are also likely to forget that speech can be a kind of action if we suppose that speech is used primarily to inform. Often it is not. When I say to a dear friend, "I love you; I love you; I truly do," I do not mean merely to give information on my state of mind or on the composition of my affections. Informing is not my aim. My saying "I love you; I love you; I truly do" is already and by itself an act of love. When you step off the curb into the street and someone shouts, "Look out! Look out!" inform-ing you is not their aim. Warning you is. And by uttering those words, that is what they do. Such speech is an act of warning as surely as if the words had been just that—"I warn you!" By saying "Greetings!" to friends and strangers, they are greeted. Saying "Greetings!" and greeting our friends are not separate things. They are one and the same. The speech simply is the act.

That is the way things are with warnings and welcomings, but also with promises and pledges. By saying "I promise," I forge a promise. By saying "I pledge . . ." (my allegiance, say, or my troth), I pledge. The speech and the act are not two things, but one. In this respect, speech is no mere *flatus vocis*, a simple snorting that happens to agitate the air. Speak and the world is changed. Remain silent and the world remains just as it is. Speak and you alter things. By speech, people are loved and warned and greeted. Promises are made and so the future becomes fixed; pledges are pledged and with them fidelity comes to matter in places and among persons where before it mattered not at all. By speech, obligations are created and assurances are offered and received. By speech, charity is extended and grace makes its appearance. These are more than merely acts of speech. In the language of philosophy, they are 'speech acts'.

This performative function of speech works also for curses. "Be damned!" Except when uttered in the first person, as in "Well, I'll be damned" (and perhaps even then), this expression, originally resident in a theology and cosmology now for the most part vanished, was never meant to assert anything that could be true or false. It was not meant to inform. Here was a speech act by which it was intended, I suppose, that someone actually be made to reside eternally in some netherland, a Sheol or Hades. Like "Bug-out!" and "to hell with you!" such expressions, as William Gass suggests, are "thrown" at people like rice at the bride and groom.[2] And just as rice at a wedding was not originally meant simply to *say* "Be fruitful," but to actually fructify the pair, so also these curses are meant not simply to say "You are unwelcome here," not simply to announce a fact, but to make unwelcome any there may be on whom these missiles might fall. Note the sweep of these acts, what a vast region they cover. They range over acts of love and banishment, grace and assurance, as well as condemnations and guarantees. If these are things brought forth by speech, then is it so difficult to see that speech, that is, public speech, is what brings forth the public?

A third foray. In the ancient world it was believed that words, once uttered, go forth into the world with power of their own. This was especially true of curses, oaths, and blessings. Such words were sent forth and could not be called back. Think, for example, of Isaac's blessing of Jacob (Gen. 27). Given under false pretenses, undeserved, unintended by

Isaac, and evoked by deception, nonetheless being given, that blessing could not be retrieved and annulled. This, of course, is the basis of one biblical argument underwriting the gravity of speech or, in other words, the obligation to speak the truth. If words go forth with power to do their work and cannot be returned and swallowed,[3] then we had better be careful what we say. Best get it right the first time.

In Isaiah we read, "so shall my word be that goes forth from my mouth; it shall not return to me empty, but shall accomplish that which I purpose, and prosper in the thing for which I sent it" (55.11). True and false prophets could be distinguished, in the biblical view of things, because if the prophet indeed spoke the Word of God, then things would happen. The Word would "prosper in the thing" for which it was sent. Proof that false prophets were indeed false lay in the fact that the word they pronounced did not so prosper. God speaks and it is so. Let there be light! And so there was. But false prophets speak and it is not so. Jeremiah complained that though he spoke truly, the power of the Word tarried. It delayed, and that delay, which should not happen, became reason for him to doubt even his own credentials. It is, I suppose, the central claim of the Gospels that proof of God's fleshly visitation is found in the fact that Jesus spoke and things happened. The claim advanced in those texts is that He was the Word, and the proof provided is plainly that his speech accomplished those things that God's Word always does accomplish, namely, the lame walk, the hungry are fed, the sick are healed, and hope is brought to the oppressed.

Whatever you may think of the argument, I ask only that you detect its texture. In these texts the theory of words and of speech is the theory of speech acts. This ancient belief that words go forth in the world to do their work is often presented as the view of a primitive people. But such an appraisal only reveals our vanity. It shows how much our own modernity pleases us. From the facts, we could as easily conclude that finding this view of speech in the ancient world shows how primitive we moderns are or how modern those primitives were, for we have by no means abandoned this ancient outlook. Consider, for example, what we mean by saying "His words are empty words," "Those are vain words," "His is empty talk." What of seriousness is intended when we say "I give you my word," "Her word is good"? These common ways of speech reveal our conviction that words ought not be empty or vain, but should be full and valid or effectual. They should go forth from our mouths, prosper in what we purpose, prosper in the thing for which they are sent. What else could we intend except that the words we speak should have their effect? Speech is formative. It is what makes the world, what creates the world. That is the biblical point of view. It is also ours. The fact needs only to be noticed to be granted.

As a fourth foray I appeal to common experience with the reflexive consequences of speech. Speech acts are both performative and educative. They shape not only the world but ourselves. Words publicly spoken form speaker and hearers alike, but perhaps speakers even more than hearers. In Alcoholics Anonymous the initial step in recovery is for the alcoholic to state aloud, publicly, and in the first person, "I am an alcoholic." The affirmation itself is therapeutic. It is vital to note that this therapeutic power is partly a consequence of the fact that these words are said in a company of people who also can, have, and will say the same thing. But such speech gains its therapeutic value even more from the fact that these words are spoken in public. It is nothing to say these things privately, to one's self, or in silent thought. That kind of speech conducted in the closet of the soul leads not to recovery but to an ever deeper descent into an ever darker night. Such public speech changes not simply the world, but the speaker. Public speech is formative. In this case, it forms the self even as it works to constitute the group within which such speech is offered.

This effect of speech upon the speaker is recognized in other practices. It is the psychological and educational principle involved in the Bar Mitzvah when he affirms, "I am a child of Abraham, Isaac, and Jacob. I was in Egypt." It is the principle underlying the conservative Christian tradition of offering testimony, describing how things were, what happened, and how things are now; and it is part of what underlies Catholic practice in the sacrament of confession. Preachers, priests, professors, and politicians, all in their own ways, know that to say what one believes, earnestly and in public, strengthens belief. Speech, public speech, forms the speaker. I have often pondered what seems to me transparent fact, namely that it is easier for me to forgive my neighbor when I have been wronged than for my neighbor to ask forgiveness. In short, asking forgiveness is more difficult than giving it. Why is this? It is so, I surmise, because to ask forgiveness is already to have confessed to fault, not something that most of us are easily given to do. Furthermore, repair is present already in confession provided it is made to the person one has wronged. To say "Please forgive me" is already to say "I am at fault," and in this speech act there is already all the redemption possible short of forgiveness. Such speech repairs the speaker.

"Sticks and stones will break my bones, but words will never hurt me." This school-yard chant of many generations (here slightly modified) is almost certainly false, but even more certain is the fact that its recitation is a useful tool. The repetition, as a mantra, that "words will never hurt me"—such an act of speech is a tool for survival. Hateful words, in fact, do hurt. Perhaps they hurt the speaker even more than those against whom they are hurled. Hateful words are not simply the words of hateful persons; they are words that make persons hate-full, filled with ugly hate. Speech shapes the speaker. Speech, in all these ways, is formative.

III. A Theory of Public Speech

I offer these forays, as I have called them, not because I think they are completed arguments that stand beyond rebuttal, nor even because I suppose they are altogether clear. Neither do I think they offer proof of anything. Let them remain quite plainly what they are already, simple pointers to facts about this peculiar human capacity for speech, simple reminders of the ordinary ordinarily overlooked, each offering a small window on the claim that the public is created by public speech. Still, the central question remains. Just what is meant by 'public speech'? Or, to be more specific, *How* does public speech do its public work? What makes public speech public?

The Question Examined

I shall offer an answer to this question and then try to unpack it. But first, consider the question itself more closely. What makes public speech public? To ask this question is not to ask for a definition, so giving a definition will not provide an answer. There is no point in offering an ostensive definition. Nobody would be satisfied. And there is no possibility of getting away with a stipulative definition. Nobody would follow it. Conceptual analysis will not help. The answer will not simply drop out of an analysis of how the word 'public' is used. Nor will the question be answered by finding some expression identical in meaning to the phrase 'public speech'. Neither is any research method likely to yield an answer. Maybe there is a Marxist answer and a capitalist answer, a liberal one and a conservative one, a feminist one and a chauvinist one, a theistic one and an atheistic one, and who knows what others, maybe a quantitative one and a qualitative one. Still, I suggest that these answers be set aside, at least for the moment, on the grounds that without exception, in matters such as this, they aid understanding far less than they obstruct it.

Try simplicity! Extreme simplicity. Studied simplicity. I am reminded of a student who, in a discussion on the logic of knowledge-claims, pronounced the currently popular constructivist thesis. "Of course," she said, "all knowledge is subjective and socially constructed." I asked her whether she was wearing shoes. She allowed the question, and said without a moment's hesitation or shred of doubt that she was. I asked whether she thought *that* knowledge was subjective or socially constructed, and she declined to answer. The answer doesn't matter anyway. The point does. To tell what it is that makes public speech public, I propose a return to innocence of a sort that I am inclined to think my students have been trying for years to overcome. We need the innocence of knowing that right now I'm wearing shoes counts as a genuine case of knowing, whereas believing that all knowledge is subjective and socially constructed requires a lack of innocence, a substantial effort, perhaps even a graduate course, if anybody is to actually believe it. In contrast, I urge you to make the effort to recover an uncommon naiveté. If it helps, please be assured that you have my permission to indulge the luxury of letting *yourself*, your very own purposefully naive self, be the judge as to whether what I am about to say fits your experience. Let that be the test rather than whether these remarks fit somebody's research program.

The Auditory Principle

What makes public speech public? My hunch is that *public speech occurs when what is said in one person's speech is heard by others as candidate for their own speech.* Call this the auditory principle. It states that speech, to be public speech, requires an auditor. *Public speech occurs when what A says is heard by B as a candidate for B's speech.* This principle points to hearing as the font of public speech rather than to any array of actions by the speaker, that is, hearing *in a certain way* . If this principle is correct, that public speech is public by virtue of the acts of auditors, then it may be tempting to suppose that any speech is public speech, if it occurs in some plurality, some crowd, some forum, or as we say, some public setting. But again, I caution. Don't reduce 'public' to 'plurality' or confuse public speech simply with whatever talk goes on in public places where speech, as it were, is disclosed.

That speech is aloud instead of silent and is within earshot of others will make speech public only in the sense that traffic sounds, being unavoidably disclosed, are public. Disclosure is at best only contingently re-lated to the sense of 'public' invoked when we refer to public speech. Consider the following fact. In any society there may be persons who mean to speak to others, but there are no others who listen, no auditors, and thus, none who hear. Declining to listen or to hear another is among our more efficient ways of denying that those others even exist. It is one way of killing them. By rendering such persons inaudible, we make them invisible and, in effect, nonexistent. That is part of what multicultural-ism in education is about, insisting that voices heretofore muted should be heard and hence allowed entry to the domain of public speech. It is not enough that there be freedom of speech if nobody listens or if nobody listens *in a certain way* .

That 'certain way' I describe as hearing the speech of another as can-didate for one's own. I admit that not much is explicated by the phrase it-self. I don't mean, in any case that we have a duty to listen to one an-other. I don't mean that public speech must be a dialogue. I mean only that public speech cannot occur unless statements about the world, as the speakers know it and announce it, are entertained by others as candi-dates for the way those others might see the world. Where speech is not heard in that way, then we have something only *potentially* public, a kind of talk that is public in contrast to private only in the sense of being dis-closed, like traffic sounds. This is not public speech; it is simply back-ground noise. Even though aloud and voiced in the midst of some plural-ity, it is not yet public speech because there is as yet no auditor.

Martin Luther King Jr.'s "I Have a Dream" speech deserves careful study as an example of public speech. It works partly because it is framed in ways that encourage listeners to entertain every step of that speech as a step that could be uttered as his or her own. It is framed in a homiletic style, familiar in the African-American churches, a style that invites the congregation to affirm what is said at each step.[4] In this way, what is said by one is entertained by others as candidate for his or her own speech. "I have a dream" becomes "Here is the dream that *we* have." What comes forth from the voice of one comes to be owned as it were by others, not as doctrine or belief, not as truth claims, but simply as candidate for some-thing that might be framed by each in his or her own voice.

Thus, speech is public when, as auditor, one thinks things like

> I *could* say what she has said
> I *do* say what he has said
> I *might* (*might not*) say what she has said, because. . . .

Each of these is a kind of interior comment that can enter into the process of hearing the speech of another as candidate for one's own. Notice especially the last of these—"I *might (might not)* say what she has said, because. . . ." The word 'because' is the prelude to reasons. How many kinds of reasons are there that can complete this 'because'? Not everything will count. Not everything goes. The 'because' might call for truth claims, reasons of the sort that enter into arguments and counterarguments. But it might call instead for reasons neither truth-functional nor even framed in the language of argument. It might call for reasons offered in the language of umbilical stories.

IV. *Types of Public Speech*

The Forum

"Here are my reasons. . . ." These are words announcing an effort to assess the *truth* of speech or the *validity* of argument. And even though our question at the moment is not what makes public speech true or valid, but what makes it public, still, when truth claims are offered as reasons, they can result in making speech public by making it subject to assessment by public standards. If I entertain the speech of another as making truth claims upon me, then I am, in fact, considering that speech as candidate for something I might say. It does not matter to what makes public speech public that I agree with what is said. Nor does the auditory principle demand agreement. It calls instead for hearing in a certain way, and this certain way of hearing without which public speech is not public is precisely the same condition without which public disagreement cannot be responsible. I can responsibly disagree with or reject the speech of another only if I entertain the claims of that speech as candidates for my own. And one way of doing that is to entertain the reasons given for their truth and evaluate the inferences for their validity.

Yet the auditory principle is only partially the same condition without which public disagreement cannot be responsible. It is only one way in which the speech of another is entertained as candidate for my own. The rational rejection of the arguments of another, on any other than purely formal grounds, will require that one entertain the speech of the other as candidate for one's own. That seems true enough. Thus, it seems that if conditions are satisfied for the use of the 'public' language of the forum, that is, the language of argument and inference, then it follows that the auditory principle is satisfied. That is correct as far as it goes, but the auditory principle can be satisfied on conditions other than those imposed by the speech of the forum. What is presented here as the conditions making public speech public is much broader than the rules of argument in some kind of forum. The forum is rooted in rational standards of inference and in evidentiary standards of truth. But the auditory principle captures a much larger and more inclusive matter of 'hearing in a certain way'.

So when 'because' is followed with truth claims, speech becomes public by being subjected to public standards of assessment. It is not a necessity, however, that this 'subjecting speech to public standards of assessment' is demanded by the need for objectivity. It is not essential that public speech be objective speech, and, in that respect, like scientific speech, subject to standard evidentiary canons.[5] Objectivity is not a standard of what makes public speech public and the auditory principle does not demand that kind of standard.

The importance of truth claims for public speech lies neither in their objectivity nor their intersubjectivity, but in the fact that by learning to frame truth claims of public speech, we learn to formulate our views in one of the ways that makes it possible for them to be entertained as candidates for the speech of others. If I announce to you, "I don't want to pay higher taxes," I say something about myself that you might say about yourself. You too could say, "I don't want to pay higher taxes."[6] Thus, it may seem that in your reiteration of my speech we have something that falls under the auditory principle, something that counts as entertaining the speech of another as candidate for one's own. That would be a mistake, however. But why? The heart of the problem lies in the fact that these statements are mere expressions of desire.[7] The 'polity of desires' is distinctly egalitarian, even anarchic. Desires, in other words, are inherently equal. There is no natural hierarchy among them, no authority that does not stem entirely from brute strength, nothing in their nature sufficient to rank them and to say that some are better than others, or that some ought to be heeded and others not.[8] So when A says "I want . . ." and B says "I want . . .," neither has said anything that bears yet upon whether what they want would be a good thing or whether they have any claim on the rest of us to grant what they want. Neither has said anything that nears public speech.

Such separate and discrete statements of desire coming from many

people may add up to a political constituency, but the sum of such statements, however enormous, will not add up to even a fragment of public
speech. For public speech, according to the forum view of things, we have
to move from statements of personal desire to public claims upon one another, from "I want X" to "we need X" or from "I want X" to "X is a good
thing for us."[9] And the disciplines of making this transition from private
desire to public affirmation are precisely those that lead us into public
discourse of a sort that makes use of truth claims, canons of evidence, and
standards of argument. These are the disciplines needed for entry to the
forum. We do not enter a public at all, however, if we come to one another simply with our separate bundles of desires and complaints. If that
is the best we can do, then we come to public speech not as adults ready
to plead a case, but merely as petulant children. Nor is it enough that I
can voice your desires also as mine. That is not what is meant by 'entertaining the speech of another as candidate for my own'. And it does not
result in public speech.

Umbilical Stories

It seems clear, then, that in the interior conversation going on as the
speech of another campaigns as candidate for my own, some reasons offered may be clothed as arguments, but others arrive simply as umbilical
stories. They stem from a narrative of memory, and their recitation presents neither arguments nor truth claims. It simply calls forth objects of
recollection, making them present to some community of memory. Their
recitation by some invites their recitation by others. Thus, public speech
is not limited to truth claims. *This narrative way of entertaining the speech
of another as candidate for one's own is what I have in mind primarily as 'public speech'.*[10] When someone like Martin Luther King Jr. says, "I was in
Egypt," we do not expect people to say "No you weren't" or "When was
that?" or "How were things along the Nile?" This statement, drawn from
a biblical narrative, is uttered, as it were, to announce one's credentials
and to tell us within what story we are to entertain what follows. These
words announce what genre of speech we are about to enter, just as "once
upon a time" and "I have yours of the 26th" announce others. We do not
treat the words "I was in Egypt" as a truth claim, and we are invited not to
treat the words that follow as truth claims either. Yet they can be and are
heard by others as candidates for their own speech. Some among those
others can respond with "I too, was in Egypt." This is public speech but it

is not the speech of argument, evidence, and the canons of inference. It is not the speech of the forum. I realize that such speech is successful only if addressed to those who know the story or the litany and those who, better yet, count the story as their own. In short, that this is public speech is dependent upon there being members who hear such speech as their own and are thus persons for whom the candidacy of speech for status as their own is short and direct. This, in other words, is the speech of members and the friends of members, a company who can be gathered by speech into a community of memory around an umbilical story.[11]

This kind of public speech has its own objectivity or intersubjectivity, but not the kind that belongs to truth claims and investigations of science. This is not the speech of inquiry; it is the speech of membership. It is the speech of some public, not because it pronounces public truth, but because it appeals to an umbilical story of some membership. So there are these two versions of public speech, one associated with a kind of forum and the other with some umbilical story.

How are we to understand the relation between these two versions? At various points in these chapters I have hinted at an answer, namely, that public speech rooted in some umbilical story is the more fundamental of the two and that the persistent images of the forum as a public arena, the normative ideal of which is rational deliberation—this image of the forum is itself a vision that draws its life from one or another umbilical story. This dependence is quite like the dependence encountered in Durkheim's distinction between mechanical and organic solidarity. The argument ran that any world in which relations of utility, contract, and ties of interest provide the integuments of solidarity, must depend for its persistence upon sustaining the shared norms that contracts should be honored, promises delivered on, and that the conditions of trust be realized and jealously preserved—none of which can be understood to emerge out of transient interests, willed agreements and other ties of convenience or social function. As Durkheim would have seen it, the world of weak normation is a world that depends for its persistence on the prior and continuing existence of some domain of strong normation. Likewise, the worldly possibility of public speech as the rational enterprise of a public space is dependent upon the viability of an umbilical story of normation to a public space where such reasonings are called for. If public speech, in short, is the speech of persuasion in a public forum, then it is already the speech of an umbilical story by which persons are normed as members to the excellent practices of such a forum.

Consider once again the example I cited earlier of a society in which there are speakers, but no auditors, those who speak, but none who listen to their speech as candidates for their own. In such a society, even one that prides itself on freedom of speech, there will be no public speech at all and hence no public to speak of. If public speech occurs there at all, it would have to occur in settings that most would view as private, like the family. Yet, what kind of family could it be in which public speech, in this sense, does not occur? It would be a setting where some speak of family affairs, but none entertain what is said as possible candidates for their own speech; a place where no one's speech enlivens the memory, stories, or convictions of others. If we ponder what this means, we may doubt that on such assumptions we imagine a family at all. There would be, for one thing, no parents—at least none who enact the role—in a family where nobody entertains the speech of others as possible candidates for their own.

V. Fallacies of Public Speech

The 'because' clause might be completed either by speech appropriate to public claims or by speech suitable to some narrative of antecedents. These ways can succeed in making public speech public. But other strategies will fail. Their various failures may be gathered as the fallacies of role, position, and motivation, as well as the fallacies of explanation and misplaced discourse.

Fallacies of Role and Position

I cannot count the times in recent years I have heard such rebuttals as "You just say what you do because you have tenure" or "because you are male (or female)" or "because you are a corporate executive" or "because you are white" or "because you are an economist" or "because you are impetuous" or "because you are a politician" (That's the kind of thing we expect from politicians) or "because you are a Christian" (or a Jew, or a fundamentalist, whatever that means). Examples are quite beyond enumeration. Each of these ways of speech constitutes not simply a failure to enter into public speech, but a quite explicit refusal to do so, a declaration that one will not entertain the speech of another as candidate for one's own. Each reveals an explicit technique for rejecting the speech of another in a way that makes it unnecessary even to think about what has been said, much less consider its truth. Thus, each has the capacity not merely to stop public speech, but to destroy a public. Such speech creates division as surely as public speech creates a public. Such rejoinders are neither prelude to nor any part of public speech. They shape no entry into entertaining the speech of another as candidate for one's own. They add up to the defeat of public speech.

Fallacies of Explanation

To these fallacies of role and position we may add a kindred set, the fallacies of explanation. Why, we might ask, is it so easy to commit the fallacies of role and position and even commend them as good practice? I believe it is because we confuse the role of auditor with the role of sympathetic listener. We confuse entertaining the speech of another as candidate for one's own with the quite different practice of listening to the speech of another in order to understand the speaker. Thus, we aim to understand the speaker, not the speech, to grasp not what the other is saying, but simply to explain his or her saying it. We seek to *explain* the speech of others under the false impression that in doing so, in trying to understand *why* a speaker speaks as he or she does, we are being sympathetic auditors.

This is a dangerous misconception. Public speech is defeated and the public destroyed, or at best severely eroded, whenever we accept or reject the speech of another on grounds of some psychological, sociological, or merely preferential explanation as to why the speaker has spoken thus. To grasp such an explanation has almost nothing to do with entertaining the speech of another as candidate for one's own. Suppose you turn to me, for example, saying, "I understand, Green, why you say these things. You talk this way because you are a philosopher" (or a professor, old-fashioned, male, of another generation, or whatever). Were you to say that to me, I would know immediately that you had not seriously entertained any word I had addressed to you. Moreover, were you to say that to me in an unctuous tone of sympathy and gentle understanding, then you will have deeply insulted me, an insult made all the more painful by coming to me clothed in kindness, by arriving with the moral endorsement of a plainly benevolent spirit. Say that sort of thing and I shall look you in the eye and say, "But I didn't seek to be understood; I merely wanted to be heard. Don't confuse the two. I don't hanker after understanding; I hanker only for a hearing." A therapist must seek to understand the speech of a client as a step toward understanding the client. But the exchange between the two is not public speech and the listening that goes on there is not the listening demanded by the auditory principle. The therapist does not entertain the speech of the other as candidate for his or her own. Public speech is not counseling, nor is counseling public speech, and being member of some public is not a matter of being in therapy.

I wish not to be misunderstood. It often happens that our public speech, the speech of one to another about our common affairs, is biased, expressing our personal histories and private preferences. No doubt, we speak from our several positions. We could hardly do otherwise. Because interest often, perhaps always, governs in the affairs of human beings, and because interests are bound to be parochial, a hermeneutic of suspicion is a good thing. Often it is more than a good thing. Sometimes it is a necessary thing. But it cannot be viewed as the only thing, because the hearing it engenders, when supplemented by no other, is precisely the kind of listening to another that makes public speech impossible.

What I object to, in short, is not a hermeneutic of suspicion, but an entirely different thing that I believe we have created, namely a *culture* of suspicion, a culture of public speech in which it is simply assumed that because of role or position, because of the partiality or brokenness of reason, nothing any of us says can be entertained at face value. All must be explained and hence nothing that you say, for example, need be entertained by me as candidate for my own speech. If I adopt that attitude, or if you adopt it, then our joint membership in a public, yours and mine, has come to an end. Make the move from a hermeneutic of suspicion to a culture of suspicion in your relations to your friends, and you will have no friends. Do it with your family, and the family will vanish. Nowadays, apparently, we need not be tutored to hear the other with suspicion. Doing that often seems simply to be doing what comes naturally. Within a culture of suspicion, we need to listen to the other with a hermeneutic of affection. Listen to the loves of the other. Can they be yours? Can they be candidates for your own?

Fallacies of Misplaced Discourse

To these fallacies of role, position, status, and explanation, we may add a third group, the fallacies of misplaced discourse. Justice Holmes, in his famous speech "The Path of the Law," said, "The law is simply what the courts decide and nothing more."[12] Holmes offered this observation as part of a general resistance to a certain kind of natural law tradition. It was his way of cautioning practicing attorneys to pay attention more to the court and less to the arguments of philosophy when pleading a case. The aim, after all, is to win the case, not to win adherents to a theory. Persuade the judge or the jury, not the American Philosophical Society, since they are not assembled in the court in any case. This is good advice for the practicing attorney. It helps to focus thought upon the task at hand. But this is useless counsel to the judge whose problem is not to plead the case, but to decide it, not to convince the jury, but to guide deliberation. When one *is* the court and must decide, neither guidance nor solace can be drawn from the dictum that the law is whatever the courts decide and nothing more. Useful on that side of the bench where it is framed, the principle is worse than useless when transported to the other side. It sits well at counselor's table, but not in the chair behind the bar.

No genius is needed to find the fault. It is the same as would be noted were we to confuse the book review with the book, the critic's analysis with the poem, the commentary with the text, the analysis of public speech with the speech, or the anthropologist's report of life among the natives with life among the natives. Public speech is living speech, the speech of members. How do we become members? By acquiring the disciplines of public speech, that is, by allowing the speech of the other to candidate as one's own. I shall try now to offer proof as much as the case allows for proof.

The *New York Times* for August 28, 1963, contains a story by James Reston, portions of which bear to be repeated:

> Abraham Lincoln, who presided in his stone temple today above the children of the slaves he emancipated, may have used just the right words to sum up the general reaction to the Negro's massive march on Washington. "I think," he wrote to Gov. Andrew B. Curtin of Pennsylvania in 1861, "the necessity of being ready increases. Look to it." Washington may not "look to it" at once, since it is looking to so many things, but it will be a long time before it forgets the melodious voice of the Rev. Dr. Martin Luther King Jr. crying out his dreams to the multitude.
>
> It was Dr. King who, near the end of the day, touched the vast audience . . . with a peroration that was an anguished echo from all the old American reformers. Roger Williams calling for religious liberty, Sam

Adams calling for political liberty, old man Thoreau denouncing coercion, William Lloyd Garrison demanding emancipation, and Eugene V. Debs crying for economic equality—Dr. King echoed them all.

"I have a dream," he cried again and again. And each time the dream was a promise out of our ancient articles of faith: phrases from the Constitution, lines from the great anthem of the nation, guarantees from the Bill of Rights, all ending with a vision that they might one day all come true.

Dr. King touched all the themes of the day, only better than anybody else. He was full of the symbolism of Lincoln and Gandhi, and the cadences of the Bible. He was both militant and sad, and he sent the crowd away feeling that the long journey had been worthwhile.

Reston offers here a report of public speech. Yet there is neither argument here nor any report of one. There is no forum. Better to evoke the vast and rich resources of umbilical stories, allowing others to take possession of these tokens of memory by virtue of which we are a public, an inclusive public, and best to do so within a liturgical setting, with Lincoln seated, "presiding from his stone temple" one hundred years more or less from emancipation. But now introduce to this scene and to this speech the academic, acerbic talk of deconstruction and critical hermeneutics, speech that belongs in the Academy and not on the steps of that stone temple, and one detects immediately the fallacy of misplaced discourse. Principles of research and practice that serve well in the context where they are formulated may serve badly as guides in any other place. The rule may sit well in the chair at counsel's table, but not well at all behind the bar. Forgo the critic's comment. I'll take the poem, the music, the memory every time. Give me the text liturgically situated and alive, not its classroom decomposition which is worthless either as public speech or as instruction in public speech unless it is taken as it resides within the context of the full story and its delivery.

But I pass to another scene, in 1863, and from that to still another eighty-seven years earlier. I refer first, of course, to Lincoln at Gettysburg. Garry Wills has written an account[13] that helps us 're-member'. Again, recall the liturgical setting, the circumstance, the act, the aim, to consecrate the ground and to remind us of its placement in a larger territory. Lincoln's constant policy, politically delicate to maintain, had not been so much to free the slaves as to secure the Union and preserve the Constitution. Yet his first utterance at Gettysburg harkened not to the Constitution but to the Declaration of Independence "four score and seven years ago." The Constitution says nothing about being created equal. The Declaration does. It was precisely because, by this speech, Lincoln brought the two together that he was criticized. "All men are created equal," indeed. Who says this nation was dedicated to any such proposition? By what right does he alter the Constitution in this way? complained the Chicago papers. But he did bring these two texts together, and did so, moreover, in a single sentence. And Wills observes, no doubt with some but not too much exaggeration, that those who heard this speech that day went forth changed. They gained a different ear and would not hear things the same way again. It was the union of these two texts, Constitution and Declaration, and a public changed by speech, that made "I have a dream" something accessible to speaker and to hearers alike. Speech offered by one became not simply candidate, but actually resident, in the speech of others. The public was formed and changed and formed again by public speech.

I do not want to leave the impression, however, that public speech is only the speech of heroes and orators, that it occurs only, as it were, on high liturgical occasions. The centrality of liturgy is a topic for another time. Liturgies have to do with seeing more than with hearing. Their educational power resides in the peculiar fact that they change nothing in the world, yet they allow us to see everything differently. Liturgy is the true instrument of deconstruction. The point I wish to stress about public speech is not its liturgical setting at moments of high drama, but its essential nature: public speech resides in our capacity to entertain the speech of others as candidate for our own. By this auditory act, public speech is permitted and we are joined even in our disagreements. The public is formed and reformed again and again.

Chapter 7

Public Policy and the Office of Citizen

I. The Office of Citizen

If moral education is construed as education for a democratic order, then its first aim must be to prepare people to assume public office, specifically, the office of citizen. It is a political office, and its exercise is a public affair, including, as it does, participation in shaping public policy. Yet, it must seem increasingly apparent to any who have lived in the twentieth century and thought about the matter at all, that whatever connection may once have existed between being a citizen and being a participant in shaping public policy, that connection is no longer obvious. It must seem, at best, a remote and fragile link. This reluctance to view citizenship as a public office flows partly from the fact that we have come to think of citizens primarily as the bearers of rights—rights, moreover, that run mostly against the various organs of government, but also against our neighbors. Citizens, by such a view, are therefore understood first as persons granted a passive and protected status. Only later, if ever, are they understood as being the active agents of some public.

By describing such a role as passive, I do not mean to suggest that all is peace and calm. To the extent that citizens, conceived simply as the bearers of rights, become active agents, their activity will be aimed primarily at defending their protected status, that is, defending their rights. Such a conception of citizenship can produce a flurry[1] of political activity, but it is likely to be activity aimed not so much at advancing the common good as at securing their rights against any invasion by their neighbors' needs. Such a portrait captures all the warm congeniality and neighborly affection of a person perched on a stool, distant from all others, and with clenched fists, glancing furtively from side to side muttering

168

through a firmly set jaw, "I know my rights!" To whatever extent such a portrait captures the prevailing view, it will seem madness to suggest that being a citizen is anything like holding a public office, much less an office engaged in forming public policy. After all, it may be argued, only those actually elected or appointed to one or another public office—legislators, judges, county executives, and the like—are in positions to make public policy in any strict sense. To the claim that being a citizen is to hold an office that calls for forming public policy, it is easy to respond, "We turn that over to others, to our elected or appointed agents. The grubby business of public policy is their affair, not ours."

To this response and to its part in making such phrases as 'the office of citizen' sound archaic, must be added the current debasement of 'politics' and 'political'. These words used to refer to a worthy service, but no longer. "He's playing politics with peoples' lives." "That has become such a political game." Expressions like these now constitute, I would guess, the primary context in which persons acquire whatever initial sense they have of the terms 'politics', 'policy', 'polity', and 'political'. In common parlance, these words now refer to a corrupting, narrow-minded, purely self-interested and partisan activity endangering the integrity of any who venture to enter it. How can anyone suggest that to be a citizen is to oc-cupy an office requiring such activity, much less an office for which preparation is an essential component of moral education? These will seem outrageous claims.

Yet, how else are we to frame our grasp of 'citizen' in a democratic order except as 'party to the formation of public policy'? It is as public actor and not as the locus of rights that we are defined as citizens in any order where the *demos* rule. Under monarchic arrangements, things are otherwise. Monarchies do not have citizens. Monarchs have subjects. Those subjects may be granted a long list of rights enforceable against the crown, but they remain subjects still, until their being subjects extends to their being party, in some way, to the formation of public policy. To the degree that subjects of the crown become party to the shape of public pol-icy, the idea of 'the crown' or 'the ruler' begins to appear archaic and un-real. Subjects, under such altered conditions, may still be described as 'subjects', but everyone will know that in speaking thus they utter fiction. It is precisely through some such transformation of status from being sub-jects to becoming citizens that the crown, though continuing to be im-portant, becomes, nevertheless, more and more symbolic until reduced to an essentially ceremonial fact of life. A democratic order always emerges as companion to the reality of the citizen as public official, that is to say, as occupant of a public office.

Remarks analogous to these about citizens and subjects under monarchic arrangements also describe the lack of fit between the notion of 'citizen' and the status of persons in various fascistic, tyrannical, and oligarchic versions of political life. There is nothing new in this observation. It was well understood among the ancient Greeks. They had their tyrants. Some, they thought, were good, and some, they thought, were not so good; but whether a tyrant is judged good or bad, the Greeks remained uneasy in describing such tyrannical arrangements as properly political. In short, there is and always has been a peculiar affinity between the idea of 'citizen' and the establishment of democratic political arrangements. Indeed, that affinity is partly implicit in the very notion of a political relation. The relation of master to slave has never been construed as political. It is a relation more akin to that of a farmer to his chickens, a relation by which the farmer is authorized to reach into the flock at any time and pluck one out for dinner. It is thus no modern invention or momentary enthusiasm that leads me to insist on the fact that being a citizen in a democratic order is to hold an office, a public office, occupied by a public agent engaged as participant in the formation of public policy.

Excellence in the practice of that office, moreover, requires the exercise of certain disciplines and hence presumes their acquisition. To speak thus of disciplines and practices is, of course, to speak in yet another way of norms and their acquisition. Among the disciplines of the office of citizen are those governing the patient exercise of reason expressed in public speech. Excellence in the office is not excellence in the office of scientist, or teacher, or priest, or athlete, or a variety of other expansive roles. It is an office that imposes its own demands. Proposals advanced for public consideration, as already noted, must be framed, for example, in a language suitable for public speech. The plot devised in the clandestine intrigue of some coterie may be conceived to serve the most partisan and narrow interests, but if such a plot is ever to be hatched and 'go public', then it must be framed and cast in reasons appealing to some common good, the good of a context much more inclusive than any mere cabal.

From the discussion of public speech, the fact emerged that simply because 'the people' *want* to pursue a certain course or would feel better if their government did so, is not yet a public reason to adopt it. The claims of mere desire for this or that must be converted somehow into the claim that this and that would be good things to do. What is wanted, wanted even by substantial numbers, is often not a good thing to do. Bare appetite and ambition must compete openly with knowledge and reason. Nor is it an objection to the necessary exercise of reason in the office of citizen that the reasons offered frequently—perhaps even always—conceal private interests. The idea is not that people are ever entirely freed of private interest, but that private interest must at least wear the garb of public reason and thus submit to public examination. To engage in such practices of patient reason and to do it well are among the disciplines of practice entailed by the office of citizen.

I have described such disciplines as the 'patient exercise of reason' first because they engage the capacity to listen not simply to the desires of others, but to their public reasons, and second, because such disciplines also involve a patient deference to the future, even to successive generations. Any course of action pursued because it appears to be good by present lights may soon be regretted when judged in the light of experience. To exercise this kind of rational patience amounts, for some, almost to an act of heroism. To exercise such patience is a moral discipline and only one of many imposed upon us by the office of citizen. However uncertain is the spread of such a discipline, its exercise is nevertheless essential because it restrains the free and unreflective passage of impulse into action. There are other such moral disciplines to explore. For the moment, however, let it suffice to note from this one alone that the office of citizen is more complex than the office of any civil servant in whatever degree it requires that one be more than an administrator, more even than an evaluator, more than a voter. It requires nothing short of becoming a policy analyst and a participant in forming public policy.

Thus, in this chapter, as in the previous one, I wish to extend the account of that seamless transition in our grasp of conscience from the inward struggles of reflexive judgment in the individual, and to extend it even beyond the practices of profession and the disciplines of public speech. I aim to extend the reach of conscience to conduct in the office of citizen. I call this an extension of our grasp of conscience because it gives the notion a reach larger than we are accustomed to entertain. It stretches our habitual ways of thinking about conscience, and for that reason may suffer abrupt rejection. Yet I also describe that extension as 'seamless' to guard against its being viewed as anything added or tagged on to what has been said already. It is not a thing of a different order. Indeed, this extension is properly described as seamless because the demand for normation to the office of citizen is implicit in what has already been learned about the formation of conscience in its various voices. The need is not to add on, but only to unwrap the ordinary.

Even in the first analysis of norm acquisition, the appearance of a critical attitude and a 'caring to be correct' turned out to be essential to the judgment that, in any specific case, a norm had come to govern conduct. These sensibilities of reflexive judgment are presumed in any claim that conduct is governed and not merely shaped. There it was discovered, moreover, with all the strength of immediate inference, that no norm can be said to govern in any person unless the guiding rule is regarded by that person as a rule of rectitude for others. Conduct cannot be regarded as governed at all unless it is governed by public norms and not by mere desires. Even in the case of the conscience of craft, governance of conduct was traced to standards of excellence in some guild or public within which norm violations provoke the emotions of self-assessment. And so it was with each of the other voices of conscience—membership, sacrifice, memory, and imagination. These points are enriched, but remain unaltered, when the analysis is unpacked with an eye on conduct in the office of citizen. To explore the point further, familiar themes will need to be revisited. Beginning with the nature of policy itself and its origins, we shall return to the difference between practical and theoretical reason, the conflict of public goods, and the dangers of turning to utopia and away from the practice of politics. These points, examined already in other contexts, will now be cast in a slightly different light. Finally, we shall have to examine a matter not yet touched upon at all, namely, the specific disciplines needed in the office of citizen and how they emerge from the central business of that office, namely, the formation of public policy.

II. Policy Questions

It is folly to undertake the project of framing a single answer to the question, What is public policy? Wisdom will resist any such approach. No single definition of 'policy' can mirror the full range of ordinary usage. Usage is too diffuse for that. Such a definition would have to capture the similarities and differences between managerial decisions, guides to practice, and rules of thumb as well as rules of conduct embodied in legislation, all of which can be described sometimes as policy. It would have to

capture the difference between basic and procedural policy, between prescriptive and permissive policies and policies simply expressing the bare
application of standard administrative requirements like, "No one gets
unemployment assistance for more than X weeks." It would have to subsume matters that fall under "Standard Operating Procedures" (File ex-
pense accounts within ten days with receipts), and matters of personal
practice (I don't answer the phone at home because it is never for me).
Although each item in the full range of these examples can be called 'policy', the term has, in each case, a slightly different meaning. I propose a
more devious approach. Instead of asking straight out, What is policy?
I aim to search for the features of policy *questions*, focusing especially upon
public policy in contrast to what might be thought of as personal policy.

Instead of asking, What is policy? suppose we ask, What kind of question is a policy question? What is the need out of which a request for policy emerges? It may be fairly argued, at least for starters, that a policy
question is a request for a fairly stable, but modifiable, line of action
aimed at securing an optimal adjustment of the conflict between different goods, all of which must be pursued, but which cannot all be maximized. We do not have a well-formed policy question or a fully formulated statement of a policy problem until we can state the set of values or
goods from which the question arises, and do so, moreover, so as to reveal
their mutual inconsistency.

The problems of education finance provide about as clear a model of
policy questions generally as it is possible to shape. The policy issues are
always 'nested' within a set of mutually incompatible values or goods, in
this case:

- equal educational opportunity for children,
- an equitable distribution of the tax burden,
- local control of education,
- responsible management of the state budget

Maximizing any one of these goods will obstruct advancement of the others. The policy problem is generated by the fact that we accept all four of
these aims and yet they cannot all be maximized. We cannot have all the
local control possible, for example, because doing so—at least in a system
of partnership between local districts and the state—would mean allowing the local district to write the bill for education and oblige the state to
write the check. Either the state would have lost control over its own

budget or else it will have to abdicate any role in preserving one of its most compelling interests, namely that the nursery be emptied and the commons inhabited. Maximizing local control would probably also mean getting less equity for children and taxpayers and less equity among districts than would be good. On the other hand, if we maximize equity for children, then we are likely to get more inequity in the spread of the tax burden and less local control. The problems of financing education, in short, do not arise merely from the need to establish a more equitable system for taxpayers and children or increased control in the hands of parents and families. They arise rather from the need to secure these things within a system of public goods that aims to do it all—produce greater equity, preserve local control, and encourage responsible public management. The policy question will always devolve into a question as to how such *sets* of goods are to be balanced.

Virtually all issues of public (or even personal) policy have this feature. Such questions are nested in a set of social goods all of which must be considered, but which are at some point mutually incompatible. Consider the issues surrounding the imposition of exit standards at the level of the secondary school. Here we seek the mutual benefits of:

- universal levels of attainment,
- high academic achievement, and
- culturally pluralistic communities

The first two present the familiar conflict between quantity and quality, the old puzzle as to whether education can be universal, equitable, and at the same time excellent. Problems in trying to balance the entire set are illustrated by experience in Florida and Virginia. Not many years ago, in an effort to raise the standards of high school achievement, these states introduced uniform examinations as a requirement for exit from high school. Once a decision is made to raise standards in that way, the next question will have to be: Where should we place the cut-off score? In Virginia, the cut-off was set by the legislature without much attention to relevant data. As a result, the attainment rate declined. That some students would fail the exit examination was acceptable in prospect to those who thought such results would signal a rise in academic standards. That would be progress toward one goal. Indeed, were there no difference at all in the attainment rate following the introduction of such an examination, that might be taken as proof that the standard had been set too low. To many, however, including, presumably, many who had approved of the new policy, such a result was less pleasing because it produced what was, for them, an unacceptable decline in the level of attainment. That meant retreat from another goal. Thus, the cut-off was adjusted in an effort to find a balance between high standards and high attainment rates. The new policy turned out to be different from the old one only in appearance, not in results.

Such advancements and retreats, stories of steps taken and then taken back, are quite usual in movements of school reform or in efforts at change in public policy generally. Such adjustments are likely to result more from the collision of incompatible goods than from administrative bungling or blindness, inefficiency, political chicanery, or legislative incompetence. Neither the most efficient action nor the most technically proficient analysis is likely to resolve the central discord among the social aims in which policy questions are rooted. In general, there is no technical solution to a policy question. There are no technical means of evading the fact that if exit standards are raised, for example, then at least in the short term, one cost is likely to be reduced attainment levels. Two goods will contend.

Policy Questions, Practical Reason, and the Technicist Delusion

This conclusion, that there is no technical solution to policy questions, deserves exploration. Note first that policy questions are always questions of practical reason, never of theoretical reason. What counts as an answer to a policy question is always a statement of what to do, never a statement simply of what we know. Policy is a guide to conduct, not a proclamation of truth. In any public forum where policy is shaped, only questions of practical reason are admissible, never those of theoretical rationality. And this is fortunate because it means that in the domain of policy we are able to arrive at agreement on what to do without having to agree on the reasons for doing it. We are able to agree on a line of action and stick to it, even when we have different goals and when we do not agree on what is good.

Are we to suppose that human beings will agree on what to do only if they agree on what is good? It seems unlikely. Where does this leave us? The argument, on the one hand, is that we can agree on a course of action even when we disagree on what is good; but also that when we do agree on what is good, that is, even when we share the same goals, it does not follow that we will agree on a course of action. If these are the facts, then it does not seem obvious that theoretical discussions about the nature of the good and the good society can ever be enough to determine what ought to be the course of public policy. Think for a moment about political coalitions. The formation of coalitions is an illustration of people agreeing on a course of action without having to agree on their values or what is good or on their reasons for endorsing a course of action. Coalitions come and coalitions go, and their coming and going manifests one feature of the fact that an agreement on what to do is always a practical question and never *determined* by answers to theoretical questions of value and public good.

Answers to policy questions always propose a line of action: they identify what to do. Answers to theoretical questions, on the other hand, always advance truth claims: they announce what is known. Policy deliberation is aimed at action, not at the acquisition of knowledge; theoretical questions are aimed at the acquisition of knowledge, not at action. I do not mean by this that we can or ever should make public decisions without knowledge. Social action should be informed. Nor do I mean that we can ever gain greater knowledge without action. Research, the search for answers to theoretical questions, is itself a kind of action. I mean rather that in any policy debate the thing to be decided is what we should do, not what we must believe. Wise policy is never made with enough knowledge to *determine* a decision, and policy questions are never asked out of a primary interest in adding to our knowledge.

These days, when a return to paradise seems often to be viewed as a mere technical difficulty shortly to be overcome, it is easy to imagine someone saying, "If we just had methods sufficiently sophisticated and relevant data sufficiently refined, we could answer whatever policy questions might come along."[2] Such a person has fallen victim to an illusion, the illusion that policy questions are theoretical. Whenever we suppose that a policy question can be resolved by some addition to our knowledge, we suppose that what presents itself as a problem of policy is in fact a problem of management or administration.

My point is not that we should abandon all attempts to improve our methods of evaluation or policy analysis. It is rather that since indecision in matters of policy does not arise primarily from the lack of such methods, it is unlikely to be laid to rest by their development. When facing matters of policy, we face indecision because we confront a kind of question that, *in principle*, cannot be answered simply by any increment or improvement of knowledge. Answers to policy questions may be improved by better information and better analyses only in the sense that such gains will make our answers rationally more persuasive. But policy questions can, will, and usually are answered even without such information. Furthermore, it is not always obvious that the answers given in the absence of such analyses are worse than or even very different from answers that would be given in their presence. Answers might be better grounded rationally without being better or even different in any other sense.[3] We can, no doubt, do something rationally more persuasive than consulting chicken entrails, but we are unlikely to get anything quite as decisive. And this is so because of the properties of policy questions, not because of deficiencies in policy evaluation or policy 'science'.

III. The Etiology of Policy Questions

Scarcity

This last observation opens a second way to grasp why there are no technical solutions to policy problems. In addition to this matter of policy questions arising from a conflict among goods being sought (one kind of necessity), we may wonder whether there are other features of human life that inescapably produce such questions, aspects of the human condition out of which such questions emerge from another kind of necessity. Consider a *Gedankenexperiment* aimed at exploring circumstances in which questions of policy are simply ruled out. The case arises from the certainty that in paradise there are no policies—except, perhaps, admissions policies. Policy questions do not occur there. Why not? What is there about paradise that makes policy unnecessary? Ideas of paradise have appeared in great variety, but I am inclined to the view that, whatever the detailed differences in their views, humans conceive of heaven (and they will inevitably conceive of it in some way) as a perfected state of affairs, one in which desires presently denied in this imperfect world, somewhere, sometime, will be satisfied.[4] What else could paradise be, except a condition in which all human yearnings are satisfied and the deepest ones most deeply? This suggests, of course, that problems of optimality, and therefore the need for policy, would be banished from any world in which human desires are perfectly matched by satisfactions near at hand.

Ask and it shall be given. Yearn and you shall be gratified—given and gratified, moreover, in an instant. That might well be heavenly!

Let us test the idea in some detail. Two general strategies exist for arriving at such a state. The first lies on the side of increasing the satisfactions available to human beings (increased productivity); the second lies on the side of doing something about their desires (improved moral education and discipline). The first view holds that desires and satisfactions can be balanced under conditions of abundance. Wherever there is enough of everything, including enough justice, enough virtue, and enough bread and wine, there is no allocational problem, no problem of scarcity, and hence, no question of policy.

The other strategy is the converse of this one. There is no scarcity of what nobody wants. Thus, for Ghandi, one supposes, diamonds and mink were plentiful, not because they were any the less scarce, but because they were not wanted. Not being wanted, they were abundant. So desire and satisfaction can be balanced not by satisfying desires, but by adjusting them, composing them, bringing them into accord with the available possibilities of a world already given. If heaven is that condition in which the desires of persons in an imperfect world are satisfied in a world like this one, except perfected, then there may be abundance in heaven not because goods are maximized, but because wants are composed, not because the world is improved, but because *we* are improved in ways that better accord with what the world provides. In neither case do problems of policy arise, and they do not arise simply because such a bounty, secured by either strategy, makes choice redundant. In paradise, there is neither discord among the goods that humans seek nor among the human beings seeking them. Neither is there any delay between desires and their satisfaction. That is why under such conditions there is no place for policy. There is no need for it.

Conflict of Goods

Short of utopia, that is to say, in the ordinary world of kitchen sinks and Euclidean geometry, in addition to this discord of desire and satisfaction, strife may arise either among human beings or, as already hinted, among the goods themselves that human beings seek. We cannot imagine paradise to be so corrupted. Yet the question remains, Why in this way do we exclude interpersonal conflicts of wants from the composition of paradise? The answer is easy. Omit such an exclusion and you introduce to paradise the judgment either that wants are improperly controlled or that goods are too meagerly supplied. Paradise would no longer be this world perfected. It would be this world still unperfected. It would *be* this world, not paradise. It would contain the problem of devising the most satisfactory composition of what goods exist, who should get them, and in what degree. In short, such a condition would introduce into paradise precisely those circumstances that make both policy and politics inescapable, circumstances that dictate the features of a well-formed policy question, namely, What are the goods in conflict? What is their best *possible* adjustment? How can we reach it? What are the trade-offs?

The force of this conceptual incursion into the territory of heaven is to show beyond any doubt that problems of policy are an immediate and direct reflection of some immensely basic features of the world and of human existence within it. It is almost as though public policy, and therefore politics, is metaphysically necessary. The world cannot do without either.[5] Policy questions arise not simply because of the conflicting desires of individuals, or interpersonal conflicts among them, but also because the goods themselves that human beings seek are interdependent and often jointly discordant, not all of the time in every respect, but all of the time in some respects. Only in paradise can we imagine all human goods *simultaneously* in sufficient supply so that there is no conflict in their allocation. As I have suggested already, however, this is a consequence not of their scarcity, but of their very structure, a matter to which we must now return.[6]

Policy, Politics, and Utopia

It is one thing to deal with the foundations of policy questions by revealing their origins in the discord of satisfaction and desire and in the scarcity of goods. It is quite another to unravel the sources of policy in the interdependence of goods. When problems of scarcity are resolved—as in heaven—then no policy problems arise. But such a pronouncement presupposes some coherence in the idea that all human goods can exist in abundance simultaneously. Imagination poses the simplifying assumption that a plenitude of some goods secured by some can exist without reducing the chances of others securing other goods. And this assumption is false. 'Utopia', after all, is still 'nowhere' even when spelled backwards.

Human goods do conflict. They conflict, moreover, in such a way that they cannot all be present in sufficient abundance to satisfy human desires. The point is central. Human discontent, one might say without exaggeration, is genetic. Goods conflict so that the cost of securing the abundance of some is always, sooner or later, the failure to secure as much as we would like of some other. Succeed in providing as much equality as is wanted, and you are unlikely to have as much liberty as is wanted. Develop all the tolerance for ambiguity you can imagine, and shortly we shall complain about an insufficiently robust distribution of courage and excessive disarray in our libraries. Balancing the goods that human beings seek in all their resplendent variation is something that, having been done, will have to be done again, and again, and then yet again. It is a task not only inevitable, but enduring. This fact, together with the *hope and expectation* (not merely the wish) that the infection can be overcome by some form of social gene therapy, offers insight into the roots of the abiding human tendency to engage in utopian thinking.[7]

The view is that human goods conflict because they are not always structurally consistent with one another. They cannot all be maximized, even in paradise. Conflicts of interest may produce political problems, but conflicts among human goods produce policy problems.

Politics and Policy in Utopia

That the ultimate solution of policy problems is to be found only in paradise, may be exactly what gives rise to the enduring human impulse to think of social solutions to policy problems in utopian terms, rather than in the proximate terms of politics and policy. However, utopian thinking as a guide to policy is faulty, not simply because it attends too little to what is feasible, but because it does not attend at all to politics. It is an oddity, and an oddity of large significance, I think, that no well-developed literary utopia has ever included an account of politics. Management yes, but politics no. The promise of utopia lies firstly in an account of how the conflict among goods—the very source of policy questions—is to be resolved, and secondly, in the unstated claim that the equilibrium so established can be made to hold. It is precisely the resolution of this conflict among goods that makes any subsequent consideration of policy unnecessary; and it is the assumption that such an adjustment can be maintained that makes politics undesirable. Politics, after all, is the continuous opportunity of a people to reconsider. That is why in utopia, politics would threaten the good life, not contribute to it.

Problems of policy can appear there only as stepchild to household management, which is the literal and original meaning of 'economics' (οἰκόνομέω), an etymological deconstruction that ought to be recovered. All that remains, in that case, is to monitor the society and manage its affairs. In utopia, politics is thus replaced by administration.

The very idea of such usurpation exposes an affair of confused and averse affections. It offers proof, of a sort, that we yearn to be done with politics, but also that we fear any and all measures strong enough to accomplish the deed. We favor the cure, but not the remedy. If politics is a peoples' chance to reconsider, and if the reconsideration is more than superficial, then it will surely stir the basest human interests, passions, and sentiments. That is always the risk in reconsideration when the things at issue are things that really matter. Paradise and utopia offer pictures of our most cherished dreams, but they remain distant and improbable. It is unlikely that arrangements for reconsideration can ever be crafted that will suffice to cool the human passions out of which the need for politics emerges, arrangements that will curb the ambition, the lust for power, the egotisms, and the evangelical impulses to convert the whole world to this or to that opinion. If the arrangements for our reconsideration are designed only to suppress these human capacities instead of harnessing them to the service of some public good, then the results are apt to bear a striking likeness to the political arrangements that always seem to accompany the sovereignty of oligarchs, monarchs, priests, and generals. Such rulers inevitably favor political arrangements designed to leave unchecked among themselves precisely those base capacities that their regimes are designed to check in all the rest of us. Moreover, any people who give up the chance to reconsider, who seek escape from politics out of weariness or fear or from the illusion that they need not be bothered, have by this very abdication started a walk down the path that leads to friendly fascism.

Any portrayal of perfection will illustrate the human hankering to do without politics because any such full-blown vision of perfection will omit politics and then count the omission as part of the improvement. This which we seek to do without we cannot avoid, or will avoid at the peril of our own well-being. Here then is that mix of affections and fears that seem implanted in human kind, a mix quite sufficient to make education for the office of citizen an essential consideration in any adequate moral education in a democratic order, any order where the *demos* rule.

IV. Other Presuppositions

To these comments on the human and worldly origins of policy questions must be added others, stemming less from the nature of public policy and public goods and more from the relation of policy questions to moral questions, constitutional questions, and research questions. Failure to mark the differences among such questions can be a source of considerable mischief. So can the failure to note how such questions are related to one another. Some of the necessary distinctions will emerge by taking into account the relation of such questions to constraints of time and uncertainty.

Constraints of Time

Like a reporter filing his story for the evening edition, whoever will answer a policy question in the real world must do so within strict constraints of time. The reporter meets a deadline, but always in the knowledge that there will be a next edition. Another day, another rewrite. Today's story is amended by the next as events unfold and other facts emerge. Note two points: first, policy questions are answered always in anticipation that the answer will be revised, and second, such questions have to be answered on time, even when the information needed for the answer is not on time. Both points arise from temporal constraints, but they have different implications.

The first implies simply that policies are impermanent. We expect them to change. Often, they are not even very durable. They are not supposed to be. In that respect, they are like the reporter's story and unlike constitutional and moral questions. If we imagine some institution or government in which policies change with speed and frequency—every three months, say, or worse, every week—then we imagine circumstances in which there is no policy at all. Policies are guides to action. They are subject to amendment, but not that often. They should be durable, but not final.[8] Consider, for example, the American foreign policy of containment in confronting world communism as proposed by George Kennan in the 1940s. Here was basic policy that remained in force for nearly fifty years. Policy as durable as that, like policy that changes every week, tends not to be viewed as policy at all, but simply as a given in deliberation, a condition of the world, like the seasons, something that life must take into account, but which is not subject to change. Permanence and transience are equally alien to the idea of policy.

Policies, in other words, are more durable than whim, but less durable than constitutional rules which, in turn, are perhaps, less durable than moral standards or principles. We do not expect persons to change their moral principles as rapidly as they change policy. The offense involved in even describing moral principles as policies offers stark evidence of how different are the two. No person for whom honesty is merely a good policy is to be trusted on matters of much gravity precisely because although it is acceptable for policies to change fairly often, it is abhorrent that our moral principles do. We expect policy to change with experience and to change fairly often. We *are* entitled to reconsider. This dimension of limited durability is among the defining features of policy questions. To discern the proper placement of policy questions somewhere between the constancy of laws of nature, rules of morality, and constitutional provisions, on the one hand, and whims of the weekend, on the other, is central to grasping what can and what cannot be framed as a policy question.

Just as it is better for the reporter to file a story on time without all the facts than to get all the facts and file the story too late, so also, in the case of policy, it is better to make a decision on time but without all the facts, than to get all the facts and make the decision too late. Policy decisions have to be made within large limits of uncertainty. Some reduction in the degree of uncertainty will be helpful, but the substantial reduction normally required for academic research is unlikely to extend to policy decision and would often be undesirable even if it were probable. Crude data arriving on time are always to be preferred over refined data arriving too late. So it is acceptable, even fortunate, that research methods required for policy decision are crude, even when the standard methods of academic research are highly refined.

To answer a question of research, we are cautioned to get as much data as is needed to arrive at a reasoned conclusion and to formulate no conclusion until the data are at hand. Caution is among the virtues bred into the researcher. In answering a policy question, however, the constraints are different. In that case, we need as much information as we can get, but this usually turns out to be less than we could get if we had more time, and, at the same time, more than can be used and more than will make a difference to the decision. A major aim of academic research is to reduce the levels of uncertainty enough to justify knowledge claims. Policy questions, on the other hand, are always answered in the midst of uncertainty, and there is always a point beyond which more information—however more excellent—will do little to reduce the uncertainty and nothing to alter the decision. All this is simply another aspect of the claim that policy questions are practical rather than theoretical. They are questions of the sort that will be answered even when we do not know, with anything nearing certainty or assurance, which among alternative answers is the best. If these observations are credible, then it is possible to understand the claim, sometimes advanced, that academic research is useful for policy decision inversely to its academic excellence.

Policy Decisions and Moral Judgments

Policies and moral rules or principles differ in their relative durability, but they are also linked. Policies are always drawn from within a set of alternatives all of which are either morally indifferent or capable of evoking broad moral approval. The set may be established, partially at least, by what are sometimes called peremptory rules, that is, rules, usually unstated, that certain kinds of things just are not done. Such rules tend to frame the moral limits within which policy can be selected, but, at the same time, they tend to guarantee that policies are chosen from among alternatives all of which are morally permissible or widely agreed to have some worth. To that extent, defining the *set* of policy choices is the expression of moral conviction and estimates of value, but selecting from within that defined set is not. Thus, two quite different questions are generated. One question asks, What alternatives can be included among the set of choices? The other asks, Which among that set shall we adopt? The first of these questions already narrows the scope of choice, and that is partly the reason why, with even the best evaluation data, we are unlikely to arrive at policy choices substantially different from those we would arrive at without such data.

It follows that in policy debate, moral argument is unlikely to pick out which policies ought to be adopted. It is more likely to aid in determining what alternatives can be included among those available for choice. If policy choice were actually *determined* by moral argument, then policy debate would be transformed more easily than in fact it is, into a debate among adherents to competing moral principles. At risk would be the fundamental notion that we can agree on what to do without having to agree on our moral principles.[9] It would turn out that what is to be de-

cided in policy debate is not our policy but our moral principles, not
What should we do? but What must we believe?

Post-hoc Determinations of Policy

All arguments aimed at identifying a policy by its consequences are necessarily weak. They are all subject to what might be called 'the policy
form' of the fallacy of *post hoc ergo propter hoc*, "after this, therefore, because of this." In other words, claims of the form "It must be A's policy to
X because X is the result of his actions" are weak claims. They assume
that because certain results follow upon A's action, therefore, it must
have been A's policy to produce those results. If we find that high rates of
failure occur in a particular school system, the inference is that it must be
the policy of that school system to produce failure.

There are several difficulties in such an inference. First, it obscures
the fact that identifying a policy always implies the identification of intent. Failure may occur frequently in a given school system, but it cannot
be concluded from this fact alone that producing failure is anybody's intent. It cannot follow that producing failure is basic policy. A more decisive fault of all such arguments, however, is that by allowing them, we
render it logically impossible ever to speak of failed policies. Every policy
has its social consequences, however modest and however desirable or
undesirable, but we cannot reason from the presence of a certain state of
affairs that it was policy to produce that state of affairs. The most we can
say, to return to the example, is that frequent failure is probably the persistent consequence of measures that *are* matters of policy or of circumstances that in the real world are beyond the reach of policy to resolve.

Although the logic of such *post hoc* reasoning is objectionable, there
are circumstances in which it would be foolish to press the objection. If
extreme and undesirable consequences are publicly evident and persist
over a long period of time, then the appeal that such effects are unintended, that is, are not matters of policy, becomes less and less credible to
any reasonable person. Consider the case of a local chemical plant engaged in the production of salts, which process over the years has seriously polluted a nearby lake. To announce "We don't pollute the lake, we
simply produce salts" is to stretch the credulity of the average citizen beyond the breaking point. But how could we describe this situation? I propose that however strongly we may incline to the view that polluting the
lake is official company policy, still we would do better to locate the

problem in another way instead of adopting the familiar *post hoc* argument. The more complete account would be that in determining policy, the mix of goods included in the 'nest' of the policy debate is impoverished. It omits matters that ought to be included. It excludes attaching any weight, for example, to the externalities of continued pollution of the lake, both as costs to the public in destroying a natural asset and costs to the industry by eroding public acceptance.

In short, such *post hoc* arguments, judged simply on grounds of logic, always fail. From time to time, however, they appear to succeed, and when that happens, success is likely to occur not because the argument is sound, but because the initial mix of goods competing in the policy debate is too limited. We may reject all such *post hoc* arguments without rejecting the normal view that policy implies intent and that policies sometimes fail.

V. The Policy Process

The office of citizen as participant in the formation of public policy involves discrete practices, each with its own disciplines. Between policy analysis, policy formation, policy decision or promulgation, and the political analysis of policy, there lie clear differences, and exercising the office of citizen will relate differently to each. It would be misleading, however, to view these four activities—analysis, formation, decision, and political analysis—as discrete steps in the policy process. They are activities never fully discrete in practice. Nor do they occur in any settled sequence. Nevertheless, there is a distinction of practice corresponding to each activity, and each practice, moreover, has its distinct set of disciplines, each its distinct excellence and virtues. Although the questions asked in each practice are here examined mostly in the context of government, and particularly in the state or federal apparatus, they are, nevertheless, implicit in the office of citizen. They are examined here as they appear within the formal apparatus of government, only because that is where they are most clearly discerned. They are implicit, however, in the disciplines practiced, whether poorly or well, by every citizen in a democratic order.

Policy Analysis

Policy analysis can be defined as the rational or technical assessment of the net marginal trade-offs between different policy choices. The question becomes, Which among the implicit set of goods will be advanced, which will not, and with what net benefits? This is the same kind of question that we confront, say, in the design of a hand drill. What should be the design? The question can be examined only within a nested set of goods. We want low cost, high safety, ease of handling, and durability. We can ask and rather precisely determine what marginal gains in one of these values will produce what corresponding costs in the others. If we choose greatest durability, then we are likely to get higher cost and less ease of handling. If we prefer the lowest cost possible, then we are likely to sacrifice something in the way of durability and safety. The design problem is to discover a balance between these competing values.

Enter the problem of incommensurabilities: How do we determine which among competing goods is to be given greatest weight? Which has the greatest worth—low cost, durability, safety, or ease of handling? Not even the most refined analysis of costs and benefits will solve such a problem. That kind of analysis gives us a list of possibilities or a set of choices, but it does not pick out any preferred answer from within the set. Yet we need some procedure for doing just that, a procedure for picking out one among the set. In short, we need a market *decision* and getting a market decision is, no doubt, going to require a market *analysis*.

Is our market made up of professionals? Or does it consist essentially of amateurs and household craftsmen? If the former, then the problem is likely to be resolved on the side of durability and safety with a slightly higher price. If the latter, then, by all means, the decision will probably be to minimize cost and sacrifice durability and, to some degree, safety. But then again, the market decision might be to go for the whole range of the market. Produce a variety of designs representing the full range of choices revealed by the analytic exercise. Something for everybody!

These activities are roughly analogous to the distinctions I want to make in the case of policy. Merely setting forth the marginal costs and benefits of a range of choices is one thing—*policy analysis*. This will establish the relative merits of several possible lines of action. Proposing one alternative or range of alternatives from among the possibilities is a different kind of task, one that initiates the actual formulation of policy—*policy formation*. The decision as to which choice or choices to make is still another matter—*policy decision*. This kind of decision is usually a political decision and it requires a political analysis.

Consider an example used earlier to illustrate the idea of conflicting goods. Financial assistance in higher education can be distributed either directly to students or to institutions. Suppose we entertain the prospect of distributing it to students and that we resolve to do so on the basis of need. In that case we require access to financial information, and not simply on groups, trends, or categories of persons, but on each actual individual. If we propose this kind of policy as more fair or just than others, then, in the name of justice, individuals will have to reveal personal information that before may have been regarded as privileged. Two goods conflict. We extend justice but diminish privacy. To secure a definable gain in one, we pay a definable cost in the other. Policy *analysis* asks, What is the net marginal gain? A truly refined policy analysis—something that almost never exists except as a normative ideal for reflection—would tell us how much we are likely to gain in the advancement of justice for each corresponding cost in privacy. We cannot bring much precision to bear in answering that kind of question, but that should not obscure the fact that the question is of the sort that we seek to address.

No such analysis, however, no matter how refined, will tell us whether the gain is worthwhile. That fact alone is sufficient to demonstrate that this second question is of a sort entirely different from the first. The answer to the first question, however crude or exact, will not constitute an answer to this second question. For it, we need something like a market analysis and a market decision, that is, a political analysis and a political decision. 'Policy' implies 'polity' and 'politics', just as 'good industrial design' implies a structure for marketing analysis and marketing decision.

Consider another example. Let us suppose that a congressman asks whether pass-through requirements for allocating Chapter I school aid should rest on tests of educational instead of economic need. The answer comes couched not in terms of whether we should, but in terms of what is likely to happen if we do. That's policy analysis. In either case, the funds would go to roughly the same places, but not quite. What's the margin of 'not quite'? Is 'not quite' very much? Is it enough to matter? And even if it is 'not much', would the change create incentives for local school districts to pay more attention to educational need in answering allocational questions? If so, would the incentives be enough to make a difference? And if so, then (here we are again) how much of a difference? That's policy analysis.

But policy analysis does not and need not stop there. It can ask not simply what the net consequences would be of doing X, but what those net consequences would be compared to doing Y, where Y is either what we are doing already or some alternative. The question for policy analysis is not whether doing X is a net improvement over doing Y, but simply, what are the net effects? Whether it is better to have a drill of low cost instead of high durability will not be determined simply from an analysis of the trade-offs. It requires a marketing decision. Similarly, whether given the different consequences, it is better to do X than Y will not be determined by a policy analysis. It will be determined by a political decision resulting from a political process involving a political analysis.

Policy analysis is that rational, technical, analytic performance in which the central question is not whether X is a good thing to do, but rather what are the marginal effects of doing X, and what are the marginal effects as contrasted with doing something else instead. Hence policy analysis is simply an activity *whose theory is the theory of marginal utilities*. It is, by all accounts, an activity that consists in the exercise of theoretical, rather than practical, rationality. It assumes that the policy question is nested in a conflict of values present as objective states of affairs in the society. It is an activity in which evaluators and other researchers may take a leading role, provided they do not suppose they are actually evaluating policy, as opposed to merely recording—either in prospect or in retrospect—the consequences of doing X or Y. But this is also a process in which ordinary citizens participate. Attend any Central School District budget meeting in the state of New York, for example, and you will hear one or another proposed course of action being debated. Shall we enlarge the computer facilities for all and reduce the program in literature for those who especially want it or need it? When parents argue "Instead of adding two more teachers to the program in biology, we need tympani, tubas and trombones for the band," and when that is countered by the claim that such a course of action will mean lower examination scores and fewer chances for future education, citizens are engaged in policy analysis, assessing the marginal net gains of doing X rather than Y.

Policy Formation

Policy formation is of a contrasting genre. It is that activity by which we seek agreement on what form a specific policy can or will take, as opposed to what form it ought to take. Not even by the most refined policy analysis will we have actually formed a policy. Policy analysts are not typically in a position to formulate policy. To actually form policy, we need to engage in conversation, persuasion, argument, and (seemingly) endless meetings with those who will actually pen the regulation, mark up the bill, establish the procedures, write the guidelines, and so on. *The theory of policy formation can then be discerned as one aspect of the theory of governmental management and rhetoric.* At the federal level, to whatever extent there is or can be a theory of such matters at all, it will turn out to be the theory of interagency politics. "Don't fight over turf; just take up space" is a rule for the conduct of policy formation. I include here the theory of rhetoric because clearly it makes a difference what things are called. The same policy that under one name may never see the light of day, under another name, will pass without objection. Calling it school aid may defeat it, but calling the same thing national defense may ensure its acceptance. "If it matters what you call it, then call it something that matters" is another guiding rule in the theory of policy formation. Call it government spending and you may face political difficulties. Call it public investment and you may have more success.

Policy Decision

Policy decision can be described as the authoritative action of some office—administrative or legislative—by which a line of action, for the moment at least, is established. Policy decision is not so much an activity or process as it is a momentary endpoint in the continuing conduct of government, an endpoint, however, that unfortunately is often thought to represent the policy process entirely—as though making policy could be reduced to a simple decision, an act of will, or the result of divination. *The theory of policy decision is simply the theory of the polity itself,* that is, the political and legal theory by which authority is distributed, obligations for decision are assigned throughout the structure of political institutions, and agents of authority are enjoined to act.

Political Analysis

Policy analysis contrasts starkly with political analysis. Policy analysis may be concerned with determining the net benefits of a given course of action, but political analysis attends to estimating their political weight.

The aim is not to determine the net social benefits of a particular policy, but to identify its constituency. Policy analysis has to do with establishing what course of action has greatest worth in the assemblage of public goods, but political analysis with estimating who will vote for it, whether, in short, the best thing to do is the same as the best thing that can be done. Often it is not. The theory of political analysis, in short, is the theory of political behavior.

We may gather these thoughts in a brief culminating summary. The theory of policy analysis is the theory of marginal utilities. It aims to rank available alternatives according to the estimated net utilities of each. The theory of policy formation is the theory of interagency politics, the process of government by which a course of action comes to be selected and is actually framed. The theory of policy decision is nothing less than the theory of the polity itself, the theory underlying the placement of authority, what passes for investiture. And finally, the theory of political analysis is the theory of political behavior. When we view these activities together, not as discrete steps in the policy process, but as distinct facets of a social process, now one feature predominating and now another, then we can discern more clearly where the practices of evaluation and policy research fit, what may be their relevance to the creation, promulgation, and implementation of public policy, and what virtues are required for the actors in this drama.

Evaluators, policy researchers, academics, and politicians all contribute something to each of these activities, but not to each in the same way or in the same degree. The rational standards of policy analysis are the standards of theoretical reason. That is what academics, researchers, and students of social affairs are good at. They may all contribute at this point. But the rational practices of policy decision and political analysis employ the standards of political judgment, something that academics and social researchers are not typically good at. How political judgment is acquired, much less exercised is, at least in my mind, something of a mystery. It is a peculiar kind of wisdom, a kind that one distinguished public servant of long experience once described to me as "a kind of Byzantine black magic." These are activities of practical reason. This difference may help to explain why it is that when the question, What should we do? is given a policy analysis, we may get one answer, and when given a political analysis or when rendered in a policy decision, we may get an entirely different answer. In short, the exercise of political judgment is a practical activity. It is also an evaluational activity. But the result of that evaluation may differ from or even contradict the results of policy analysis. What we should do—even the best thing to do—may turn out to be one thing by policy analysis and a very different thing when it comes to political decision.

Professional evaluators and policy researchers can contribute in the context of government, but will contribute to *all* of these activities only to the extent that they become also politicians and political advisors. Consider, for example, the case of policy formation. The evaluator, as professional, can contribute, but that contribution will be substantial only when he or she becomes a student of bureaucracy and a trusted counselor to authoritative leadership.

Each of these activities involves research and a kind of technical expertise in some broad sense of those terms. Each involves evaluation and research in the sense, say, that buying a camera does. But only in the case of policy analysis is the expert's role undiluted by the need to take on the burden of other practices. The evaluator, *as evaluator*, is likely to make a contribution only to the conduct of policy analysis. In government as elsewhere, the possession of knowledge can bring with it a certain kind of power. To the extent that the evaluator and policy researcher goes beyond his or her professional practice and earns the confidence of political leaders, exercises political judgment, and acquires the additional skills of a practiced political observer of the present bureaucracy and an uncertain future, then he or she will contribute to *every* facet of the policy process. But in doing so, such a person will also become less an evaluator, a researcher, an academic in any limited professional sense, less a technical expert, and more a political leader or public servant in a quite old-fashioned and conventional sense. The exercise of technical skill is not the principal asset that such a person brings to the policy problem. His or her main asset will be the capacity to combine technical expertise with the exercise of a particularly important kind of civic virtue or political judgment, not different in kind from the sort of virtue we have always called upon citizens to exercise. Indeed, it is just this combination of skills, acquired over time, that is needed for the activities engaged by participation in the office of citizen.

VI. Normation to the Office of Citizen

Michael Walzer offers a suggestive account of the relation between citizens and their political leaders in a democratic state, an account that frames precisely the metaphor I have been reaching for in this extended account of the office of citizen. He writes:

> It is a special feature of democratic government that the experiences of leaders are not alien to ordinary citizens. . . . With only a modest imaginative effort, the citizen can put himself in the place of his elected representative. . . . Because he can do that, and commonly does it, he engages in what I want to call . . . anticipative and retrospective decision-making. He asks, "What would I do in his place?" and then, later on, he asks, "Would I have done what he did?" In a democracy, decisions are anticipated before they are made and reviewed after they are made, and these anticipations and retrospections play a large part in determining all those subsequent actions—voting, contributing money, demonstrating—to which political scientists normally devote their attention. Vicarious decision-making precedes and follows actual decision-making. In our minds, if not in fact, we imitate the Aristotelian ideal: We rule and are ruled in turn.[10]

This "anticipative and retrospective decision-making" involves disciplines that can be practiced well or badly. In short, their conduct is norm-governed. To be educated to the office of citizen is to become normed to the excellent practice of its disciplines, and those are the disciplines I have outlined already as salient within the policy processes of public service.

Throughout these essays, the argument has been that the voices of conscience are various and that no one of them can be made entirely subservient to any other. Even less could all be bent to the service of a single voice. Still, it has not been argued that the domain of each is entirely discrete. Instead, the argument has been that these voices will quarrel. The voice of duty, for example, is important, but not all-important. It will yield, for example, to appeals of loyalty and to other claims of conscience. It is a useful injunction that I should do my duty though the heavens fall; yet if their fall seems imminent, then perhaps I should be prepared to reconsider. If I seriously entertain what I would do were I the chancellor of the university, then my loyalty to my own academic department or school will have to suffer some adjustment. No academic department offers a suitable vantage from which to survey and grasp the good of the whole. If I cannot or will not make such adjustments, then I cannot have considered well what I would do were I the chancellor. In my prospective rehearsals or in my retrospective judgments, I would not have acted well within my office as citizen of the university. Similar remarks apply when I consider in prospect what I would do were I the mayor or the governor or a member of Congress. The claims of family and neighborhood or region must be bent, from time to time, by the claims of memberships progressively more extensive, because it is not simply my will or yours, but the will and well-being of those larger associations that anyone in such positions of leadership will have to consider.

Whatever may be my utopian and untested visions of what I would do were I this public officer or that, those imaginary acts will have to be balanced against the claims of others in those more extended memberships. But they will also be subject to the various voices of conscience, the conscience of craft, for example. In my prospective role, if I enact it well, I will not propose to act the fool. I will have to consider the craft of that larger office. But then craft, as I have abundantly noted already, can turn to craftiness and craftiness to cronyship, at which time the peremptory claims aroused by other forms of membership, or by the conscience of sacrifice or of memory and imagination, will surely be enlisted to rein in the otherwise unbridled march of appetite and ambition. Even more fundamental is the simple fact that my own desires, if they enter at all into this interior rehearsal and retrospective judgment, must 'go public'. They cannot be presented simply as *my* desires or even as the collective desires of a large population all of whom happen to want just as I want. Needs may be limited, but desires are not. In that imaginative rehearsal, my desires must be clothed in terms that equip them to enlist the rational yearnings of others to a joint enterprise. Those hankerings must be given credentials so that they can appear not simply as my yearnings or as yours, but as something of value for us all. Otherwise they will fail as policy considerations and will appear instead simply as the poor, impetuous longings of a child. In other words, even in such anticipatory rehearsal and review, I am called upon to practice that rational patience of which I spoke. It goes with the territory. Its exercise is implicit in the practice of the public office of citizen.

So all the voices of conscience will speak at one time or another in the office of citizen. The problem is to discern *case by case* just how the argument among those voices will proceed. In this respect, the office of the citizen is casuistic. It goes case by case in these practices of preview and criticism because that is the way that policy formation generally advances. In just that degree, it is like the practice of law which also goes forth case by case. It too is strikingly casuistic.

There are three points implicit in this observation. The first is that the office of citizen is casuistic partly because it is impossible to balkanize the voices of conscience. We cannot frame a division of labor sufficient to say that standards of craft will govern in these contexts and rules of duty in these others, and that membership and loyalty will be granted a dominant voice in still other cases. Such borders, even if they could be framed, would themselves be subject case by case to prospective and retrospective judgment. From this it follows, secondly, that conduct within the office of citizen will be casuistic also because it is impossible ever to formulate a policy to include the details of its own administration. It is folly to attempt it. Policy formulations, like many (not all) moral rules, must be open-textured. Are we to suppose *ahead of time* that exceptions, without exception, must be disallowed? The distinction between a rule of justice and its just administration will extend as well to the formulation of policy and its application. My own experience has led me to believe that too often people seek to frame policies, for example, like those guiding the assignment of grades and promotion within the academic institution, and to include within their formulations apparently endless subsidiary rules for the administration of policy. The process is meant to take account of every contingency that can boil up within a mind fearful of the future, suspicious of strangers, and distrustful sometimes even of what may turn out to be one's own future self. Such timorous creatures constitute a tribe of little legal minds.

Finally, it needs to be noted that these aspects of conduct within the office of the citizen that make its practices curiously casuistic—that the voices of conscience cannot be balkanized, that argument among them cannot be stilled, that rules of policy, like rules of thumb, are open-textured—these features of the office of citizen reflect a property of norms generally, namely, that being situationally specific is not a deficiency of norms, but merely added evidence that norm acquisition entails the formation of judgment in finding the fittingness of conduct to context.

Notes

Preface

1. I would adhere strictly to the advice of Thomas Aquinas, and do so in the spirit of Aquinas, who advised that "an argument from authority which is based upon human reason is the feeblest" (*Summa Theologica* I, q. 1, art. 8, reply 2), implying thereby that there are no authorities in philosophy, and who admonished us that when we hear a certain view expressed, we should pay no attention to who is propounding it, but concentrate only upon what is being said (*De modo studiendi*). Cf. Timothy C. Potts, *Conscience in Medieval Philosophy* (Cambridge: Cambridge University Press, 1980), p. x.

1. The Project: A Matter of Governance

1. See chapter 5, "Teaching Values: The Grand Delusion," in which this approach, together with its origins, is examined in detail.

2. *Reflections on the Revolution in France*, in *The Writings and Speeches of Edmund Burke*, vol. 8, ed. L. G. Mitchell and William B. Todd (Oxford: Clarendon Press 1989), p. 216.

3. From William Lee Miller, *The Business of May Next: James Madison and the Founding* (Charlottesville: University Press of Virginia, 1992), p. 16.

4. This groundless expectation that instruction in moral philosophy will make whoever engages in it morally better is apparently an expectation, foolish or not, that is shared by many but, oddly enough, in a way that seems to strengthen the central point. There is, in fact, a growth industry arising from the assumption that teaching moral philosophy to physicians (as well as to engineers and civil servants) will, at minimum, contribute to the formation of morally sensitive physicians, engineers, and civil servants. So somebody apparently believes what it is here claimed that nobody ought to believe. Still, it is doubtful that what is taught under the rubric of medical ethics ever is or ought to be called moral philosophy. It falls more accurately under what has historically been viewed as casuistry. See Albert R. Johnson and Stephen Toulmin, *The Abuse of Casuistry: A History of Moral Reasoning* (Berkeley: University of California Press, 1988).

5. Bernard Williams, *Ethics and the Limits of Philosophy* (Cambridge, Mass.: Harvard University Press, 1985), pp. 6–7.

6. See Robert C. Roberts, "Will Power and the Virtues," in *The Virtues: Contemporary Essays on Moral Character*, ed. Robert B. Kruschwitz and Robert C. Roberts (Belmont, Calif.: Wadsworth, 1986), pp. 123–136. Roberts argues that "the virtues of will power are in an important aspect skills or skill-like powers," and he describes some of the tools "of self-management" that are available for their acquisition.

7. According to Kittel and Friedrich [and also Liddell and Scott], *Theological Dictionary of the New Testament* (Grand Rapids, Mich.: Eerdmans, 1964–1976), vol. 7, p. 898 *passim*, the term *syneidesis*, among the Greek parallels of 'conscience', referred, in an early form, to acts already done, and thus, conscience was construed as having a primary, perhaps exclusive, association with bad actions in the past. Hence, 'conscience' was apparently concerned primarily with what nowadays we might refer to as 'bad conscience'. Matters in prospect, apparently, were not covered. Thus, it was not always that conscience could be construed as associated with a capacity for reflexive judgment both in prospect and in retrospect. An entire system of motivation and self-judgment, now largely extinct, is connected to this fact. Still, the idea here of conscience as involving judgments of actions both past and future seems familiar in the modern world.

8. The more common—we might even say 'instinctive'—view is that conscience is not *reason* commenting, but mother or father, teacher or aunt, preacher or politician, etc. The basis for this view, that is, what constitutes its appeal and may make it seem instinctive, will be discussed below together with what may constitute the error implicit in it.

9. *Summa Theologica* I, q. 79, art. 13. Aquinas distinguishes conscience from any innate faculty or power. It is an act of reason, he says, expressed in three ways: "insofar as we recognize that we have done or not done something . . . insofar as through the conscience we judge that a thing should be done or not done . . . and insofar as by conscience we judge that something done is well done or ill done." This last kind of judgment, that something is well done or badly done, is what extends the reach of conscience to judgments of excellence in practice, to standards of craft, for example.

10. Immanuel Kant, *Lectures on Ethics*, trans. Lewis White Beck (Indianapolis: Hackett, 1963), p. 129.

11. Ibid., p. 131.

12. John Stuart Mill, *Utilitarianism* (London: Longmans, Green and Company, 1895), chap. 3, pp. 41–42. Italics added.

13. This distinction between attention to conscience already formed and conscience in formation is the central difference between moral philosophy and a philosophy of moral education.

14. The term 'normation', I am told, is not a part of the standard sociological lexicon. Perhaps it is not a part of any standard vocabulary used in discussing these matters. I introduce it here because the term 'socialization' is so loosely used, so vague and ambiguous, so misused in educational discourse, that

some fresh approach, hence some fresh and therefore more adaptable terminology, is needed. As I shall argue, 'socialization' is not an adequate substitution for 'norm acquisition'. Thus, I defend what would otherwise be no doubt a foolish step and introduce yet another piece of technical jargon.

15. In the *Encyclopedia of Philosophy* (New York: Macmillan, 1967), for example, there is no entry on 'learning' at all. Yet it is, or ought to be, among the most contested concepts of philosophical interest. By contrast, in the *International Encyclopedia of the Social Sciences* (New York: Macmillan, 1968), pp. 113–197, there appears an extended article of some twelve sections.

16. As far as I know, the description of these as the emotions of self-assessment originates with Gabriele Taylor. See her *Pride, Shame and Guilt: Emotions of Self-Assessment* (Oxford: Oxford University Press, 1985).

17. For a more extended account of how the emotions of self-assessment are structured in normation, see chapter 2, "Moral Education as Norm Acquisition."

18. In Hebrew, I am told, *davar* (word) has alternative renderings—word, event, act, deed, thing, matter, process. In such a view, the Word of God is more than an act of saying. It is efficacious, a power. Its utterance makes things happen. An event, for example, is 'a word'. This understanding of 'word' lends increased seriousness to such things as giving one's word, or uttering false words or impulsive words that, literally, cannot be taken back. Curses are not just words; they hurt. They are actions. See Susan A. Handelman, *The Slayers of Moses* (Albany: State University of New York Press, 1982), p. 32. "The Hebrew God," she points out, "though invisible, did not just statically exist, but *spoke*" (p. 17). See also Thorlief Boman, *Hebrew Thought Compared with Greek* (London: SCM Press, 1960), pp. 57–67. See also chapter 6, "Public Speech."

19. Vicki Hearne, "Can an Ape Tell a Joke?" in *Best American Essays 1994*, ed. Tracy Kidder (Boston: Houghton Mifflin, 1994), p. 204.

20. It is a tenuous point, but one that should be left open for study, that entirely different moral worlds are defined by the ways that verbs are handled in pedagogy. But beyond the usual distinction between active and passive voices of verbs, one needs to acknowledge how important it is that thought, in the classical pattern, is based upon the copula, a verb form not simply tenseless, being neither past, present, nor future, but also voiceless, neither active nor passive. It is essentially this tenseless and voiceless character of the copula that renders discourse suitable for philosophical expression making matters appear to be eternal (hence beyond time and detached from particular voice). In Hebrew, I have been led to believe, there is no such copula. Thus, reasoning in the texts of the Hebrew Bible does not consist of such joinings of propositions as are afforded by Western logic. In "The cedars of Lebanon will stand forever," 'stand' should be read as an active verb. Durability, i.e., constancy, is an activity not a property, a verb not a predicate. It is a feature of faith. The famous response to Moses, "I am who I am" might better be rendered as "I will do what I will do." See Handelman, *The Slayers of Moses*, chap. 1, esp. pp. 23–24.

2. Moral Education as Norm Acquisition

The central argument of this chapter appears, in an earlier form, in "Education as Norm Acquisition," in *Pragmatism, Reason, and Norms: A Realistic Assessment*, ed. Kenneth R. Westphal (New York: Fordham University Press, 1998).

1. There is an important peculiarity, however, in such a portrait. For anyone so alienated, that is, anyone who would actually say, "nothing vital is at stake," much of great importance is at stake. The very statement "nothing serious is at stake" may constitute a kind of tool for dealing with serious matters, making their gravity clear, and proclaiming to others how well one can 'get along' without submission to *their* sense of what things matter. And as for any to whom such words are directed—for them as well—a great deal is at stake. Such an agent must proclaim his or her independence of the norms that 'they' prescribe. Yet the use of such verbal clues as a tool for proclaiming that independence betrays one's observance of those rules even in the act of protesting against them. The protest is an announcement that independence of the norms, their full detachment, is incomplete.

2. *Acedia* is the term translated as 'sloth' among the traditional so-called seven deadly sins. For an interesting account of how these emotions or states of being are related in a constructivist view, see Claire Armon-Jones, "The Thesis of Constructionism," in *The Social Construction of Emotions*, ed. Rom Harré (New York: Blackwell, 1986), chap. 3.

3. This anomic perspective is not always to be decried. See Joseph Mercurio, *Caning: Educational Ritual* (New York: Holt, Rinehart and Winston, 1972), chap. 5, esp. p. 55. In this participant-observer study of caning in Boys' High School in New Zealand, one cannot help being impressed by the degree to which the practice of caning, though persisting, becomes irrelevant to the lives of the boys subject to it, and the degree to which their withholding of authority from the practice can be viewed as a mark of maturity in them, a point at which they begin to "take their lives into their own hands" and withhold authority from the adult community. This is alienation that can also be viewed as a step toward maturity.

4. Hope is not an emotion structured by normation in this way even though it is central to any adequate view of moral education. Hope, although forward-looking in its object, is always dependent upon memory for its foundations and thus is backward-looking in its formation. See "Hope" in chapter 4.

5. *Oxford Latin Dictionary*, ed. P. G. W. Glare (Oxford: Clarendon Press, 1982).

6. See Robert Dreeben, *On What Is Learned in School* (Reading, Mass.: Addison-Wesley, 1968), pp. 66–67.

7. See "The Conscience of Memory and Imagination" in chapter 4.

8. The possibility of framing such inclusive and therefore exhaustive guides to action is what underlies the fantasy of computerized decision trees,

bureaucratic manuals, the expansion of wills and legal standards to cover every possible contingency, and, I presume, the fantasies of military command and control, insofar as such efforts aim at replacing the uncertainties of practical judgment.

9. Frederick L. Will, *Beyond Deduction: Ampliative Aspects of Philosophical Reflection* (New York: Routledge, 1988), p. 135.

10. Ibid., p. 136.

11. It is a matter of considerable interest that such contexts, namely those in which norm acquisition is taking place by a process of formation, are also the settings in which case studies and casuistry seem to emerge most naturally.

12. Ferdinand Tönnies, *Gemeinschaft und Gesellschaft* (1887), 8th ed. (Leipzig: H. Buske, 1935).

13. Ferdinand Tönnies, *Community and Society*, trans. Charles P. Loomis (New York: Harper and Row, 1963), p. 192. Emphasis added.

14. Robert A. Nisbet, *The Sociological Tradition* (New York: Basic Books, 1966), p. 76.

15. Henry J. S. Maine, *Ancient Law* (Boston: Beacon Press, 1963).

16. Nisbet, *The Sociological Tradition*, pp. 85–86.

17. Emile Durkheim, *The Division of Labor in Society*, trans. George Simpson (New York: Macmillan, 1933), p. 277.

18. Talcott Parsons, "Emile Durkheim," in *The International Encyclopedia of the Social Sciences* (New York: Macmillan, 1968–1979).

19. And it is here that we shall discover the parameters of the 'collective conscience' in Durkheim's sense.

20. Emile Durkheim, *The Rules of Sociological Method*, trans. Sarah A. Solovay and John H. Mueller (New York: Free Press, 1965), p. 13.

21. See "Individualism and the Intellectuals," trans. Mark Traugott, in *Emile Durkheim on Morality and Society: Selected Writings*, ed. Robert Bellah (Chicago: University of Chicago Press, 1973), pp. 43–57. A slightly different translation with comment by Steven Lukes is found in *Political Studies*, 1969, vol. 17, part 1, pp. 14–30, reproduced in *Emile Durkheim: Critical Assessments*, vol. 4, ed. Peter Hamilton (New York: Routledge, 1993), pp. 166–183. A valuable discussion of this piece is found in Ernest Wallwork, *Durkheim: Morality and Milieu* (Cambridge, Mass.: Harvard University Press, 1972), pp. 166–170.

3. The Voices of Conscience I: Craft and Membership

1. Joseph Townsend, *A Dissertation on the Poor Laws by a Well-Wisher to Mankind* (Berkeley: University of California Press, 1971). This small and nearly forgotten book was first published in London in 1786. Both Malthus and Darwin owe much to it.

2. Ibid., pp. 37–38.

3. Karl Polanyi, *The Great Transformation* (Boston: Beacon Press, 1957), p. 114.

4. Cited in John F. A. Taylor, *The Masks of Society* (New York: Meredith, 1966), p. 258.

5. Senator Alan K. Simpson, Republican of Wyoming, announcing his retirement after eighteen years in the United States Senate, *New York Times*, Sunday, January 21, 1996, sect. A, p. 14.

6. R. R. Palmer, *Twelve Who Ruled: The Year of the Terror in the French Revolution* (Princeton, N.J.: Princeton University Press, 1969), p. 19. Quoted in William Lee Miller, *The Business of May Next: James Madison and the Founding* (Charlottesville: University Press of Virginia, 1992), p. 11.

7. Miller, *The Business of May Next*, p. 11.

8. See chapter 7, "Public Policy and the Office of Citizen," where these issues are discussed at length.

9. *Politics*, 1253a 25–35.

10. Emile Durkheim, *Moral Education* (New York: Free Press, 1961), chaps. 2–6.

11. See chapter 6, "Public Speech," in which it is argued that the public forms a capacity to entertain the speech of the other as candidate for one's own, a significant test of empathy, and also chapter 7, "Public Policy and the Office of Citizen," in which it is argued that the need for policy arises not from a conflict of human interests, but from a conflict of goods, and that the policy process aims to discover a suitable balance among such goods.

12. Adam Smith, *The Theory of Moral Sentiments*, chap. 2, part 1, sect. 1, p. 260, in *British Moralists*, ed. L. A. Selby-Bigge (Oxford: Clarendon Press), vol. 1, p. 266.

13. See Jeremy Bentham, *Introduction to the Principles of Morals and Legislation*, esp. chapter 4.

14. *De inventione rhetor.* II, 53.

15. *Summa Theologica* II, part I, q. 57, art. 6, reply 4.

4. Voices of Conscience II: Sacrifice, Memory, and Imagination

1. Henry Sidgwick, *The Methods of Ethics*, 6th ed. (London: Macmillan, 1901), preface, xvi–xvii. Bracketed text is an insert of the editor in a manuscript that was unfinished at Sidgwick's death.

2. Ibid., xviii.

3. Joseph Butler, *Fifteen Sermons* (London, 1914), preface, 39. See also Sermons I and II.

4. See Henry Sidgwick, *Outline of the History of Ethics for English Readers* (London: Macmillan, 1906), chap. 4. For a historical account of arguments relating to self-interest and benevolence from Hobbes to Adam Smith, see Milton Meyers, *The Soul of Modern Economic Man* (Chicago: University of

Chicago Press, 1983). See also David Hume, *A Treatise on Human Nature*, book 3, sect. 2, on greatness of mind. "'Tis necessary," he writes, "to feel the sentiment and passion of pride in conformity to it, and to regulate our actions accordingly."

5. John Dewey, *Democracy in America* (New York: Free Press, 1966), chap. 26, pp. 350–354.

6. It is worth a reminder that here, as elsewhere, I am concerned with the formation of conscience, an educational problem, and thus, with the order of learning, not the order of being. The question is how we come to see truth telling as a duty. It is worth noting that within the metaphysics of morals, Kant distinguishes between the metaphysical principles of right and the metaphysical principles of virtue. In connection with the principles of virtue, and in particular with the didactic of ethics, he says, "The moral capacity of man would not be virtue if it were not actualized by the strength of one's resolution in conflict with powerful opposing inclinations. Virtue is the product of pure practical reason insofar as the latter, in the consciousness of its superiority, gains mastery over the inclinations." "The Elements of Ethics, First Section of the Methodology of Ethics, The Didactics of Ethics," no. 49, in *Kant's Ethical Philosophy* (Indianapolis: Hackett, 1983).

7. It is hard to know what such a discussion would be about, i.e., whether it could itself be a morally serious discussion if it arises from a genuine doubt that one should tell the truth *in this case*. Presumably, such a discussion cannot arise from a troubled conscience *in that case*. The very possibility of discussion, in other words, presupposes agreement that one should tell the truth.

8. See Basil Mitchell, *Morality, Religious and Secular: The Dilemma of the Traditional Conscience* (Oxford: Clarendon Press, 1980), pp. 4–6.

9. Arthur E. Murphy, *The Theory of Practical Reason*, ed. A. I. Melden, Paul Carus Lectures, series 10 (La Salle, Ill.: Open Court, 1965), chap. 4, "Right in General and Moral Right in Particular," p. 81.

10. See Edmund Pincoffs, *Quandaries and Virtues: Against Reductivism in Ethics* (Lawrence: University of Kansas Press, 1986), esp. chap. 4, "The Justificatory Powers of the Standard Theories," for the distinction between explanatory and justificatory functions of such theories.

11. Pincoffs describes it as mandatory. Ibid., p. 85.

12. Michael Walzer, *The Company of Critics: Social Criticism and Political Commitment in the Twentieth Century* (New York: Basic Books, 1988), p. 20.

13. Ibid., p. 230.

14. John F. A. Taylor, *The Masks of Society: An Inquiry into the Covenants of Civilization* (New York: Appleton-Century, 1966), p. 250.

15. Edward Shils, *Tradition* (Chicago: University of Chicago Press, 1981), p. 32.

16. Walter Brueggemann, *The Creative Word: Canon as the Model for Biblical Education* (Philadelphia: Fortress Press, 1982), p. 52.

17. Walzer, *The Company of Critics*, p. 209.

18. See John Kekes, *Moral Tradition and Individuality* (Princeton, N.J.: Princeton University Press, 1989), esp. chap. 1. In this book, I believe, Kekes has provided the strongest argument in contemporary philosophical literature on the essential place of moral horror in providing the foundations of objective self-judgment.

19. Ibid., p. 12.

20. *The Ethics of Aristotle,* trans. J. A. K. Thompson (Harmondsworth, England: Penguin, 1955), book 3, chap. 2, p. 83.

21. This assertion that hope can only take things future as its object may seem rebutted by examples such as "I hope that my father (now dead) knew that I loved him." "I hope that I had enough sense to turn off the stove." What to make of this! Perhaps it is worth noting, however, that even such expressions as these are employed always with some concern in prospect. "I hope that I turned off the stove and that the house will not burn down."

5. Teaching Values: The Grand Delusion

Less developed versions of the central argument in this chapter have appeared earlier as "Values: Linguistic Conjecture, Constructive Venture," in *1993 Proceedings of the Philosophy of Education Society* pp. 68–75, and "The Value of Values," in *Career Development Quarterly* , vol. 38, no. 3 (March 1990): 208–211.

1. Citations to the *OED* are to *The Oxford English Dictionary*, 2d ed. (Oxford: Oxford University Press, 1992).

2. Eric Partridge, *Origins: A Short Etymological Dictionary of Modern English* (New York: Macmillan, 1966).

3. The phrase 'taking unfair advantage of neighbor' has the force of a moral prohibition. But to what extent is this rhetorical force produced by the presence of the word 'unfair', a term that carries with it already the idea of unjust? To say that 'unfair' is redundant is to imply that taking advantage of neighbor is already a moral breach, and to say that the term is essential is to imply that taking advantage of neighbor is morally acceptable provided it is done fairly. What is it to take advantage of neighbor fairly? Neither alternative—redundancy or not—seems to offer a satisfactory interpretation.

4. Of its formulation, Jevons wrote in a letter to Herbert Jevons in June 1860: "in the last few months I have fortunately struck out what I have no doubt is *the true theory of Economy* so thorough-going and consistent, that I cannot now read other books on the subject without indignation." *Papers and Correspondence of William Stanley Jevons* (Clifton, N.J.: Augustus M. Kelley, 1972), vol. 2, p. 410.

5. Cf. William Stanley Jevons, *The Theory of Political Economy* (London: Macmillan, 1924), p. 52. Marshall used the now more familiar term, 'marginal

utility', and in a note says, "The term *marginal utility* (*Grenznutz*) was first used in this connection by the Austrian Wieser." See Alfred Marshall, *Principles of Economics*, 9th ed. (London: Macmillan, 1936), p. 93.

6. Ibid., p. 93. This, of course, was Marshall's rendering of the familiar notion of *declining* marginal utility.

7. Cf. Robert L. Heilbroner and James K. Galbraith, *Understanding Microeconomics*, 9th ed. (Englewood Cliffs, N.J.: Prentice-Hall, 1990), p. 133.

8. Jevons, *Theory of Political Economy*, p. 43.

9. This 'discovery' (or better, 'invention', since we are not speaking here of nature) of marginal utility is at the root of what Maurice Dobb has called 'The Jevonian Revolution', which at heart is the shift in the history of economic theory from the factors of production to the theory of consumer behavior. See Maurice Dobb, *Theories of Value and Distribution since Adam Smith: Ideology and Economic Theory* (Cambridge: Cambridge University Press, 1973), chap. 7.

10. For a useful and detailed account of this development in economic thought, but without the implications that are drawn here, see Joan Robinson, *Economic Philosophy* (New York: Doubleday, 1964), chap. 2 and 3, and also George Soule, *Ideas of the Great Economists* (New York: Viking Press, 1952), chap. 6.

11. Something that Kierkegaard dreaded and Nietzsche celebrated.

12. George P. Adams, "The Idea of Civilization," in V. F. Lenzen et al., *Civilization* (Berkeley: University of California Press, 1959), pp. 57–58.

13. That children are more experienced with pluralism than their parents, curiously enough, is a judgment likely to be offered only by the parents, however, and not by the children. This is probably true, however, not because the children are less experienced, but because the multiplicity that adults are inclined to think expresses the value, pluralism, will be experienced by children as simply another given of the world they inhabit, nothing to be remarked upon as special.

14. See chapter 7, "Public Policy and the Office of Citizen," for a fuller discussion of these points.

15. Note how odd it is to suggest that such loves, always akin to *agape*, are to be understood as measuring the marginal utility of some object or person *to* someone. It accords more with common sense to suggest that such loves bring just that kind of value into the world that cannot *in principle* appear in the market at all.

16. It is worth a reminder, perhaps, that this shift of focus to a preoccupation with behavior echoes a similar shift of attention central to these essays, namely, the focus not upon the logical or ontological status of norms but upon their acquisition. There is this important difference, however. The shift of thoughtful attention to evaluational behavior may result in a kind of 'evacuation of value' from the world. But the shift of attention to norm acquisition has no such consequences.

17. Consider, for example, the notions of 'economic man' and 'the corporate person'. Lon Fuller in his treatment of legal fictions distinguishes between expository and persuasive types of fictions in law: "The expository fiction of corporate personality serves to preserve the premise that only 'persons' can have rights. The persuasive fiction of the 'acceptance' of a gift delivered out of the presence of the donee operates to keep intact the assumed notion that no one can secure a title without an expression of his will." *Legal Fictions* (Stanford, Calif.: Stanford University Press, 1967), p. 55. A significant contrast, however, is that in the case of law, none of the litigants believe that the donee is actually present or that corporations are actually capable of, say, weeping, whereas in the case of 'having values', the presence of the fictional entity is often taken quite literally and is even presumed, apparently, to be causally efficacious.

6. Public Speech

This chapter is an extended version of a talk framed originally as the DeGarmo Lecture for the Society of Professors of Education, delivered at the annual meeting of the American Educational Research Association in Atlanta in 1993. It has its origin, however, in meetings of the National Faculty Seminar on Religious Education convened over several years at the Christian Theological Seminary in Indianapolis, Indiana, under the aegis of the Lilly Endowment. In a form only slightly modified, it appeared also under the same title in *Teachers College Record*, vol. 95, no. 3 (Spring 1994), and also as electronic text in *Education Policy Analysis Archives*, vol. 2, no. 5 (February 6, 1994), an electronic journal at Arizona State University, http://olam.ed.asu.edu/epaa.

1. The amusement betrays our common ambivalence between myth and literalism. Why are we amused? Because we had not noticed? Does our amusement prove that we insist on taking the story literally?

2. William H. Gass, *On Being Blue: A Philosophical Inquiry* (Boston: David R. Godine, 1976), p. 47.

3. We have a rich vocabulary for "taking one's words back." It includes "eating crow," "eating hat," "gagging in the process"—and what else?

4. The speech has the structure of a multiple-choice question, i.e., a stem and then a series of declarations following from that stem. I say nothing here as to how this style of speech and its content is rooted in the voices of memory and moral imagination. In the case of this speech we have not only public talk, but congregational and prophetic talk.

5. My impression, perhaps erroneous, is that the 'critical thinking movement' in education tends to present the practices of public speech as primarily in need of adherence to such evidentiary canons, drawn either from formal

logic or from science. If this is a fair appraisal, it points to a mistake. Such evidentiary canons have the consequence of making speech public because such canons are themselves public standards. But this identification obscures what it is about such standards that has that effect. It is a view that misrepresents what makes public speech public.

6. Note the indexical reference of the first person pronoun in these statements of desire. These are statements *by* different persons *about* themselves. They are not statements about any *joint* concern, much less any common good. And if pronomial reference is any part of the meaning of such statements, neither are these statements about the same fact.

7. They are not even *about* our desires. "I don't want to pay higher taxes" is a statement even more primitive than "I know that I don't want to pay higher taxes." The latter is a statement about my desires, of which the former is a mere expression. "Ouch!" might be the expression of pain, "that hurts" a statement about a pain.

8. I am aware that there is such a thing as a hierarchy of desires. I can have a desire to have other desires than those I have. We might say, "I wish I didn't want that so much." But these 'higher order desires' are invariably the consequence of some order in the self other than desire itself. It was this absence of a *natural* hierarchy of desires that led to Plato's anti-democratic sentiments. He thought of the order of polity always as akin to order in the soul. And when desires alone rule, there is no order. The natural equality of desires is akin to anarchy in the self, he thought.

9. See Joseph Tussman, *Obligation and the Body Politic* (New York: Oxford University Press, 1960), p. 78. Tussman marks a useful distinction between the assertive mood and the claiming mood of discourse, suggesting that "'I believe P' is related to 'P is true' as 'I want X' is related to 'I am entitled to X'." This advancement from belief to knowledge (truth) and from blind assertion to grounded entitlement is akin to the transition I am referring to here as moving from the expression of desire to public claims.

10. The illustration and much of the analysis at this point I owe to Emily Robertson.

11. It is worth noting that this is the point at which John Dewey's conception of the public fails. In *The Public and its Problems*, Dewey's principal treatment of this problem, he defines a public as consisting of those effected by the consequences of actions taken. He distinguishes between nascent publics, whose members are unaware of how they are effected by actions taken, and self-conscious publics, whose members are aware of how they are implicated. But the crux of the matter is that for Dewey, belonging to a public is a purely consequential matter, entirely contingent upon the nexus of act and consequence. There is, for him, no such thing as a community of memory, one defined by recitation of an umbilical story.

12. Oliver Wendell Holmes, "The Path of the Law" (address delivered at

the dedication of the Boston University School of Law, January 8, 1891). Published first in *Harvard Law Review* 10 (1897): 457–458. See Max Lerner, ed., *The Mind and the Faith of Justice Holmes* (New York: Modern Library, 1954), p. 75. Holmes wrote, "The prophecies of what the courts will do in fact, and nothing more pretentious, are what I mean by the law." He actually believed that the tangled relation of law and morality was far more complex than so simple a rendering would suggest. He no doubt believed, however, that such a claim was a useful heuristic.

13. Garry Wills, *Lincoln at Gettysburg: The Words That Remade America* (New York: Simon and Schuster, 1992).

7. Public Policy and the Office of Citizen

This chapter is a substantial adaptation and extension of an earlier paper, "Policy and Evaluation: A Conceptual Study," *Paper and Report Series*, no. 52, Northwest Regional Educational Laboratory, Research on Evaluation Program, 1981, pp. 162–187. That paper was turned in another direction and published as "Policy Questions: A Conceptual Study," in *Education Policy Analysis Archives*, vol. 2, no. 7 (April 15, 1994), http://olam.ed.asu.edu/epaa. The current version is constructed upon these earlier drafts.

1. Those devoted to quantitative measures may find some pleasure in the equation that a flurry of political activity equals one-half a hostility but only about one-quarter of an actual belligerency.

2. When interviewing an economist as a part of preparing a paper commissioned by the World Bank, and in response to the judgment that the Bank should reinstitute something like a research center for economic analysis, I asked, "Do you mean that if we could achieve gains in economic wisdom, equal to the gains made from the study of human investment, then we might dispense with political judgment altogether?" The immediate answer, offered in tones of astonishment, was "Of course." The answer did not surprise me, but the speed of the response did, because it seemed to betray a remarkable lack of awareness of what policy questions are about, to say nothing of a failure to grasp the nature of politics.

3. Notice that 'rationally more persuasive' may imply neither 'politically more weighty' nor even 'politically more wise', a point that, as we shall see later, figures prominently in understanding the different facets of policy formation.

4. A compilation of eschatological visions would reveal a great deal about this human tendency to form images of perfection, and about how the inclination persists, even as the content changes. The border types of such a collection might be found in two visions of heaven, one from the twelfth century in southern France, one found in Marx's *Lectures on Political Economy*. By the first of these, heaven is understood as a kind of life in which one works and works

but does not weary, a life in which the rest and fellowship at day's end are like a candy that is sweet but never satiating. In this it is easy to discern the principal failures of the world, the things most fervently longed for, by those standing within this tradition. On the other hand, when Marx observes that bourgeois society is the last stage of *prehistory*, we know that we have entered a world entirely different from medieval France, a world in which the *eschaton* comes not at the end of history but at the beginning, a world in which the condition of human beings as the objects of social forces has yielded to a day in which they are the actors. Even in Marx's secular world, images of paradise prosper.

5. On the necessity of policy and politics, William Lee Miller offers an alternative view in an entertaining note. Beginning with James Madison's remark, "If men were angels, no government would be necessary," Miller remarks, "Government is necessary even for angels because the essence of government includes not only coercion but also consent, not only restraining order but also clarifying order. When the angels play serious volleyball someone will need to say when to start and where the lines are and what the score is and whether the ball is in or out, even though there will not be any argument (each side yielding always to the other would be as confusing as each side always claiming its own). Order is a social good, a need of all creatures, dangerous though it be; we *want* and *need* it, and so would angels. . . . even angels could not build a transcontinental railroad—assuming angels would want to do that—by a Quaker meeting." Miller, *The Business of May Next*, p. 167.

6. See chapter 5, "Teaching Values: The Grand Delusion," and especially the section "Social Values as Social Structure." What will become more apparent later should be reiterated here. The argument was that such goods (read 'values' if you must) as security, health, privacy, liberty of many sorts, work, and the like are not so much attitudes or dispositions of persons as they are objective social structures, the arrangements of social life. If public policy aims at an enlargement of liberty, then it must nurture those economic, social, and educational, arrangements by which liberty of movement, of conscience, of speech, of inquiry, and the like are nurtured. It is these *arrangements* that conflict in such a way that they cannot be jointly accessible.

7. This combination of vision, hope, and expectation also offers a clue to the peculiar American impulse to engage in complaint, even to the point of elevating lamentation to the level of an academic discipline, or, if not that, then to the level of a literary genre. Probably no society in the world is so given to lament as the American. For Americans, there is always *something* wrong, seriously wrong, that needn't be. The solution always seems to be more fidelity, more benevolence, more liberty, more education, more pride, more modesty, more time, or more leadership. Lamentation, it has been observed by many, is a national recreation. It is, perhaps even more than baseball, the true American pastime.

This peculiar mark of national character makes sense if we see it as the underside of American optimism, nurtured by life in a land of material abundance that provides for endless moral possibilities. As everyone knows, it is easier to adjust competing claims to a growing budget than to a shrinking one. Where goods conflict, the law of abundance would resolve the matter by allowing all competing claims to have their way enough to scatter discontent widely, thereby assuring that it cannot concentrate and thus, like manure, become pestilential.

8. See Lon Fuller, *The Morality of Law* (New Haven, Conn.: Yale University Press, 1964), in which he argues, successfully I think, that durability is an essential condition without which law could not exist. Without durability, it cannot be known, and thus cannot be public.

9. An important caveat: the policy *choice* is likely to occur in consequence of a kind of utilitarian calculus refined through several stages of the policy process. But it seems odd to regard this utilitarian calculation as in any sense a process of moral reflection, so thoroughly infused as it is with considerations of aggregate efficiency and net benefits. The so-called right-to-life position, for example, is not grounded in such considerations. It is grounded rather in convictions concerning what is morally right, wrong, or evil, and hence is concerned not so much with what policies should be adopted as with what courses of action should be excluded from among the set of viable choices. Here is a clear case where the moral deliberation occurs outside the realm of policy debate. Which is where it belongs.

10. Michael Walzer, "Political Decision-Making and Political Education," in *Political Theory and Political Education,* ed. Melvin Richter (Princeton, N.J.: Princeton University Press, 1980), p. 159.

Index